LEGACY

THE SUSTAINABLE DEVELOPMENT GOALS IN ACTION

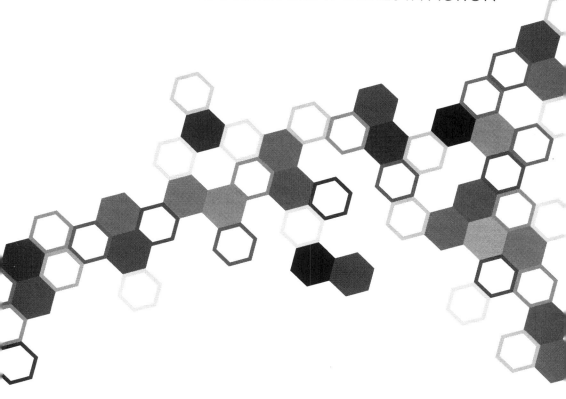

First published in 2019 by Dean Publishing
PO Box 119
Mt. Macedon, Victoria, 3441
Australia
deanpublishing.com

Cataloguing-in-Publication Data
National Library of Australia
Title: Legacy: The Sustainable Development Goals In Action
Edition: 1st edn
ISBN: 978-1-0772936-9-4
Category: Business/ Personal growth
Alexander Inchbald, Andrew Bachour, Ben Walker, Bernadette Sarginson, Brian Keen, Catherine Yang, Cheryl Angela, Chris Beks, Christopher Wick, Craig Doyle, David Keith, Deanne Firth, Deborah Harris, Douglas Barra, Dr Hanan Al-Mutawa, Dr Madhav Narayan Sathe, Gary Tho, Goh Swee Chen, Harvee Pene, Heather Yelland, Helen Campbell, Jamie Selby, Jeannie McGillivray, Jeremy Bentham, Joanna Oakey, Jody Ann Johnson, Joshua Ngoma, Karen Longwith, Karina Grassy, Kirsten Hawke, Kristy Castleton, Linda Saddlemire, Louisa Lee, Masami Sato, Mathew Colin Davis, Monty Hooke, Natalie Jameson, Pam FeatherstonePaul Polman, Richard Flanagan, Robert Lee, Russell Byrne, Shane Black, Shannon Burford, Sian Conway, Stacey Kehoe, Stella Petrou Concha, Steve Pipe, Susie Hutchison, Susan Dean, Paul Dunn and Yves Daccord.

CONTENTS

> *"...business can be the catalyst for the transformative progress the world desperately needs."*
>
> **— Paul Polman**

 Paul Polman is Chair of the International Chamber of Commerce (ICC) and The B Team and Vice-Chair of the U.N. Global Compact. As CEO of Unilever (2009–2018), he demonstrated that a long-term, multi-stakeholder model goes hand-in-hand with good financial performance.

In recognition of his commitment to driving transformational change, Paul was appointed to the U.N. Secretary General's High-level Panel, which developed the Sustainable Development Goals. He has played a leading role since in highlighting the business case for the 2030 development agenda.

FOREWORD
Paul Polman

At times, our biggest challenges can seem insurmountable. Runaway climate change, deforestation, plastics in our seas, and the extinction crisis. Not to mention gross inequality, poverty, disease, and human rights abuses. Our natural world and civilization appear to be under constant attack. On a downward spiral that is impossible to abort.

Yet, the great irony is, we already possess the means and solutions to solve these critical issues. Greater energy efficiency and use of renewables; more sustainable land use and food systems; smarter infrastructure and city planning; deployment of the circular economy; and more investment in education, healthcare, and diversity.

So, what's holding us back from making more progress?

Unfortunately, our global governance system is under significant strain. Many governments are retrenching from their responsibilities, looking inward, and questioning the benefits of multilateral cooperation and globalization.

This has led to a vacuum in international leadership — so often the prerequisite and essential ingredient for solving these multifaceted and interconnected problems — leaving the door open for the rise we have seen in nationalism and populism.

To correct course, this void needs to be filled. And we have no time to lose, as the cost of inaction is now higher than the cost of action.

This is perhaps the business community's biggest opportunity. To step in at this crucial time and de-risk the process for politicians by demonstrating there are more advocates for change than there are detractors. The scale, resources, and innovation of business make it ideally placed to have an out-sized impact.

The best contribution any business can make is by putting its full talents and expertise behind the United Nations 17 Sustainable Development Goals (SDGs). These act as a bulwark for long-term, sustainable, and equitable growth and provide an ambitious blueprint for a better world.

And in case there are still some companies that do not buy the moral case for action, perhaps they should consider the economic imperative. Investing in the SDGs promises to unlock economic opportunities worth at least $12 trillion a year and generate up to 380 million jobs.

There is also increasing evidence that supporting this agenda enables organizations to better manage risks, drive innovation and growth, access new markets, and recruit and retain talent. This new way of doing business is consequently fast becoming a matter of corporate self-interest.

We must however acknowledge there will always be limitations in the ability of any one company to act alone. Leaders must look beyond their own operations and take a share of responsibility across the total value chain. They also need to collaborate and partner with other organizations to move at scale and maximize impact.

By putting itself to the service of others, by putting purpose above profit, and by putting shared responsibility and prosperity as the kitemarks of success, business can be the catalyst for the transformative progress the world desperately needs.

Therefore, the central message of *LEGACY* could not be more pertinent. Business truly can change the world. And, as this book shows, everyone can make their own individual contribution.

WELCOME TO LEGACY
A note from the curator

The first definition in the dictionary defines "legacy" as *money* or *property that someone leaves behind when they pass away.*

And while you can find tens of thousands of book titles on Amazon around the topic of the money and property that you might leave or give one day, this book is not about those things.

This book is about a different kind of gift. It's a gift you live each day. A gift that you craft masterfully, share with others generously and pass on to your children, to your grandchildren, and to the world.

And interestingly, you alone cannot become a master of this "gift-craft" no matter how good you are. Because the gift you create alone is not impactful unless everyone else starts creating, appreciating, and sharing their gifts as well.

In the next seventeen chapters, you are presented with unique gifts of all varieties. And as you uncover and open the gifts you see a precious gem of a message in each one. These gems work together to form a foundation — one set back in September 2015, when, after 3 full years of highly-focused work, a group of global leaders worked with the United Nations to launch the 17 Sustainable Development Goals.

This marked the beginning of a new era. Something that had never been done before. It marked a turning point in business, a time when global leaders (and the UN) recognized the importance of businesses in setting the roadmap toward true and collective success.

It also acknowledged that one approach or one big plan alone couldn't create the true sustainability of this planet. It needed participants of the greatest diversity.

Now it's time that each of us discovers the unique gift we individually have so we can successfully identify the opportunities we are given to create a greater future.

We're so fortunate that 52 changemakers have come together in this book with their own gift of researching, of experiencing and of writing. And we're also pleased that global leaders like Paul Polman, Goh Swee Chen (President, Global Compact Network Singapore) and Yves Daccord (Director General, International Committee of the Red Cross) have added in their inspiring insights, the latter two — as you'll discover — as guest writers in some of the chapter introductions.

This entire book invites leaders and team members of businesses (small and large) to join the movement. This book is a call to us all — corporations, businesses, governments, NGOs, and individuals — to align together.

Together, we really can create, leave, and live the LEGACY our world needs.

Masami Sato,
Founder and CEO, B1G1 (BUY1GIVE1)

P.S. This book is powered by B1G1, the global giving initiative working with businesses around the world to make giving an integrated part of everyday business. As a result of the publication of this book, one entire community in Ethiopia receives a life-giving well. Every copy sold or given also gives to a uniquely selected SDG project. You'll find out more about that and the B1G1 initiative in the closing chapter.

CREATE AN ABUNDANT WORLD

1 NO POVERTY

HOW YOU AND YOUR BUSINESS CAN HELP END POVERTY IN ALL ITS FORMS EVERYWHERE.

"Overcoming poverty is not a gesture of charity. It is the protection of a fundamental human right, the right to dignity and a decent life."

— Nelson Mandela

THE CHANGEMAKERS

BECOME A BUSINESS FOR GOOD
HARVEE PENE

Harvee Pene is a four-times author, TEDx speaker, and co-founder of Inspire — Life Changing Accountants. His book, *Cashed Up*, outlines the seven-step method to draw more money, time, and happiness from your business, enabling business owners to have more, so they can live more and give more. Harvee and his team are on a mission to become Australia's most impactful accounting firm by giving 1 billion days' access to food, water health, and sanitation by 2030.

inspire.business

THE THOUGHT THAT CHANGED MY BUSINESS
JOANNA OAKEY

Joanna Oakey is the owner and director of Aspect Legal, a commercial law firm with a difference. She is a mother, author, lawyer and podcaster with a passion for people, business, and global issues. Joanna and her team provide a range of proactive and commercially driven legal services to support growing businesses in building their business machine, from acquisitions through to exit and everything in between.

And while doing that, Joanna and her team give to worthy causes to reduce world poverty.

aspectlegal.com.au

THE BUTTERFLY EFFECT IN BUSINESS
KIRSTEN HAWKE

Kirsten Hawke is a chartered accountant and CPA. She is the founder and CEO of Astill Hawke & Associates Accounting and the driving force behind BUSINESS *buddy*. Kirsten had the vision to create an accounting practice focused directly on its clients, and this led to BUSINESS *buddy* becoming the number-one provider of accounting in the cloud, an approach that's revolutionizing the accounting world.

businessbuddy.co.nz

CREATE AN ABUNDANT WORLD

Bangladeshi social entrepreneur, economist, and leader Muhammad Yunus said, "Poverty does not belong in civilized human society. Its proper place is in a museum."

Imagine if poverty was among other ancient fossils — that its only purpose was to tell a story about the past, like dinosaurs and Neanderthals and the Ancient Egyptian pharaohs. Imagine if poverty was something more of myth and legend, a tale about the "old days" and how horrid those times must have been for those who lived them.

Sadly, that's not the case. Those horrid times are happening now. Poverty is a living, breathing organism that exists and breeds in our world today. It's a life-inhibiting virus that has not been eradicated. As Einstein pointed out, "The world is a dangerous place, not because of those who do evil, but because of those who look on and do nothing."

But, does it have to be this way? Of course not.

In fact, statistics prove that we are moving in the right direction; more people are being lifted from the cycle of poverty. However, the statistics also reveal that too many remain there.

Almost half the world survives on less than $2.50 a day. That's equivalent to half a cup of coffee for some people. In Sub-Saharan Africa, 42% of the population lives on less than $1.90.[1]

But what we must remember more than these alarming statistics is that behind every number, every dollar value, and every country — is a person. A real person facing desperate situations. A real person who is not only facing poverty but often facing discrimination and feelings of low self-worth because of it. And more often than not, that real person is a child.[2]

---

1   World Poverty Statistics: Global Poverty Report 2018, The World Bank.
2   World Bank Group and UNICEF

Changemaker Harvee Pene encourages people to travel, to visit developing countries as a way to shift perception; to understand the limits poverty imposes but also the difference any contribution can make.

Changemaker Kirsten Hawke helps us realize that poverty is not neatly boxed into the category of economics and average household incomes, but it greatly inhibits access to things such as water, health, education, housing, and security. Ending poverty is all about finding ways to give people their basic human rights.

And we can do that. Together, we can give back the basic right to everyone. World Bank Group President Jim Yong Kim said, "Over the last 25 years, more than a billion people have lifted themselves out of extreme poverty, and the global poverty rate is now lower than it has ever been in recorded history. This is one of the greatest human achievements of our time."

This means that not only is there less poverty in the world but, the average life expectancy has increased significantly and the gap between rich and poor is slowly closing.

As wonderful and promising as these results are, we must ask: can we lift the benchmark from out of "*extreme* poverty"?

Sure, "average" poverty is a step up from extreme poverty, but is that what we want for others? Our children? Should poverty really have "acceptable" sub-categories? Can we be as bold and as brave to move from poverty and go all the way to equality?

This is our aim. The aim of these changemakers and of many people, business owners, organizations, and families. To close the gap between rich and poor.

Each country has its definition of poverty, its own "danger line" that qualifies its citizens as above or below standard. But let's be honest, many of these invisible lines and figures don't really hit home. Most young people won't have a clue that 100,534 pesos a year is the national poverty line in the Philippines. After all, 100,534 sounds like a lot of numbers. Or that the poverty line in Mexican pesos is defined as no more than 2,542 pesos ($157.70) a month in cities and 1,615 pesos in rural areas. What about the Albanian lek or Indian rupee?

To make these numbers mean something, it's converted to the international poverty line, which is currently set at $1.90 a day. This is classified as the international measurement of global poverty. This helps measure and compare levels between countries.

According to the United Nations, poverty is:

> ...the inability of having choices and opportunities, a violation of human dignity. It means a lack of basic capacity to participate effectively in society. It means not having enough to feed and clothe a family, not having a school or clinic to go to, not having the land on which to grow one's food or a job to earn one's living, not having access to credit. It means insecurity, powerlessness and exclusion of individuals, households and communities. It means susceptibility to violence, and it often implies living in marginal or fragile environments, without access to clean water or sanitation.

As you can see, poverty means a lot.

Poverty crosses into every part of a person's life. *Every* part. It affects health, wellbeing, education, nourishment, self-esteem, violence, relationships, and families; it even means that someone may or may not get clean water. As the famous quote says, "Poverty is like punishment for a crime you didn't commit."

No human should pay a price because of where they're born.

Global leaders and business leaders are now banding together to face poverty as one major entity to ensure this unjustified suffering stops. Conscious business leaders, such as Paul Polman, are advocating strongly for businesses to change their business models and align them with the SDG goals. Businesses can provide a deeper and more powerful impact than ever.

Changemaker Joanna Oakey is testament to this. She has changed the nature of commercial law simply through aligning her values and those of her team with global goals.

Business is a multi-tool, the ultimate Swiss army-knife against poverty. A business has the power to hire and provide ongoing employment to others. It has the power to drive economic growth and make decisions about who it buys from and who it doesn't.

It has the power to make headway where more formal institutions or governing bodies can't. It has the power to train others and provide them with tools and education.

Inspiring business leaders around the world encourage us to take a more active role in society and stress the point that we can all make a difference. They show us that an entirely new business model can be a savior to both humanity and the business itself. That business and global poverty are not poles apart but in fact married together in a perfect and positive union.

It really is possible now to see growth and prosperity for all. As Paul Polman says, "The real purpose of business has always been to come up with solutions that are relevant to society, to make society better."

Every business can contribute to the greater good. Every person. By joining together, by forming alliances and partnerships, we can not only become a stronger business force, but we can become a stronger force for good in the world.

Harvee, Joanna, and Kirsten show us that conscious entrepreneurship is a threat to poverty. We ask people to become an active threat to poverty. To become a threat to the fact that a third of the entire urban population is living in a slum; to become a threat to the fact that children suffer simply from being born in a particular place in the world.

To end extreme poverty worldwide in 20 years, economist Jeffrey Sachs calculated that the total cost per year would be about $175 billion. What this breaks down to is less than 1% of the combined income of the richest countries in the world.

Let's say that again:

To end extreme poverty in 20 years, the cost per year is less than 1% of the combined income of the richest countries in the world.

This reeks of possibility. Extreme possibility. To end extreme poverty, we already have extreme possibility. Now, all we need is extreme action.

BECOME A BUSINESS FOR GOOD
HARVEE PENE

I was born into a poor family in a very poor town in New Zealand. My mother was thirteen when she had my sister and sixteen when she had me. When we moved to Australia, "the land of opportunity," we had no money, no friends or family, no education, and no hope. Mom would take us through a basic grocery store, called Franklins, and we had to steal food for dinner because we had no money. Stealing to survive isn't a great feeling. Desperation makes people do desperate things, and poverty forces people into desperate situations.

I started business at fourteen, and if there's one thing that I've learned since being in business it's this — business is tough! I've experienced what it's like to grow up with nothing and get into business as a way to survive. Yes, I got into business long before Gary Vaynerchuk made the hustle of entrepreneurship cool. It was my tool for survival, for making ends-meet, for providing for my family.

Fast-forward decades ahead and I spend my time helping young families use their small business to get *Cashed Up*, to be free from the worries and burdens that I know only too well. Business can be the ultimate vehicle for rising out of poverty. It was for me. In 2018, our business Inspire gave 3 million days' worth of life-changing help to families across sixteen countries.

Sadly, even in a country as wealthy as Australia, small businesses are notoriously failing to reach their full potential. When a business fails to reach its potential, it fails to make its ultimate difference in the lives of its owners and others.

There are almost 1.9 million small businesses around Australia, and of those, 60% either:
- earn less than $200,000 in revenue,
- cannot afford a team,
- are unprofitable, or

- don't even pay themselves a decent salary.

These small businesses have big goals but often fall short of achieving their deepest desires. I dedicate my days and brain-power to ensuring families and small businesses don't fall into the "just-make-ends-meet" category.

I believe every business should be a vehicle for success, to thrive and enjoy. At the nucleus of every business should be positive impact.

Think about this:

If you're a dentist, you help people smile.

If you're a teacher, you help people learn and grow.

If you're a financial planner, you help people gain freedom.

If you're a real estate agent, you shelter people.

If you're a restaurant owner, you nourish people.

If you're a psychologist, you help people gain peace of mind.

So why not link your business' direct impact with an additional impact to help families in need? I call this, becoming a Business for Good.

For example:

- Become a **Dentist for Good**. Every time someone gets their teeth cleaned, you provide a regular check-up for someone in India. Only $2 via B1G1.
- Become a **Teacher for Good**. Every time someone completes your course, you provide teaching materials to an Ethiopian nursery school. Only 3 cents via B1G1.
- Become a **Restaurant for Good**. Every time someone enjoys a meal, you give seeds to nourish a child in Malawi. Only 1 cent via B1G1.

Another great thing to consider is taking a Holiday for Good. Let me explain...

The Reason I Said 'No' to Necker Island

In November 2016, I got an invitation to go to Necker Island and meet Sir Richard Branson. A week-long invitation to collaborate with other life-affirming entrepreneurs at the top of their game. Its core focus was on how we could use business to make a bigger impact on the planet. While it was the "golden ticket," it also came with a golden price tag. We decided to say "no" to Necker Island and instead focus on making a bigger impact.

It was this moment, where the #GIVE1MDAYS campaign was born. Our bold and audacious idea — to give 1,000,000 days of life-changing water to families in need in Malawi. We figured that the opportunity at Necker Island may be there for some time, but the 1.7 million people at risk of disease and even death may not be. There was really no time to lose. Saying "no" to Necker meant we could say "yes" to other people, those that really needed a yes in their lives.

Take a Holiday For Good

Choosing holidays can actually play a vital role in ending poverty. I suggest that people plan a "Holiday For Good." An unforgettable, perception-changing holiday.

This idea became clear to me while in Bali. I took a few days to go visit a B1G1 cause — The John Fawcett Foundation, a humanitarian not-for-profit organization that helps restore sight to those in need. This project was close to my heart because I grew up both poor and blind in one eye.

We spent time in the villages helping restore sight for those both poverty-stricken and blind. It blew me away! Changed me. For a mere $50, I could give someone a lifetime gift — vision. A wish that for me would be priceless. $50! Often, we spend $50 on a nice breakfast, or a few drinks on a Friday afternoon, or a quick massage. But to our friends in developing countries — $50 can mean their entire life. Restoring sight also restores confidence and a chance for employment and independence. This was a major turning point for me; it ignited my drive to become a massive force for good.

We recently returned from a Holiday for Good in Cambodia, one of the poorest and least developed countries in the world. Many people there still lack some basic necessities and live in appalling conditions. It was also an eye-opener for my children (six and ten) who now understand that they already live in Disneyland every day, but other kids, far too many, aren't as fortunate.

Bono said it best when he said, "Where you live should not determine whether you live, or whether you die." Nor should it determine whether you get access to water, food, and shelter, but sadly, it still does.

We may not choose where we're born, but for those of us who have our basic needs satisfied, we can "Live to Give." I believe this is the change we need.

A Holiday for Good does many things:

- It shifts attitudes and perspectives. When you see conditions that many developing countries are in, you can't remain the same.
- It helps children who aren't living in poverty understand global issues quicker than any school assignment.
- It gives money to the countries and people that need it more than Disneyland (though I do like Disneyland, too).
- It inspires people to be the change. We have seen firsthand the change our business has brought about in these countries, and it's the key to long-term motivation.
- It gives you and others a lifetime experience and a holiday that helps others.

If you want to double your impact overnight, then book a holiday that contributes to others. Take the family. Take the kids. Take the team. Take your clients. Take your alliance partners. Damn, take your competitors! You might just come home as collaborators. A Holiday for Good is life-changing, not just for the families in need, but for you and your family, too.

Imagine going to Ethiopia, Laos, Moldova, Morocco, Kenya, or Lebanon for a once-in-a-lifetime experience. It doesn't mean you can't go anywhere else; it just means that you balance your lifestyle with giving.

So, if you want to be part of the global change,

1. Become a Business for Good.
2. Take a Holiday for Good.
3. And Live to Give.

After you do that, tell everyone. My dear friend and mentor, Glen Carlson (co-founder of Dent Global), said, "It's not about how much you're giving, it's about how effectively you are engaging others to give as well."

Once you've decided to become a Business for Good, I recommend you tell everyone. Yell it from the mountains. Share your vision. Engage others to join the giving movement, and inspire everyone to bring their biggest game to the table.

At Inspire, we define our values as "Dream Big. Make an Impact. Remember Your Roots." So every time we make an impact, we are reinforcing our core values to the team, giving them real reason to feel part of something bigger than themselves.

To illustrate this in practical terms. To date, we've proactively saved our small business clients' more than $7 million in tax, which means that our Day for Dollar initiative has given over 7 million days of help to families in need, across sixteen countries. That's the power of business aligned with giving.

Our goal toward ending extreme global poverty by 2030 is by giving 1 billion days of life-changing help to those in need.

This is our legacy, and we will never stop. Our global friends are counting on it.

THE THOUGHT THAT CHANGED MY BUSINESS
JOANNA OAKEY

I remember the moment well. Seven years prior, I had begun my own law firm, Aspect Legal, and then had two delightful children. Between running and growing a business and being a mother, my thoughts and energy were solidly occupied.

After having my second child, I returned to work, but something inside of me had changed. Some may call it an existential crisis, but I was thinking differently. Very differently. Asking questions like: "What's this all about? How am I helping the world? What am I doing that's useful? How should I live in a way that matters?"

This type of deep inner questioning ruminated inside me for the next six months.

I looked at the world around me and felt deeply connected to it, so lucky to be in this safe and beautiful country, Australia. So lucky to have every opportunity available to me. Yet, I also saw the massive global issues — everywhere — and felt that I wasn't truly helping anyone or doing anything about them. There was a lingering uneasiness inside, and I evaluated my life and business practices.

I looked first at my legal firm. We worked really hard to deal with our clients' issues to protect them through the storms of business, but could we be doing this in a better way? How else could we help the world? Was there more depth for us than just being in business?

I started to think deeply about these bigger questions. It was something that I knew I really needed to pay attention to and work out. I knew now that I just couldn't get fulfillment from life or business until I had worked out how to make good use of my time on this planet.

I had a meeting with my team and suggested we find a good project to give to. To find a way to give back in a way that we all felt good about. The question was, "How could we as a legal firm, as a business, use our privileged position to help people in the world and in our community?" Sure, we participated in community appeals and charity days, but I felt we could do so much more.

I wanted to find something that we all felt connected to, something that connected us to the world and our community in a deeper way. And so, the search began.

We looked and looked and looked. It was really important to find projects where the money went directly to people who needed it most. We tried a few different things, but they just didn't feel right. And then we found B1G1, and our giving journey finally began. We focused on poverty and rallied our team. Everyone felt connected. And we involved our clients, and referral partners, and suddenly we had inadvertently triggered this deeper connection with them as well! And once we started, it just multiplied.

Now, every time we receive a client referral, we give 20 days of school fees for disadvantaged children in Thailand and 20 days of support to keep a family together in times of poverty. And only a few months down the track, we've given more than six-and-a-half years' worth. And for every single email I send, we give a day's worth of grain seed to nourish kids in Malawi. I now have a deeper reason to email. This is now equivalent to 14 years' worth of grain seed. We also provide support to subsistence farmers in Cambodia, life-saving water to families in Ethiopia, and access to income-generating tools for women in Bangladesh — all connected to stages of our business journey with our clients and partners.

This is business success amplified with meaning.

I must admit that at first, I saw other businesses, inspiring businesses that had been giving to charitable projects for a long time. And in many ways, I felt we just weren't doing enough and perhaps just couldn't meet those lofty standards set by others. But later, it occurred to me that perhaps we are representative of those who are at the beginning of their journey. That's our story, because even though we don't have notable awards or epic numbers yet, like some other major companies, we do represent the importance of starting. The most important decision a business can make. To begin to give. This simple choice is transformative because it not only gives people in poverty a chance, it gives our business and team a sense of worth and meaning in their daily jobs. It takes the grind out of work and ignites it with gratitude.

Different Dimensions of Happiness

When I was young, my parents reminded me that I was lucky. And I believed it. When I was quite young, we had foster children in our home, so I grew up with a good understanding that some children didn't always have the level of love that we had in our family. I simply saw the benefits of being in a family that could share love. But I always had this lingering concern about global poverty; it was always there hovering in my mind.

After I finished school, I went traveling with my sister. We went on a big round-the-world trip, and the first place we saw was Indonesia. I remember thinking that this could be really confronting because I knew there would be many people with less opportunity and more difficult lives. The interesting thing was, everywhere I looked, I saw really happy people. The people who didn't have much seemed to have something I valued — really deep happiness. This was repeated again a few times in my life later when I visited places such as Cambodia and Laos. I met very, very poor people but was taken aback by the joy and happiness they exuded. It made me look at the many dimensions to life and happiness. While it certainly never took away from my feeling that we have gifts that we have to share, and help to give, it did help me view people and poverty in a new, multi-dimensional way.

In many places around the world, happiness is attributed to "things," and often these things are neatly packaged so we believe they make us happy. Some people are still really sad when surrounded by so much and others find happiness in very simple things. There are many deep dimensions to life, and sometimes growing up blessed means that we don't fully see or appreciate other dimensions. The true happiness we are all fundamentally seeking is to feel connected. To feel connected to others and the world. That's really what underpins it all. And I believe that giving is the perfect conduit to connection.

Reflect To Connect

A client once sent me a little line that struck me. He said, "When I'm dealing with you, I absolutely know that you have my best interest at heart."

I thought, this is it. This is truly who we are, and what our company stands for. In many instances, we help our clients make decisions that will earn us far less money, but for us, at the end of the day, the absolutely critical question is: "What is the absolute best thing for our clients?"

I'm not saying that lawyers intentionally make decisions to push their clients into paths that cost more money, I think there are very few lawyers who would do that, but lawyers sometimes forget to step back and look at their clients and their clients' businesses from a human perspective. To cross-check their heart and ask, "Is this really the right thing, and the best way?" It's vital to ask this without stepping first. I believe this is true for many things.

It's about looking intelligently at the whole perspective and asking yourself and your team:

- Why are we doing it this way?
- Is there a better way to do this, or a different way that works?
- Can we innovate this idea?'

In law firms, everyone gets a bit freaked out when I discuss innovation because lawyers don't necessarily know how to innovate. But just because that's how it's always been doesn't mean that's the way it should be. We must keep fresh and continually ask, "Is there a better or different way to do this?"

I think there's a deeper connection to the world when you reflect before you step. To ask deep questions and consider new alternatives, to innovate thinking. Strategies and contributions are indeed valuable, but it's also important to find space and time to think about the best approach. To reflect on these issues, such as poverty, with an honest, inquiring mind. Are there ways you or your business could leverage the projects you're connected to for greater impact?

It is important for people and businesses to make time and space for asking questions, for reflection and deep thought. I have actually scheduled time in my busy calendar once a month to ponder such questions. To deeply reflect.

Another powerful question is, "How can we spread more joy?"

Some people may not have a lot of money, but they spread something truly valuable — joy.

I'm deeply passionate about joy and being a provider of happiness to people. Business is a great avenue for that. Not just any business, but the right business. Growing a business where clients are over the moon and staff are really happy and connected. A business that ensures family balance and happiness. A carefully thought-out business can be your happy bubble.

Because the best businesses are where the owners and staff understand what they're all about, and the happiest families are where parents and children have time and space to be their best selves. So, I believe it's about understanding what you need to be your best self and then working hard to filter that through your business and your life.

It's vital to be aware of the decisions you're making and the actions you're taking, to not just act on autopilot, but to be sincerely intentional and conscious. To give people time and space to find their happiness and best self.

We have staff in both Australia and the Philippines. I go and visit our team in the Philippines once a year, and I absolutely love it. Having diversity in people and cultures and approaches is a great strength. And our giving projects also operate on this basis. And getting the team on board to get involved in our giving projects is a big connector. It's a great connector with our clients and our referral partners, too.

I absolutely believe that implementing giving into business is the future. It's the key to happiness and sustainability. It's the key to supporting people out of poverty and treasuring their gifts. Giving has connected our clients, our team, and our culture with the world. We don't think separately; our culture is global thinking.

This is also partly due to our hiring process — we only hire people who have a high value alignment to altruism. Our choices are deliberate and conscious, such as who we're working with and who is helping to serve our clients. We value care and altruism and know that it's these qualities that will not only make our work place great but will support our endeavors to be part of the change — to help eradicate poverty by 2030.

So in the end, the existential crisis that drove my change in thinking has fundamentally changed my business, and my thought processes in business as a whole. It has helped define our core values, it has helped unite our team, it has changed how we hire, and it has helped us connect with our partners and clients on a whole new level. And it has given us an aim that feels so much deeper than just to grow a business. Because now we are on a mission to grow in order to help drive change in the world — because now our success is amplified with meaning.

As the great Helen Keller said, "*Alone we can do so little; together we can do so much.*"

THE BUTTERFLY EFFECT IN BUSINESS
KIRSTEN HAWKE

It's obvious that living in a world without poverty would be better for everyone. It seems difficult to believe that we haven't achieved this yet. As an accountant, the numbers can all point to the achievable outcome, but in reality, it isn't adding up. Why is this? Because ending poverty is not as simple as throwing money at those with less and expecting change. We need sustainable solutions that provide long-term and ongoing progress. This will achieve a happier world.

For the most disadvantaged people, it can seem impossible to break free from the cycle of deprivation. Poverty leads to health, education, lifestyle, and wellbeing inequalities, and the despair, anger, and frustration creates tension at the core of households and extends to communities and nations. Violence and conflict directly impact poverty.

We see severe deprivation and suffering around the globe but often fail to see what is happening next door. In New Zealand, for example, most people have a good standard of living, but there are still families that go without and children who need others to extend compassion. That hungry, sick, cold child will need some sort of miracle to achieve the same outcomes as an advantaged youngster on the other side of town.

Poverty and inequality are often living right under our noses, in our neighborhoods and communities. Change can be as easy as looking next door.

Growing up in New Zealand meant there were plenty of moments when you learned to have a charitable heart. At school, we were exposed to "coin trails," a school-based initiative that collected money for people in far-away countries who were suffering from drought, war, and other heart-wrenching disasters. I just grew up fully aware that there were others less fortunate than me. We were raised to know that when you can help, you should.

Growing up with this foundation meant my social conscience grew, and I came to understand the impact my parents had in various community service organizations.

I followed in their footsteps and also joined community service organizations. In my pre-teen years, I committed to 40-hour famines and other fundraising for sponsored children in disadvantaged countries.

My adult years, and becoming part of B1G1, consolidated my awareness of addressing poverty with that old cliché — give a hand up, not a hand-out. Becoming part of a collaborative global vision empowered our business to make a difference, one that perhaps would be unattainable as a single entity. The power of many far exceeds one's own attempt, no matter how positive the intention.

Even more mind-blowing is when a business becomes increasingly meaningful by contributing to a project in a developing country. Some of our clients have been so inspired by our giving initiative that they have done the same. They understand that giving impacts others and makes them feel good.

I love to share the message that *being a good business is accomplished by being in business for a higher goal.*

New Zealanders are a humble bunch, and they can often be reluctant to tell the world about great stuff they're doing, mostly for fear of appearing conceited. However, I believe that charitable organizations need to tell their stories in order to encourage others to do the same.

Our team at BUSINESS *buddy* has bravely ignored Kiwi conformity and actively shared our social enterprise successes. One of our favorite impacts is providing one year's supply of seeds to a family so they can feed their children. It's truly incredible to think our business can directly feed impoverished families.

This concept appeals to my sense of entrepreneurship because the family has the capacity to harvest seeds and use them for following years, building up their crop size and creating a business themselves.

This business model is sustainable for feeding the family and also generating potential income for other items, such as school books and uniforms. This improves education opportunities and maximizes potential for children. It helps them step out of the cycle of poverty.

The global vision to sustainably end poverty inspires me greatly. I have seen firsthand how the lives of BUSINESS *buddy* clients improve when their businesses do well. It gets me out of bed and motivated to have a great day at work. When I know what we do empowers people to live free of poverty, I know why I do what I do, and why I keep doing it. When I know I'm helping a client achieve a personal goal, which often includes doing something for their family — it means BUSINESS *buddy* is on track. That is a successful day.

The impact of being a giving business benefits generations and communities. For example, learning how to run a business profitably provides food for the table, employment opportunities, and hope. From there, economic growth supports better education, healthcare, and infrastructure, all of which improve the wellbeing of entire societies.

Then who knows — maybe the world will be a peaceful and harmonious place.

Business is Not Just Business — The Butterfly Effect

I have often heard people justify their greed or over-charging tendencies as "Business is business." But business is not just business; it's much more.

We often ask a client to see the bigger picture and understand that the wage they pay an employee is not just an expense. That pay packet could mean that a child has shoes to wear to school or a partner can afford a medical check-up. Business is much more than it seems.

Taking care of the wellbeing of your team is equally important as taking care of your clients. Working together to achieve better outcomes, which could be anything from improved profitability to less stress, makes business better for everyone. Adding social enterprise to the business mix gives greater meaning to each day and everyone on the team.

At BUSINESS *buddy*, we've always had a commitment to improve the wellbeing of our clients, our team, and our community. All team goals are set around a win for everyone — those we have immediate contact with as well as those we may never meet.

We are aiming to give 1 million impacts because this will benefit many people at different levels. It's the butterfly effect. We help our clients improve their businesses, which then has a positive impact on their families. The contribution BUSINESS *buddy* then makes to B1G1 reduces global poverty on a bigger scale.

The true impact of this means it reduces daily hardship for families around the world and reduces international tension. The good created from one simple giving action never ends. This is the true value of business.

When I had children, our family started to sponsor a child in a developing country. At first, we never really knew where our donation was going until we received a card from a boy called Oscar. That card reassuringly gave us the warm fuzzies. The money we sent allowed Oscar to buy books he needed to enroll in school. It felt incredible knowing that we had a hand in supporting his education.

We have contributed to our local children's hospital and neonatal unit. Sometimes our support was a regular financial contribution and at other times we rallied the BUSINESS *buddy* team to support larger community campaigns. A fun example was collecting pajamas for the children's hospital; we encouraged our clients and other businesses to get on board. Something as simple as a pair of warm pajamas can reduce the hospital readmission rate for children living in our city. It feels good to stop a kid from suffering and something as simple as a pair of PJs can help.

Sometimes it's not money but time that we give. Our family has a personal connection to the local Hospice, and for numerous years the BUSINESS *buddy* team has given time to collect donations at the Hospice Trees of Remembrance.

So, how does all this impact on my day? Poverty is everywhere, and being part of a bigger project makes me feel that even the smallest contribution really makes a difference to the lives of others. It can sound cliché — until you see the results. And then you know that the butterfly effect is true.

Ultimately, it would be incredibly rewarding to know that the values we instill in the next generation, including my own children and the younger people I work with, inspire them to take up the mantle for the future. That's the ultimate legacy — one that never stops.

WHAT YOU CAN DO TO
CREATE A WORLD WITH ZERO POVERTY

Lifestyle tips:
- Make your weekends "Weekends for Good". Involve others and make your weekend one that supports those in need.
- Wherever possible, choose to buy products that are produced under fair and ethical trade partnerships and employment.
- Have "SDG Learning Days" where you and your family get together to learn more about the SDGs and then plan actions that make change possible.
- Have "$2 days" where you experience what it feels like to survive on $2 a day.

Business tips:
- Enhance your business model to include giving to people in need.
- Support inclusive and sustainable businesses.
- Hire people who are willing to make a difference.
- Create opportunities for good and decent jobs and secure livelihoods.
- Link your activities to doing good in our world.

Giving tips:
- Sponsor education and ocupational training for a person in poverty.
- Donate your old belongings.
- Give leftover food and groceries to local charities.
- Crowdfund to support causes that aim to tackle poverty.

NOURISHING THE WORLD THROUGH CHANGE

2 ZERO HUNGER

HOW YOU AND YOUR BUSINESS CAN HELP END HUNGER, ACHIEVE FOOD SECURITY AND IMPROVED NUTRITION AND PROMOTE SUSTAINABLE AGRICULTURE.

"The first essential component of social justice is adequate food for all mankind. Food is the moral right of all who are born into this world."

— Norman Borlaug

THE CHANGEMAKERS

THE POWER OF UNITY AND COMMUNITY
JOSHUA CHIMAKULA NGOMA

Joshua is the Founder and Chief Enabler of Enterprising Africa Regional Network (Pty) Limited (EARN). EARN was formed with the overriding goal of creating an enabling environment for African entrepreneurs to grow profitable and sustainable businesses that would compete regionally, nationally, and internationally. A mining engineer by profession, Joshua spent almost half of his mining career building and running successful mining and mining-related businesses. He is now a trainer, business coach, and mentor. He uses his business experience to help others achieve similar business successes.

earninternational.net

YOU ARE THE ULTIMATE VEHICLE FOR IMPACT
SHANE BLACK

Shane runs a financial services business called Pearl Finance Group. They specialize in helping Gen Y business owners accumulate more assets, generate more income, and build a meaningful business and life. He has an MBA, Master of Applied Finance, and Master of Financial Planning. First and foremost, Shane is a proud family man, husband to Hong and father to William, with two dogs — Chelsea and Lily.

pearlfinancegroup.com

THE CALLING IN YOUR HEART TO HELP
CHRIS BEKS

Chris Beks is Team Leader and Principal of Ceebeks Business Solutions for GOOD. He's deeply passionate about his work with families in small businesses and creating a bigger impact together. He is a true family man, with his lovely spouse, Angela, of 20 years and three teenage daughters. Chris loves singing, the performing arts and is an avid sports fan. And in his spare time, he became a qualified fitness and aerobics instructor.

ceebeks.com

NOURISHING THE WORLD THROUGH CHANGE

Have you ever felt real hunger? Sure, you may have skipped a meal or two, cut calories or embarked on a "clean eating" regime. But that's not the same as hunger.

Thankfully, many people don't know what real hunger feels like, the type that leads to malnutrition and, for some, starvation and even death. It's not an easy subject to talk about, in fact, it's downright harrowing to investigate deeply.

Our aim is that no one will ever endure, experience, or see the effects of hunger again. What a legacy to give the world.

Most of us have seen graphic media images depicting famine and drought, such as a gaunt mother with a sunken body desperate to feed her starving children. These images burn deep into our conscience and leave us asking — what can I do to help? How can this possibly be happening in our modern world?

Most feel too small to help such a massive global issue. But the good news is … the great news is … we can do something. We *are* doing something.

Even more reassuring is that businesses are at the fore of this change.

The following three changemakers are testament to this impact. They are living proof that business owners filled with humanitarian hearts are the future for change.

Leader and social entrepreneur Bill Drayton said "Social entrepreneurs are not content just to give a fish or teach how to fish. They will not rest until they have revolutionized the fishing industry."

Let's not rest until we have revolutionized world hunger. Aligning your business, community, family, and personal practices with this SDG goals means *you* become part of this revolution.

Some argue that merely giving food is a short-term hand-out and that perhaps educating people to create their own food resources is a more viable long-term solution. Making sure every person has access to nourishing food has many dimensions. For example, the UN identified that more than half of the people in need of food live in countries with ongoing violence. More than three-quarters of the world's severely malnourished children live in high-conflict regions infested with uncertainty and violence. Then, there's the added issues of droughts, floods, and farming instability. Climate change emerges as a major problem that influences all others and has been the catalyst for the sudden rise in recent years.

As changemaker Joshua Ngoma points out, world hunger is on the rise. It's challenging to face the raw statistics he shares. However, without the major shift he's advocating, climate change is anticipated to force more than 100 million people into extreme poverty by 2030. That is, unless we seek to actively revolutionize it.

The topic, like many, is multifaceted and deeply layered. But if we stay in touch with our basic humanity, we know that everyone has the right to clean, nourishing food. When deprived of this basic right, the vulnerable only become more vulnerable. The violence only increases, and social justice is no longer just. As changemaker Shane Black points out — currently, one in four children worldwide have stunted growth due to lack of nutritional food.

Bill Gates says, "When stunted children don't reach their potential, neither do their countries. Malnutrition saps a country's strength, lowering productivity and keeping the entire nation trapped in poverty." So, when we begin with the simple mechanics of nutrition and consider feeding one child, we begin to change the world.

The annual revenues of the four main food industries (fast food restaurants, fruit and vegetable processing, bakery good manufacturing, and candy and chocolate manufacturing) total more than 1.6 trillion dollars. That's not even including all the restaurants, cafes, and sectors of the agriculture industry.

A mere glance at the revenue within these industries reflects that we really do have the capacity to feed everyone in the world.

So, why isn't this happening? You see, a global problem requires global solutions. Not just looking after ourselves but looking after each other.

Like changemaker Chris Beks who shows us through his business practices that hunger is everyone's problem to solve, not just the hungry. Hunger of course isn't only about food but about the effects of climate change and resources. Since the 1900s, around 75% of crop diversity has been lost from farmers' fields. And while our crops have vanished so dramatically, on the other end of the spectrum the Natural Resources Defense Council tells us that in the U.S. alone more than 40% of food that can be safely consumed is wasted.

So, part of the solution isn't just about generating more food, but not wasting it, growing it nutritionally, and distributing it fairly, whole-heartedly.

Embedded throughout these chapters are powerful stories, examples, and simple tips that can help anyone join the change.

Changemaker Shane Black highlights something significant — the power food plays in our lives. Shane's story points out something simple but poignant: that a good home-cooked meal can be the ultimate act of love and feel like a refuge of safety. Food not only fills our stomachs, but also our hearts. We share it with family and friends and use it to celebrate, connect, and show affection.

Yet food isn't always a cause of joy and celebration; for many it presents a puzzling dichotomy. As Joshua tells us, nearly 1 billion people suffer from obesity while another billion suffer from malnutrition. This paradox depicts a major imbalance in society, one that reflects the global imbalance. That it's *not* the lack of food causing world hunger, it's the lack of consistent health and adequate nutrition for everyone.

We all know we can feed the entire planet. We know good nutrition is important. Let's make that a daily action. As the great astronaut Buzz Aldrin says, "If we can conquer space, we can conquer childhood hunger."

And we can.

These three changemakers are already leading the way to change. Join the movement today.

THE POWER OF UNITY AND COMMUNITY
JOSHUA CHIMAKULA NGOMA

I come from a developing country with a story to tell. Though I'm now a successful entrepreneur and have traveled the world, it wasn't always this way. I was born in a rural part of Chipata in the Eastern Province of Zambia. My father, Joshua, was an ex-soldier turned businessman, so we grew up very disciplined. He started his first business when I was just born; I saw him grow three successful businesses in a short span of time. For rural standards, we were considered rich. Like most rural women at the time, my mother, Elinala, had very little education but was a great mom. She took great care of the family while dad took care of the rest.

Dad was very generous and supported all his relatives and other members of the local community well, a trait that I'm glad I inherited. However, I was only seven years old when my father was murdered by people he knew and trusted. Some of my father's relatives, most of whom he supported when he was alive, came and took everything we owned – everything! Mom didn't fight them; instead she reminded us that what they were taking were only material possessions and that with the true wealth locked inside us we would be able to find our own things.

We became materially poor overnight. We left our establishment with nothing and went to live in Mom's village. She also reminded us that despite what my father's relatives had done to us, they were still our relatives and that we should still visit them and show them our love. So, we learned to go into the world without harboring hatred. At that very young age, I decided I was not going to depend on anyone else. I started my first business when I was eight years old; ironically, it was in agriculture, growing and selling vegetables.

What was interesting in Mom's village was that people cared more about each other. They shared most things. Though there weren't luxuries, everyone had access to basic needs such as food, clothing, and shelter. Even if you were an orphan, you never felt alone. There were always people to lend a helping hand. So, young people were taken care of by the elderly people, and old people were taken care of by the young. We played and ate together. If one parent cooked food, we stopped playing and would all go and eat together. I suppose, that's where the saying "it takes a village to raise a child" comes from. Despite having little, I had a very happy childhood, full of giving and sharing. We lived in a world of abundance, and this laid a great foundation for the type of person I am today.

While the people in the village might not have been materially rich, they were spiritually very rich. They understood what it meant to be human. Many times, we look at poverty from one dimension, one of material possessions, and in the process we fail to notice all the other dimensions. We see the world only from our own material perspective. I learned at an early age that to be rich is not about what you have in your bank account but what you have in your heart. And I have always tried to relive that happy early childhood experience throughout my life.

While I may have done well for me and my family, I still don't value material wealth as much as humanity. This is because, as one great man once correctly put it, "At the end of our lives, what will really matter will not be what we bought, but what we built; not what we got, but what we shared; not our competence, but our character; and not our success, but our significance."

So, we need to live a life that matters; a life of love; a life of significance. I believe that together, we can create a life of significance and leave a legacy. And, furthermore, we can do this right now.

The SDG of Zero Hunger, which we in Enterprising Africa Regional Network (Pty) Limited (EARN) are focusing on, is truly a valuable legacy to begin with because it is a basic need for every human being.

I'm a mining engineer by profession, and people have asked me why a mining professional is more interested in agriculture. Well, if we are to help a lot of people, this is the sector to focus on for two main reasons. First, agriculture is the main source of income for rural areas in many African countries, as is the case in many other parts of the developing world. According to a recent World Bank report, farming alone currently accounts for about 60% of total employment in sub-Saharan Africa, while the share of jobs across the general food industry is potentially much larger. Secondly, we need to produce and distribute food efficiently to feed a growing population, which is projected to reach 8.5 billion by 2030, and 9.7 billion people by 2050. So, food production must be increased by up to 60% to feed every mouth. Unfortunately, according to a recent UN report, the number of hungry people in the world is also growing, reaching 821 million in 2017, or one in every nine people.

On the other side of hunger, the number of people suffering from micronutrient deficiencies is worse, currently standing at 2 billion people. Therefore, feeding the growing world population with good, healthy, and nutritious food is the daunting challenge we should all aim to meet.

However, the problem is that while the global population is going up, the overall expertise, agri-business interest, and dedicated and knowledgeable agri-entrepreneurs are diminishing rapidly. This is because agriculture is seen as old fashioned and difficult and is thus unattractive to young people. Even traditional farmers' children, like most other young people, have sought to go into other professions rather than taking over their parents' farming operations. As a result, the traditional practice where knowledge and expertise were passed from generation to generation is no longer the case.

At EARN we're looking at ways to make agri-business an attractive and viable alternative to young people. We do this in two ways:

1. Firstly, since young people love technology, we aim to introduce them to modern practices of farming that have a strong technology component; and,
2. Secondly, we have developed a novel and holistic approach to developing them into successful agri-entrepreneurs.

For the past four years, through our agriculture subsidiary African Greeneurs (AG), my team and I have been working on an effective development model. We aim to develop young men and women into successful agri-entrepreneurs through our modern agriculture training facilities.

Through a mix of practical business and technical agriculture skills training and a coordinated delivery of a customized and comprehensive range of business support services, we aim to develop a cadre of indigenous agri-entrepreneurs that will be able to establish successful and growth-oriented agri-enterprises.

Once the AG model is refined and perfected, the aim is to apply it across other geographic areas in Africa, and other parts of the world. The model is aimed at contributing toward global food security and job creation as well as the eradication of poverty and inequalities, thereby achieving the socio-economic benefits the world needs to move forward. It's a big endeavor, but one I am certain can transform people's lives.

Make the Wellbeing of Ordinary People the Centre of Your Business

Contributing to "Zero Hunger" is not just about the production of food but also the way we use this important resource. While there is an increasing number of people that go to bed without food, there is also so much food waste. A report from the Food and Agriculture Organization of the United Nations said that roughly one-third of the food produced in the world for human consumption every year gets wasted. That's approximately 1.3 billion tons. We need to raise awareness among all of finding beneficial use for food that is presently thrown away. We need to find creative ways of channeling the wasted food to those in need. We need to find innovative ways of fighting world hunger from various fronts. By working together selflessly, we can eliminate world hunger.

One thing I have learned in my many years in business is that you don't have to wait until you have made it big in your business to make a difference. You can start straight away as your business grows. If people truly want to experience a "Better Business, Better Life, Better World," I would suggest to put the wellbeing of ordinary people at the center of their business. This is the key. That's what living in a world of abundance is all about. It is not the size of the contribution that matters, but the habit, the consistency, and the spirit with which you give. By making it a habit — to consistently make small contributions toward causes you believe in — over time your contribution grows as big as any major business that gives a large contribution only once in a while.

My early childhood experience in the village showed me this firsthand. It also reminds me of a beautiful TEDx talk I watched. Spiritual guru Radhanathi Swami shared a memorable story with the audience, a story about the secret of the redwood forest. Swami and his colleague had joined a tourist group in a forest near San Francisco in the U.S. when the park ranger shared this story.

The sequoias and redwoods are the largest trees on the planet. Some of them are said to be hundreds or even thousands of years old. While the roots of these trees don't grow too deep, they have been standing for centuries and centuries, enduring raging fires, massive windstorms, frigid blizzards, and devastating earthquakes. And without deep roots one would not have expected them to have stood for all the years of these severe environmental conditions, but they have. The secret is said to be underground, in their roots. When these trees are growing, the roots of one redwood tree reaches under the ground, seeking the roots of other redwoods. And when they meet, they intertwine, making a permanent bond with each other. In this way, all the redwood trees in the entire forest are either directly or indirectly giving support to each other. Unity is their strength. They reach out to care for each other. And even little newborn baby redwoods, with their tiny roots, are given shelter by the ancient giants. In his conclusion, Radhanathi Swami advises that in these Muir woods, nature is giving humanity a very crucial lesson: that our real strength is in our willingness to care for and support each other. Whatever wealth we have is not ours. We are caretakers of divine property. Wisdom is in the understanding of this simple universal principle — that in giving we receive. By getting things we make a living, but by giving we make a life. He ends by noting that "the spiritual evolution of society can be understood when people love people and use things. But too often, in today's world, it's just the opposite; people use people and they love things." This should be food for thought!

This story also parallels my ultimate legacy, which is to contribute toward an equal society where everyone is able to afford the basic necessities and experience a good livelihood and happiness.

YOU ARE THE ULTIMATE VEHICLE FOR IMPACT
SHANE BLACK

"Finish your dinner." I remember hearing this almost every night growing up in Australia. My mother was a typical Aussie mom. Dinner would consist of meat and three types of vegetables, or as we say in Australia — meat and three veg. To my mom, making sure that her family was well fed was a high priority, and because of this, I never went hungry growing up … which might explain why I'm 190 cm tall and 110 kg+.

I grew up in a small town named Dunedoo, with a total population of 850. Dunedoo is in New South Wales, Australia and is over an hour from any major town.

Growing up in this sleepy country town meant that I wasn't really exposed to the effects that hunger had on so many people around the world. For me, there was always food on the table, and, while we struggled from time to time, we never went without. My mother, on the other hand, grew up in a family where she was often hungry. She grew up in post-World War II, so she had known hunger in her youth. I remember her telling me when I was young that she never wanted me to experience the hunger that she did when she was growing up.

My mother worked incredibly hard to make sure that there was always food on the table. My father had passed away when I was very young, and we had lost our family home, so the odds were stacked against her. She had no formal qualifications, and for most of her life, she was a stay-at-home mom. When my father passed, she had to work two jobs to make ends meet. It wasn't until years later that I realized that it was the fear of hunger that drove her to work so hard. She didn't want me to go hungry, like she had. It was around this time that I started to understand the effect that hunger can have on people.

It wasn't until my first overseas trip that I saw what real hunger looked like. I traveled to the U.S., and, while it's obviously a developed nation, there were still people living it rough on the streets. In 2010, I traveled to South Africa. The trip was planned around the FIFA World Cup, but my friends and I made sure that we traveled off the beaten track to really experience Africa.

The "low-fuel" warning light on our car wasn't just flashing … it had been flashing red for half an hour. The needle on the fuel gauge had fallen off and was pointing in a rather concerning downward angle.

My friends and I were driving through rural South Africa after having decided to "push on" until we reached the next town. We were driving from Durben to Cape Town, and we had inadequately planned for the trip. We got our hands on some maps, but they didn't really state which roads were sealed, drivable roads and which ones weren't.

It was late afternoon, and we realized that we needed to find fuel soon, otherwise we'd be involuntarily sleeping in the car for the evening. Just as we thought the car was surely about to stop we noticed a town on the horizon. It wasn't exactly on the map, and as we drove in, we could tell that this was an area referred to in South Africa as a "township." We were warned about townships — that they were dangerous and no place for three Aussies and their surfboards — but there was no choice. We could either stop here and find fuel, or we could run out of fuel just up the road and be forced to brave a night in the African wilderness.

We turned off the main road, and immediately the road became nothing more than a roughly sealed track. I was worried about the hire car, and the security bond that we had left on it!

We pulled up to a bus stop and immediately drew a lot of attention. Three Australians — surfboards, thongs. and board-shorts, in a car at least 20 years younger than any other vehicle around.

We asked a man seated on the curb whether he knew where we could get some fuel. Immediately, he jumped up and ran into the crowd, returning a few minutes later with milk bottles filled with petrol. He syphoned the fuel out of the bottles and into our car. I couldn't help but think … here was a man that was obviously living a harder life than I could ever imagine, and yet here I was, completely relying on him to be able to help us.

This simple encounter taught me a few deeper things:

- You don't need to be rich or famous to make a positive impact on someone's life.
- You don't need anything fancy to get started; just start where you are and do what you can.
- An action that may feel small to you can have a gigantic impact on someone else.

At that time, I was still in the NSW Police Force, and, while helping people was in my job description, I knew I needed to do more.

Africa was the first time that I really understood the importance of ending global hunger. Particularly in Zimbabwe, I saw that hyper-inflation had decimated their currency, leaving it valueless, meaning some of the people there took to selling their currency in exchange for U.S. dollars so that they could buy food.

I began to understand that so much of a person's wellbeing originates from proper nutrition. If people are well nourished, they can take care of their family and contribute to the wider community, not only lifting themselves up, but others, too.

I am fortunate enough to have never experienced serious hunger … but I know that not everyone in the world is that fortunate. My wife, Hong, was born in Australia, however her parents had immigrated from Vietnam. Hong has family in Vietnam, and we have visited on a few occasions. I remember that the first time we went to Vietnam, I was introduced to one of her cousins. Her cousin looked just like Hong, except she was at least 15 kg lighter. It struck me that this difference was probably caused by lack of nutrition. This prompted me to turn my thoughts to my son, William. Throughout his first year of life, he has been off the growth scale … would this have been possible if he was born in a country where hunger and malnutrition were more widespread? How many children aren't growing to their full potential due to hunger?

According to the UN, a quarter of the world's children suffer from stunted growth. In some developing countries, it's as high as one in three. And furthermore, Asia is the continent with the most hungry people, counting for two-thirds of the total.

To think that there are people, children, who, through no fault of their own, suffer from unnecessary hunger, which impacts the quality of their life. This drives me. And one avenue to help make a change is through business.

Business as a Vehicle for Impact

Business is a vehicle for creating an impact. It is completely up to the business owner as to the magnitude of the impact that the business can provide. When I describe a business that matters, I think of it impacting three groups of people: *Me — Us — Them.*

Firstly, a business must take care of the business owner and his/her immediate family. If the business owner and family aren't looked after, how can they expect to make an impact on others? This is the "Me" part of the above. Put on your oxygen mask first.

Next, a business that matters begins to make an impact on those around the community. Once the business owner is taken care of, they can begin to turn their attention to improving their community, associates, clients and customers. This is the "Us" part.

Finally, a business that really matters makes an impact on people that they are never likely to meet. The impact generated by the business radiates out from the owner, through the community, and into worthy causes that help make the world a better place. This is the "Them" part.

In my business, we align everything we do for our staff and clients with a worthy cause that sits close to their heart. For example, we have staff in India, and I provided them a list of worthy projects and asked them to let me know which one resonated with them and to explain why. I wasn't surprised when they identified some very worthy causes in India to support.

My businesses are still young; however, I always wanted to make a positive contribution through my business regardless of its maturity or size. The first initiative I launched was informing every client that I would donate to a charity of their choice on their behalf. This initiative started strong, with some clients electing to help orangutans while others looked to feed families in South East Asia. It wasn't long before some cracks started to appear in this program, though.

Even though we were asking every single new client, often they would say they needed to think about it and never got back to us. We would be chasing them down, and it was becoming difficult for my business to make the impact I wanted.

It wasn't until I came across B1G1 in 2017 that I found a way for my business to make the impact I desired. In less than a year, we have made over 100,000 positive impacts on people around the world. A particular highlight for me is providing over one hundred years' access to clean drinking water to families in Cambodia. One hundred years! That feels good. I am now planning a campaign where we will be contributing one day's worth of support to a worthy cause for every dollar my team is able to save our clients, whether it's on their home loans, investments, and/or insurances.

I believe that every dollar saved makes a small impact on the lives of my clients and their families and that these small impacts, compounded over time, have huge results.

Make a Life While Earning a Living

At the time of writing this, my son, William, is sleeping next to me, snoring. He obviously takes after me. He is thirteen months old and has his whole life ahead of him. My ultimate legacy is to instill in him the values and beliefs that will lead him to continue to make our world a better place. This is for all of us. While we can make a significant impact in our own lifetimes, the real impact we create is when we empower the next generation to also make an impact and accelerate the positive changes the world needs.

I want to know that this planet is a slightly better place simply by me being here. I want my children, and their children, to experience an amazing world full of opportunity and absence from hunger. I would love to see people live a financially fulfilling life. My father passed away when I was less than one year old, and, while I cannot remember him at all, it taught me never to take anything in this life for granted. I remember my mom struggling at times while I grew up, and if I can help others avoid these struggles, then I will see that as success.

We all need to remember to make a life while earning a living.

THE CALLING IN YOUR HEART TO HELP
CHRIS BEKS

Five years after the ravages of World War II and the devastation left behind by Nazi Germany on their homeland, three young Dutchmen boarded a KLM flight with just carry-on luggage and a one-way airfare to Australia, a trip that took five days.

They were under strict instruction from their father to check out the country and if possible to find work and a base from which to come and go. If they thought that the country was suitable, they were to send word for the rest of the family of five siblings and their parents to join them.

The third youngest was my father, who had not traveled more than 25 kilometers from home nor spoke any English.

As most of their fellow passengers were heading to the migrant camp in Bathurst, New South Wales, they had no plan of action but would at least get a bed for the night. Conditions there were very challenging — wooden benches and thin blankets constituted as bedding, and with a surplus labor pool, employment prospects were limited. These conditions forced them to pool together the last of their money and buy three train tickets to Melbourne to locate Father Maas, a Dutch priest who ran a hostel in Kew.

They had enough change to scrape together the tram fare from the Spencer Street station and then relied on their survival instincts to find somewhere to stay and scrounge a meal.

Father Maas looked on their letter of introduction favorably and provided them with a room and meal in return for washing the dishes and other odd jobs.

This kind gesture from a stranger who recognized their plight and the desperation on their faces reminded me of the Christian parable of Jesus feeding the masses with just five loaves of bread and two fish, and this inspired me to help with the Zero Hunger SDG goal.

I grew up in a one-income household of seven kids. My late father earned about $18,000 from his retail assistant's job, and my late mother was a homemaker who operated on a shoe-string budget and could make the finances stretch beyond imagination.

I saw firsthand how hard they worked and struggled to make ends meet and to provide us with a great family life, education, and opportunities that they never had. Having a regular meal was something we never took for granted, and we always had empty plates after meal times — nothing was left nor wasted. If we didn't eat what was served, one of my siblings would be happy to oblige, and there would be nothing until the morning at breakfast time.

Even when we had our friends over, relatives visited, or neighbors dropped in, I don't know how, but my mother would always be able to create something amazing to share with them.

At school, I witnessed a documentary about the famine in Africa and how many people, especially the kids, were dying from malnutrition and hunger. The sight of starving Biafrans' wide-eyed, frail living skeletons with extended bulging stomachs was forever burnt into my mind.

In 1990, when I first started our business, we joined World Vision Australia as a child sponsor with the sole purpose of helping a child receive proper food and nutrition — and I have been an active sponsor ever since. I know that Zero Hunger is an achievable goal for our modern world.

I was inspired to play a part to ensure that excess food can be repurposed and distributed to those in need in our local community with Warrnambool and District Food ("Food Share"). In 2015, a call for volunteers went out, and a "workforce" to operate was made. After discussions with our team we decided we wanted to play a role and allocated two hours per week on a Wednesday morning between 8:30 and 10:30 a.m. to help out.

In 2017, 143,000 kg or the equivalent of $1,000,000[1] in food were provided to those less fortunate in our local community alone. Our small team of five, dubbed "The Fantastic Five" by Food Share CEO Dedy Friebe, are still passionate about the small role and impact

---

1   Food Bank places a cost of $7.00 per kg on repurposed food.

we make and look forward to our turn on the roster.

This Sustainable Development Goal is of high importance to me because of my parents' early struggles to provide a regular meal for us and my early school education about the crucial work of World Vision in Biafra to help solve that crisis.

Become a Business That Matters

Every business has the power to IMPACT, to change lives and lifestyles, and that's why we make it part of our culture and embed it in everything we do — to become a business that matters. A business that matters contributes not just profits.

It's important to make this part of your everyday business practices. Simply by choosing to work with us means that our customers know they will be contributing to this growing movement of changing the world. It's a powerful way to see business. For example, for every new customer or service we provide to our existing customers, we contribute a fixed percentage of the income generated to the global giving initiative, B1G1. This allows our business and clients to contribute to services and charitable projects around the world. Even though we are only a small team of four, we are still able to make small but powerful impacts all over the world.

We are also passionate about supporting national programs and are active members and/or supporters of other Australian-based charitable, social organizations and networks, such as World Vision Australia, who we have been a sponsor of for over twenty-nine years. Despite these global changes, we also know local change is global change. The two hours each week one of our team spends at our local community District Food Share, sorting food collected from supermarkets and local farmers, stocking shelves, packing hampers, and assisting collectors is a valuable hands-on contribution. It's a simple but meaningful way small businesses can make big impacts. Giving time can be just as valuable as donating money.

Being a "Better Business" stands for more than itself and its owners — it stands for change and taking a position, making the decision to make the world a better place for the next generation. Governments have struggled over decades to find a way to deal with world issues, such as clean water deficiencies, hunger, sanitation, etc. "Better Business" takes on this social responsibility and can make significant in-roads into these problem areas where governments have failed to find solutions.

Being a "Better Business" starts with some real soul-searching and discovering. It's important to begin with the deep questions. Why does this business exist? What's its true calling? What's its higher purpose or reason for operating, far beyond the product or service it sells?

Once the business's "Why" has been developed and clarified, it's then ingrained into the business culture (the way people do things), and it becomes a standard that everyone on the team works toward and aspires to achieve.

People are drawn to those that are confident, positive, and working for a higher purpose or cause, and this is why a "Better Business" leads to a "Better Life" — including for those connected by this movement; this movement will create change and build a lasting impact for a "Better World."

WHAT YOU CAN DO TO
CREATE A WORLD WITH ZERO HUNGER

Lifestyle tips:
- Keep your leftovers for another meal.
- Buy only what you need. Enjoy simple and nourishing food.
- Buy "ugly" or irregularly shaped fruits and vegetables.

Business tips:
- Know your value chain. Partner with local producers and farmers.
- Explore creative ways to reduce or donate your wastage.
- Partner with your local FoodBank.
- Provide paid volunteer days.

Giving tips:
- Support programs that "rescue" leftover food.
- Donate to support school lunch programs.
- Clean out your pantry and donate the surplus food.

BUILDING THE FOUNDATION FOR HAPPY LIVING

3 GOOD HEALTH AND WELL-BEING

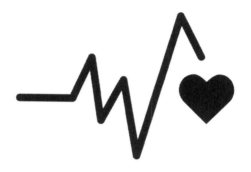

HOW YOU AND YOUR BUSINESS CAN ENSURE HEALTHY LIVES AND PROMOTE WELL-BEING FOR ALL AT ALL AGES.

> *"It is health that is real wealth and not pieces of gold and silver."*
>
> — Mahatma Gandhi

THE CHANGEMAKERS

WHEN YOUR "WHY" CHANGES, EVERYTHING CHANGES
KARINA GRASSY

Karina Grassy became a company director at age twenty-two. She went on to work for several corporations, including HIT Group and Starbucks Coffee. Following the birth of her daughter in 2008, Karina saw a gap in the baby market. Karina's love of Slumbersac products led her to become a successful distributor for Slumbersac in Germany. In 2012, Karina bought the business and has successfully increased sales from £500,000 to £7 million in just seven years. She holds an MBA in international retailing from Stirling University in Scotland.

slumbercompany.com

WELLNESS IS POWER
LOUISA LEE

Louisa Lee is an entrepreneur and educator. Her core business is DP Dental, a progressive dental practice regarded by many around the world as a leading-edge example of digital integrative dentistry. She is also the director of Progressive Practice, which provides high-quality education and consultancy services. She sits on the advisory board of the Imagine Cambodia Foundation and Connected Women and was recently co-opted as a council member of the Association of Small and Medium Enterprises (ASME) in Singapore.

dpdental.com.sg

A HEALTHY SPIRIT REDEFINED
BERNADETTE SARGINSON

Bernadette Sarginson is a former lawyer turned empowerment coach and mentor. She has coached hundreds of individuals and groups through self-awareness, personal development, and long-term change. She is the creator of the Spirit Level Success™ System — Six Secrets of Self-Esteem — gentle transformation for women and men with high success on the outside and low spirit on the inside. Bernadette is the author of *Climb Your S.T.A.I.R. ™ of Self-Confidence.*

spiritlevelsuccess.com

BUILDING THE FOUNDATION FOR HAPPY LIVING

Let's begin with a number: $70,000,000,000.

That's the amount Americans alone spent on diets, gym memberships and 'good health' in 2018.

And little wonder. We are bombarded with new diet trends, fanatical exercise options and droves of supplements, shakes, juice and detoxes. Health has never been so full of marketing hype.

Yet, in spite of that, statistics prove that two-thirds of Americans are still overweight. And it's not only a US-based issue.

But weight is not the only health issue. Health includes many factors.

So, let's define it. The World Health Organization tells us: *Health is a state of complete physical, mental and social well-being, and not merely the absence of disease or infirmity.*

Given this holistic definition, we can now look at ways we can make health accessible to all. Here are some health goals we might aim to achieve:

- Significantly reduce the number of preventable deaths of newborns and children under 5 years of age.
- End the epidemics of AIDS, tuberculosis, malaria and neglected tropical diseases and combat hepatitis, water-borne diseases and other communicable diseases.
- Strengthen the prevention and treatment of substance abuse, including narcotic drug abuse and harmful use of alcohol.
- Halve the number of global deaths and injuries from road traffic accidents.
- Ensure universal access to sexual and reproductive health-care services, including family planning, information and education, and the integration of reproductive health into national strategies and programs.
- Achieve universal health coverage, including financial risk protection, access to quality essential health-care services and access to safe, effective, quality and affordable essential

medicines and vaccines for all.

- Substantially reduce the number of deaths and illnesses from hazardous chemicals and air, water and soil pollution and contamination.
- Increase health financing and the recruitment, development, training and retention of the health workforce in developing countries.

We see in this list that what constitutes as "health" for one may be poles apart to what it means to another.

In Africa, for example, adolescent girls and young women face huge gender-based inequalities, including exclusion, discrimination and sexual and physical violence. This puts them at a huge risk of acquiring HIV. For them, health is survival; not being raped and infected. Sadly, AIDS is now the leading cause of death among adolescents (aged 10–19) in Africa and the second most common cause of death among adolescents globally.

For a teenage girl elsewhere, health may mean something different — mental health for example — understanding the pressures that consume her and result in her body image issues and depression. It may mean helping her understand that mental health and social well-being are essential to discuss and get help with.

Health means a lot. In fact, it means everything. As Gandhi said, "It is health that is real wealth and not pieces of gold and silver."

These next three changemakers weave a colorful tapestry of how our health goals can be seen, met and achieved in different ways, not only through our personal endeavors but through education, giving and business.

Louisa Lee seeks to revolutionalize the health and education systems. She sees clearly how they go hand-in-hand in improving all the Global Goals and how they can be improved through some simple and easy strategies. Louisa shares some fresh new insights and gives us tangible and practical guidance on making health an everyday experience.

Bernadette Sarginson provides us with a different yet equally great approach. She points us inward and helps us consider our own self-esteem and confidence in a healthy way. She invites us to bring our spirit into everything we do and believe in our innate skills and endeavors. She encourages us to truly know we are enough.

And Karina Grassy brings us full circle. Back to where it all began. Back to newborns. Back to the importance of getting it right from the beginning. Back to love, care, support and giving much needed health services to our vulnerable children and mothers. Her personal story along with the information and statistics she offers will inspire you to see good health in new and promising ways. As you read, you'll feel full of hope that you too can be the difference.

Because inevitably, health gives us so much. It gives us the chance to work, to play, to give, to create, to build and to share. It gives us the chance to do and become whatever our heart desires. As the Arabian proverb says, "He (or she) who has health has hope; and he (or she) who has hope has everything."

Good health gives us the chance to change the world.

WHEN YOUR "WHY" CHANGES, EVERYTHING CHANGES
KARINA GRASSY

The importance of SDG 3 became very clear to me when I became a mom ten years ago. I had a difficult pregnancy, and the support and care I received from the NHS in the United Kingdom was outstanding. Without it, I might have lost my child. I was so grateful to live in a country where my child and I could be saved.

Although the maternal mortality rate has declined by 37% since 2000, many mothers living in developing countries still do not receive the care and support they need to enjoy a healthy pregnancy and safe birth. In 2015, 303,000 women around the world still died due to complications during pregnancy or childbirth.[1] Lucky for me, my daughter was born healthy and she thrived.

Significant progress has been made when it comes to child mortality. In 1800, the health conditions of our ancestors were such that 43% of the world's newborns died before their fifth birthday. In 1960, the child mortality remained at 18.5%.

Given the decreasing poverty levels and the increasing knowledge and services available in the health sector, child mortality is declining rapidly: global child mortality fell from 18.2% in 1960 to 4.3% in 2015; while 4.3% is still too high, this is a substantial achievement. In 1970, Malawi, Afghanistan, and Yemen still suffered from infant mortality rates over 20%. Today no country experiences infant mortality rates higher than 10%.[2]

As one would expect, a country's income level correlates heavily with child mortality rates. The poorest countries have the highest levels of child mortality, and the countries with the highest incomes have the lowest rates. As a mom, and dealing with many moms on a daily basis (my employees and customers at Slumbersac), SDG 3 is very close to my heart.

---

1   World Poverty Statistics: Global Poverty Report 2018, The World Bank.
2   World Bank Group and UNICEF

Reproductive, maternal, newborn, and child health are all part of SDG 3, "Good Health and Well-Being," and align with Slumbersac's company ethos. At Slumbersac, we believe that a good night's sleep is essential to happiness and well-being. We create products that serve a vital purpose in the safety and development of a growing child. Our products are designed to make every moment special while promoting peaceful sleep for babies and parents alike. Baby sleeping bags help babies maintain a constant temperature during their sleep, which results in better, undisturbed rest. The use of the correct baby sleeping bag can avoid overheating, which is one of the main factors of sudden infant death syndrome (SIDS).

When I became a mom, I experienced first-hand how the lack of sleep can negatively affect parents. During the first few months after giving birth to my daughter Katie, I became emotional and short-tempered, and lost weight due to sleep loss. This may have been one of the primary factors contributing to the breakdown of my relationship, which saw me become a single mom when my daughter was only nine months old.

The Turning Points in Business

When you start out in business, it is important to know the *what*, *why*, and *how*, even if you do not think about these when you begin. I started my business in 2010, and I didn't have a mission statement or a vision of where I wanted to go. I launched my business because I was a single mom who rarely saw her daughter due to my long commute and long hours working in London. It was a turning point for me when my daughter started calling my au pair "Mama." I knew I had to change something if I wanted to be part of my daughter's life — this was my *why*.

The *what* came to me when other mothers began commenting on my daughter's booties, which I had purchased in Germany. I started importing them to the United Kingdom. This led me to research whether there was a market for baby sleeping bags in Germany — which it turned out there was. I contacted the owner of Slumbersac, the baby sleeping bag brand, and asked if I could become their distributor in Germany. The rest is history, which brings us to the *how*.

I bought the Slumbersac brand in 2012 and have sold baby sleeping bags and sleep-related products online ever since. From being a one-mom operation, I grew my team to thirty, with many more freelancers working in countries such as Australia, Ireland, Italy, Japan, Spain, and the United States. Most of my team are women and almost all are mothers. We offer flexible hours and a home office. It is extremely important to me that we work with factories that share our values and produce our products in an ecological and sustainable way. We regularly check the working conditions of our factories, which mainly employ women and mothers and pay fair wages so the employees can support their families.

The *what* and *how* haven't changed much, but the *why* has.

When I met Paul Dunn at a conference in 2016, my business had grown from £500,000 to £4 million in just four years, but I didn't know where to go next, or why I should continue to grow the company. I was even contemplating selling the business.

I went to my first B1G1 conference in Bali in 2016 and on my first tour of Cambodia in 2017. Both had a major impact on me. It became clear that running and growing a successful business is much more fun when you do more than pay wages and deliver a great product to customers. Being able to support so many children and their families in poverty-stricken countries has given me a massive boost in confidence and happiness. Doing so makes our growth worthwhile, and connects our customers with other moms that struggle on a daily basis to keep their children fed, healthy, and safe. Slumbersac is a brand that creates products made by moms, for moms — and now supports moms coping with difficult circumstances. We were exceedingly proud to win the Business Excellence Award for Best Online Business in 2016 and 2018.

A Business Does More than Sell

My marketing director, Elke Kramer, and I took part in the B1G1 Study Tour to Kenya in 2018. We spent two days in the village of Odede, home to Mama Ann's Community Health Centre, which is sponsored by World Youth International.

The Centre aims to provide the village and surrounding areas with much-needed quality health care, serving an estimated population of twenty thousand, the third-largest tribe in Kenya. The Odede

Community Health Centre treats up to two hundred patients a day. In addition to basic treatment and consultations, the Centre offers laboratory testing for malaria, typhoid, and pregnancy. It also has a pharmacy that provides vaccinations to babies and children. The Centre has reduced the number of malaria cases by distributing mosquito nets to the community. Expectant mothers can also deliver their babies there instead of at home, which has decreased the mortality rate of moms and children tenfold. When we visited a hospital, we were fortunate to meet a new mom and her baby, who was born there the day before.

Odede is one of the most impoverished districts in Kenya and suffers from one of the highest rates of HIV/AIDS in the country. HIV tests are mandatory at the Centre; they conduct the tests there and then, offer results within fifteen minutes. If positive, the patient receives counseling and medication. If HIV-positive expectant mothers are identified early enough, it is possible for the baby to be HIV-negative when born.

The second charity we visited in Kenya was So They Can. We went to one of the largest slums, Rhonda, an informal settlement in Nakuru with mud-thatched houses squeezed close together. Most residents are extremely poor due to lack of employment, inferior infrastructure, and sanitation. So They Can began supporting its primary school last year. The school has twelve hundred students and twenty-four teachers. Many students suffer from malnutrition, as their parents are unable to afford food due to the high level of unemployment. It was sad and humbling to see these poverty-stricken families. The clothes they were wearing were muddy and torn, and many suffered from illness. It was an extraordinarily emotional day.

We played with the children, who were so happy to see us and thanked us for our help and support. We were surrounded by at least thirty children, who wanted to play and hold our hands. They didn't want us to leave and neither did we!

We visited another school, with eight hundred students, located in the slums near a rubbish site. The school has a special facility for blind students, who also live there. It was shocking to hear that only 10% of parents could afford school lunches for their children.

The rest don't get a meal at school and search the rubbish dump every day, trying to find something to eat.

Another heart-wrenching moment was when we saw the big sign at the school gates advising children what to do when they are raped, *not if*. Being moms ourselves, Elke and I felt quite somber reading this and seeing the poverty amongst the children. However, it provided even more reason for us to do well at Slumbersac in order to support such causes on a regular basis. While we can't prevent bad things from happening to these children, we can play a small role in improving their future.

To me this is the greatest thing a business can do — change lives. I encourage anyone wanting to go into business to:

- Run your business with an end goal in mind.
- Be content with your achievements and share them with your family and employees.
- Make the world a better place by supporting those less fortunate.

Through B1G1, we were introduced to ChildAid, a charity that supports poor people in eastern Europe. The demise of the Soviet Union brought economic crisis and resulting instability to the region, and many children became vulnerable due to broken homes and extreme poverty, their parents' unemployment, alcoholism, and/or lack of care, or their own special educational needs. We have sent nearly three thousand sleeping bags to Moldova, and in response Director Martin Wilcox recently sent us this heart-warming message, "The families living in Transnistria fight for survival every day — the warmth that you have brought can literally keep families together rather than having to give their babies to the State as they cannot keep them warm enough! Thank you for such amazing generosity."

This is why we do business.

WELLNESS IS POWER
LOUISA LEE

Good health is a fundamental need for everyone, yet the current healthcare system is more a "sick-care" system in deep need of a (r)evolutionary change. We need to move away from treating only the symptoms and move toward fixing the root causes of these symptoms. This requires an integrated and holistic approach.

I think of this SDG goal as a call, not only to those in so-called developing countries, but to everyone. Modern inventions compromise the health of people living in the "developed" world too. Many suffer from chronic issues resulting from poor daily habits. It is important to recognize that the target of this goal is to ensure healthy lives and promote well-being for all of us, at all ages. In my opinion, we need to focus on seven fundamental elements — air, water, food, light, movement, sleep, and love.

The challenges of Goal 3 are so enormous that it's possible to miss the important details — the "sub-headings," if you will. We see three of those sub-headings as critically important.

Help Babies Thrive —Target 3.2
By 2030, end preventable deaths of newborns and children under five years of age, with all countries aiming to reduce neonatal mortality to at least as low as twelve per thousand live births, and under-five mortality to at least as low as twenty-five per thousand live births.

This is a massive target. And it needs new insights to get to the core.

In 2017, my husband, Dr. Yue Weng Cheu, delivered a TEDx talk focused on the impact of something practitioners in the field often ignore — the tongue. He titled the talk, "Wellness through the Power of the Tongue."

He pointed out that the tongue is one of the most underrated muscular organs in the body. It's often thought to be used only for speech and eating, but what is often missed is how it affects the delivery of air to our bodies. The tongue has a massive impact on sleep if it is physically restricted from being placed at its proper resting position against the roof of one's mouth, or if it is in a low position due to poor oral habits.

In our practice, we have come to realize that we cannot help a person get to a point of wellness if we only look at one specific area of the body and ignore the rest. When we ask deeper questions, we often arrive at the root cause of the problem, which may in fact reside somewhere else. When this happens, we need to work hard at increasing our own knowledge and understanding, and interact closely with other healthcare professionals who are experts in their fields. This is one key area in which we need to drive change in the current healthcare system — to require either expert-generalists or a team of specialists and expert providers to all look at the person as a whole and examine the issue from various angles. In order to achieve SDG 3, "Good Health and Well-Being," this must occur in "developed" countries; boutique practices like ours are already heading in this direction.

Reduce Substance Abuse — Target 3.5
Strengthen the prevention and treatment of substance abuse, including narcotic drug abuse and harmful use of alcohol.

There's so much talk now about the opioid epidemic. In April 2019, James Carroll, founder and CEO of THOR Photomedicine, briefed Congress and the White House on Photobiomodulation (PBM) Therapy as a possible solution.

Lasers have been around for more than forty years, yet the adoption rate has been relatively slow. We are slowly making headway and have developed a deep understanding of what light therapy can do, especially in the area of pain management.

In our practice, we are early adopters of technology and have used lasers and CAD/CAM for more than ten years, motivated by the efficiency and extra comfort they can yield to our patients. Technology is certainly able to disrupt healthcare. PBM is an example of how light therapy can replace drugs that have costly side effects. So why are institutions not widely adopting them? First, these go against the economic interest of existing solution providers, which is why I have come to the realization that all SDGs are linked.

The current state of poverty and hunger around the world is the result of uneven distribution. For change to take place, we need an enlightened group of leaders who are not afraid to show the way through their actions. DP Dental's partnership with B1G1 is one such example of how we commit to driving that change through our actions.

Halve the Road Toll — Target 3.6

By 2020, halve the number of global deaths and injuries from road traffic accidents.

Driving while sleep deprived can have a similar effect on the body as driving while under the influence of alcohol. What can cause a person to be sleep deprived? We must pay attention not only to the quantity of one's sleep, but also to its quality. Airway obstructions can lead to the disruption of deep sleep and affect overall health.

It is essential that we begin to solve problems at the root cause; we have realized that airway obstruction due to the tongue not being placed against the roof of the mouth is a major root cause of many related health problems, especially those affecting sleep. In paying attention to how we breathe, we are setting ourselves up for a better sense of well-being.

Living in Congruence

One of the most memorable trips I've taken was when I was a teacher. We brought a group of sixteen and seventeen-year-old students to Chiang Mai, Thailand, for a community involvement project. We were attached to the indigenous White Karen hill tribe who resided in the mountains.

We were there to help repaint their school, yet we came away with more than we sought to give. We received the gift of knowledge, the realization that people can have so little and possess such contentment and happiness. We realized that when we seek to give, we end up receiving so much more. This insight is valuable in our modern and often superficial culture.

In a world where fake news is becoming harder and harder to discern, and a perfect Instagram photo omits ugliness, we are increasingly questioning the authenticity of what we see. Trust from others will be harder and harder to achieve.

Yet, when we lead a congruent life, others are much more likely to place their trust in us. The more consistent and aligned we are in all aspects of our lives, the more we gain the trust of others. Often these values are neglected, as people feel the need to put on a certain mask in a certain situation. They just don't realize how tiring that is.

Simplify your life by following one set of rules that applies to everyone in your life — your family, your friends, your colleagues, your clients — and you will notice you are much more at ease and unburdened. You can then channel your energy into things that truly matter and make a great impact in the world. This applies in business as well.

To us, it's very simple: A business should never be set up solely for the purpose of reaping profits. Such a business is one without soul. On the other hand, when a business has a mission that is greater than itself, incredible things happen.

I recently took part in a panel discussion featuring women across all generations. One of the questions posed to us was, "What do you wake up for in the morning?" For me, it's the legacy I would like to leave behind for my children, and all the children in the world.

I am fully aware we all only have a finite number of years on Earth. My burning desire has always been to create a positive change in the way things are, so that I leave Earth having made it a better place for the next generation.

My vision of the world is one in which we have effected transformation in the healthcare and education systems, both of which will prove incredibly challenging to change. They are enormous, living systems and changing them will affect many. As such, there will be resistance, and the challenge is how we bring about a shift in the majority.

Currently, the healthcare and education systems are too compartmentalized. The way we classify things shapes the way we think, and the first fundamental question we need to ask is what and whom do these classifications serve? Why in modern medicine is the body carved into parts and assigned to different specialists?

We are not robots with parts manufactured separately and assembled together. We evolved and divided from the merger of the egg and the sperm cells. Likewise, in education, why are our children taught according to subjects, as if science and mathematics are not related to languages and the arts?

Another pressing issue is how technology and other inventions have made our lives more convenient, yet also create a certain reliance that is unprecedented. From the chair and the sitting toilet bowl, to the modern-day smart phone, we are creating postures and movements that make us inflexible and less mobile in the long run.

My goal is to start a global movement, first by raising awareness and then by inspiring others to make a concerted effort in effecting change through the formation of new habits. Through B1G1, I learned about the "power of small," and that change happens when we develop the habit of feeling gratitude and making giving a habit.

In my pursuit of living a congruent life, I have learned to apply this to all aspects of my life and my businesses, and I am realizing it is absolutely fundamental. I need to be the change I want to see. Whether it is in healthcare or education, to eradicate poverty or stall climate change, I realize it begins with self.

I am fortunate to be part of a community of like-minded people who inspire me and sweep me along, so that collectively, we are able to leave behind a *legacy* we can all be proud of.

A HEALTHY SPIRIT REDEFINED
BERNADETTE SARGINSON

I am fifty-one years old, hopefully only halfway through life. I wasted a lot of energy over the years, second-guessing myself, plagued with self-doubt and lacking in healthy self-esteem and self-worth. Yet very few people would have known. I was a lawyer and presented a positive, professional, "have-it-all-together" persona on the outside while struggling desperately on the inside.

It took me a long time to become a lawyer, but a very short time to change. It was 2005 and I was heavily pregnant with my second child. Despite my best intentions, I gained a huge amount of weight during pregnancy and developed gestational diabetes as a result. I had always told myself that I didn't want to get pregnant, put on loads of weight, and then struggle to lose it. Yet I was clinically obese, with little self-awareness, oblivious to the fact that I was inadvertently focusing on precisely what I didn't want. That was when I saw an advertisement that changed my life; it led to a permanent career change out of law and into personal empowerment. Needless to say, I never looked back.

I realized how shielded my legal education had been, and how much more there was to learn about people and what it really meant to be happy and successful. I developed an integrated approach to create a success mindset. I coached and mentored hundreds of clients to help them make the transformation to self-empowerment. In the process, I lost a significant amount of weight, reached a healthy BMI, and saw a massive shift in my own physical and mental health and well-being. All because I saw one advertisement.

I came to understand how inextricably linked *all* parts of you are in making up a healthy whole.

This is why the effort to improve SDG 3, "Good Health and Well-Being," is vital, because any effort that focuses on supporting well-being will transform lives on a massive scale in a way which is sustainable. And if we dedicate effort to transforming people and communities, this will ultimately transform our world.

When leaders and influencers have a healthy sense of well-being, this positively affects how they lead, how they form their worldview, and what their impact ultimately becomes.

I want to live in a world where politicians, influencers, and entrepreneurs start from a place of humanitarianism and philanthropic compassion, where we all take on the responsibility to say, "Enough is enough."

We cannot have children, families, and communities sick, cold, starving, or without shelter. These are our most fundamental human needs. It is widely understood that we have enough wealth and resources to feed, clothe, and house every single person on the planet. The flaw lies in how and where that wealth is distributed.

Many millionaires, billionaires, and entrepreneurs give back on a massive scale and this should be applauded. However, those who cannot contribute as much can still make a difference. This is what I love about B1G1: the ability to give a modest sum, yet make a life-changing impact, even if it's only one person — they matter. We are all part of the human race, and we can all make a difference. The question is what difference will you make?

This goal has the capacity to alter and enlighten thinking, not only in this generation, but also in generations to come. Today's children become tomorrow's parents, and they will pass on the skills and tools they learned through the successful attainment of this goal.

I am passionate about spreading the message that you are enough exactly as you are; that you are capable of change if you want it; and that changing your thoughts will change your life. With this attitude, we can change the world.

Healthy People Create Healthy Businesses

Often, it is only in their dying breath that people understand that more money can't buy what is important in life. It can't buy health or time back with your loved ones.

I believe in the power of self-empowerment, of being able to fix and heal yourself from within rather than relying on external emotional crutches. It is common to rely on food, drugs, alcohol, shopping, gambling, or whatever your coping mechanism of choice is, to deal with the stresses and strains of living in the age of technology, social media, and instant gratification. Living at this pace and in this way is crippling us, and depriving us of our mental, emotional and physical health and stability.

I believe that when you connect with a higher level of energy and consciousness, no matter what your circumstances are, you can experience life in a richer, calmer, and more appreciative way.

I suffered from social anxiety throughout my teenage years and twenties, triggered by a health issue in my childhood. I lived with an undiagnosed bladder issue that shaped how I felt about myself for many years. Living with a physical health issue isn't only about physical health, as it also contaminates our mental, emotional, and spiritual well-being.

This health issue was in fact a gift that ultimately sparked a life-long interest in self-awareness and personal development. However, we need not wait for ill health to arrive before we seize this opportunity. Often to improve our quality of life, we need to slow down, not speed up. We need to look after each other as well as ourselves.

This hit home for me in December 2012. I was expecting a large group of friends to arrive for Christmas drinks and was rushing around to get everything done. I decided to wear a new pair of black dress trousers; though they were too long for me, I thought I could manage. The clock was ticking. It was 2.55 p.m. and my guests would arrive in five minutes. I rushed downstairs to try to ice the cake before they arrived.

Six stairs from the ground, I accidently stepped on my trouser leg and hurled headfirst and backwards down the stairs. I cracked the back of my head and top of my spine on the corner of the window recess before being thrown onto the floor, 180 degrees in the opposite direction. Concussed and sore, with an egg-shaped lump on my head, I realized icing the cake could have waited. This was my wake-up call to slow down and take proper care of my health. I now walk much more slowly through life. I encourage others to do the same. Small daily changes can prevent big health problems.

The Privilege to Change
At Spirit Level Success, we strive to be a business that matters,

one driven by people and purpose, not zeros on the bottom line. While we appreciate that business is about being successful and making a profit, we believe it means accepting responsibility, both corporate and personal, to make a positive impact on the people we seek to serve. We believe that when you focus on people and purpose, the rest will flow naturally.

Why does this matter? Because it's really about contribution, responsibility, humility, compassion, connection, and humanity. Who wants to live in a world where the super-rich continue to profit, yet we have people living in poverty, people who may have fallen on hard times and can't break the cycle? I don't. Yet this is the reality in 2019. Something is broken, and as entrepreneurs, we have the privilege and opportunity to bring about change.

How have we created a "better business"? We embedded giving into our business. We created specific giving impacts based on particular product sales. We made a clear decision to be a business for good, to set up the right systems from the start, and to share our story with others to inspire change.

We know that when you feel good about yourself, no matter what your external environment or circumstances, you will be more emotionally balanced, rely less on unhealthy crutches, and will develop a more robust mindset and sense of self-esteem that will allow you to live your best life.

We support projects in developing countries and communities that involve play and education, particularly in children. We also help provide fresh, clean water, as its short supply can have devastating effects. The ability to maintain a strong and healthy sense of self, no matter what is happening in your surrounding environment, is what ultimately determines how your life unfolds, which is why we support projects that empower children and enable them to develop skills that will last a lifetime.

Tips for Creating a Conscious Business

Take time to connect with your *why*. Rise above the day-to-day workings of your business to a more existential place, and ask yourself these questions:

What makes you get out of bed in the morning?

What difference do you want to make in your business and in your life?

What touches your heart when you see, read, or hear about it? Is it children? Poverty? Food? Water? Education? Connect deeply with the causes that move your spirit.

Then ask yourself, "How can I integrate this cause into my business?" Ask your team, your mentors, and your customers for input. What is important to them?

Get into the habit of stepping outside of your own experience and see the world from the viewpoint of others. Broaden your perspective on what you think you are able to do that can have an impact on the wider global community, and commit to giving something back on a regular basis.

Your legacy awaits you.

WHAT YOU CAN DO TO
CREATE A WORLD OF HEALTH AND WELL-BEING

Lifestyle tips:
- Spread healthy habits such as healthy-eating and exercising.
- Choose products that are good for your health and the planet.
- Connect and care for others, and exercise empathy.

Business tips:
- Make your workplace safer by creating safety guidelines.
- Select suppliers that care for the well-being of their workers and the local community.
- Enroll your team in fitness and health programs.

Giving tips:
- Give a mosquito net to prevent Malaria.
- Give a cataract surgery to give vision to the blind.
- Fund a counseling session to help a person with a mental health issue or trauma.

AN EDUCATED WORLD

4 QUALITY EDUCATION

HOW YOU AND YOUR BUSINESS CAN ENSURE
INCLUSIVE AND EQUITABLE QUALITY EDUCATION
FOR ALL BY 2030.

"Education is the most powerful weapon which you can use to change the world."

— Nelson Mandela

THE CHANGEMAKERS

REFUSING THE STIGMA OF SOCIETY
RUSSELL BYRNE

Russell is the co-founder and CEO of the multi-award-winning Education Consortium (EC), the Royal Britannia (RB) Education Group, and the THRIVE Foundation. Russell has over 30 years of experience in the education, retail, and financial sectors and has served as a trusted C-level executive, management consultant, educator and "change agent." Russell's philosophy and *raison d'être* are simple, "Embolden, Engage, Empower, and Serve the community at large."

thrive.world

THE TRUE PRICE OF EDUCATION
DR. GARY THO

Dr. Gary Tho is a chiropractor, author, speaker, ex-National Australian badminton player and father of two. He is the founder of ChiroWorks, a pain relief and peak performance clinic. His clients include world champion athletes, busy executives, and super moms and dads. Dr. Gary has featured in over 600 speaking engagements and workshops. His book, *The Pain-Free Desk Warrior: Free Yourself from Aches and Pains*, teaches people how to live pain-free for life.

drgarytho.com, flipflops.asia

EDUCATION NEVER STOPS GIVING
CHRISTOPHER WICK

Christopher Wick is an award-winning speaker, bestselling author, and internationally recognized social media consultant. He is the founder of SMM International. Christopher ensures businesses online presence provides revenue growth and lead generation. Christopher and his team have helped over 200 companies "get found" online, engage their customers, and make more money. SMM International was recognized as one of the fastest growing companies in 2015 and as having the most measurable community impact in North America in 2017.

smminternational.com

AN EDUCATED WORLD

Tuesday, 9 October 2012, a bus was ferrying children home from school in Afghanistan. Within seconds, two Taliban militants jumped on board. One militant yelled, "Who is Malala?"

All eyes turned to 15-year-old Malala Yousafzai. The militant pointed the gun toward her and shot her in the face.

She was left for dead.

Miraculously, she survived and has continued to speak out on the importance of education.

Since she was 11 years old Malala had been writing anonymous online diaries. She questioned life under the Taliban and she wrote about their attempts to suppress the right to education for girls in Pakistan.

She said this about her experience:

"They thought that the bullets would silence us, but they failed. And out of that silence came thousands of voices. The terrorists thought they would change my aims and stop my ambitions. But nothing changed in my life except this: weakness, fear and hopelessness died. Strength, power and courage was born. I am the same Malala. My ambitions are the same. My hopes are the same. And my dreams are the same. Dear sisters and brothers, I am not against anyone. Neither am I here to speak in terms of personal revenge against the Taliban or any other terrorist group. I am here to speak for the right of education for every child."

In 2013, she gave a speech to the United Nations and published her first book, I *Am Malala*. In 2014, she became the youngest person to win the Nobel Peace Prize.

She reminds us that education is neither eastern nor western. "Education is education," she says, "and it's the right of every human being." She also tells people that her story isn't unique. She believes it's the story of many girls and boys. Sadly, she's correct.

Though others' stories may not be as obvious and as terrible as a shooting, the damage is the same. The lack of access to education, the suppression of the right to be educated is a silent bullet that kills a future and dismantles a life. It's a bullet that can ravage entire countries and stunt them from growing to their full potential.

The UN says that obtaining a quality education is the foundation of creating a sustainable world. It really is. Education can foster new ideas and equip people with the tools to develop innovative solutions to the world's greatest problems.

Every child is our future.

And though literacy rates and education attendance are better than before, many children are left behind. Further behind than ever.

In fact, over 265 million children are currently out of school. Imagine them all lined up. Currently, they're left behind. And 22% of them are of primary school age.

Primary school education in developing countries has reached a promising 91% but that still means 57 million primary age children remain out of school.

But these kids are not numbers. They have names and lives and emotions and dreams. Dreams that often get quashed through lack of opportunity and lack of education. Dreams that often fall short through no fault of their own.

But, here's the thing. We can all be dreammakers. We can give all children access to their dreams. To their hopes and desires. We can give them the skills, education and understanding they need to be all they wish to be.

Changemaker Russell Byrne is one such dreammaker. His Kuwait-based school RB gives all children the right to a great education. But not only a great education; they also teach them life skills and offer them holistic learning options and teach their students about the world and sustainability. Russell doesn't just settle at education; through his own inspirational personal story, he empowers others to make a life. A happy, fulfilled and educated one. Much like Aristotle meant when he said, "Educating the mind without educating the heart is no education at all."

Changemaker, Dr Gary Tho, shares these sentiments and offers the compelling view of how education can often be taken for granted by those who have the good fortune to access it. That is, until they know otherwise. Or witness the lack of it elsewhere.

Gary illustrates what a good education can do and the ripple effect it has. It gives hope and possibility. He reminds us that education isn't just an intellectual experience but a set of skills that can alter the course of people's lives.

And changing lives is what Christopher Wick is passionate about. As a wonderful connector for people to actively engage with change and do something about it, he sees business and social media as a vehicle for change; whether it be to spread a powerful message or offer a helping hand. Chris helps us see the new bridge today's media can bring to education and the world.

United as one, these three changemakers are remarkable in their personal quests. They agree that collectively, we need to make bolder efforts if we want to give everyone a great education.

We need to invest in teacher training and lift the conditions of many schools around the world. We need to ensure clean water and electricity to many rural areas to allow school buildings to be built and schooling to continue after dark.

And most of all, we must ensure no child is just a number. We must line them all up and count them all, backwards to zero. Until no child is left behind.

Malala says it like this, "One child, one teacher, one book and one pen can change the world. Education is the only solution."

REFUSING THE STIGMA OF SOCIETY
RUSSELL BYRNE

Wherever you look in our world there are disenfranchised and impoverished children — children who, due to an absence of quality education, lack a voice and a choice. I was one of these children.

By age thirteen, I was constantly being told by my teachers that I was stupid and naughty. I was "too argumentative", "asked too many questions", and "challenged assumptions". In other words, I had an inquiring mind. Unhappily, around this time, while walking home alone from school, I was attacked and molested. When I eventually found the courage to speak up about it to people I trusted, I was told to simply forget about it and act as though it never happened. I gave up because no one believed me, let alone in me. I withdrew. I quit school. I was told to get a job, so I took any job because I didn't know any better. I did everything from working in fast-food establishments to manual labor until I was old enough to drive.

I hated every job I did, so I started a few businesses — some successful, most not — until I took a chance on a commission-based role requiring community work and martial arts training. I've always loved sport and had played at state and regional levels but breaking my knee ended a potential professional sporting career. Martial arts training helped heal and rejuvenate me in ways I had not imagined. I grew immeasurably in self-worth and self-assurance. My training gave me purpose I'd never envisioned, and the opportunity to teach and lead.

Over time, I discovered that I was relatively self-efficacious and entrepreneurial, I loved to learn, and more importantly, I lived life through knowing what I did not want. I realized that I wanted to do something where I could be of value and help kids like me who had lost their way, their voice, and their choice. I wanted to help by providing quality education.

The stigma of being told I was stupid held me back for the longest time. Certain misconceptions became reality while others were simply erroneous beliefs I upheld. I knew deep down that I was smart, yet I doubted myself. I had hit multiple glass ceilings imposed by society, especially being pigeonholed for lack of education.

Later in life, I knew I could not attend classes at university surrounded by teenagers — we'd have very little in common. So, in 1999, I applied for a master's program, completed the tests and interviews, and actually got in! Amazed, I shared the news with my family but succumbed to peer pressure (to get a job) so I quit, and kept battling on. I finally learned to stand up for my beliefs and applied again in 2005, and again was accepted. At this stage, I had to divorce my family to do what I needed to do — not the best outcome, but necessary for my personal circumstances at the time.

Freshly divorced with four young children, a new business, no home and no money, I embarked on this new journey. I failed my first university unit. I was horrified — all my doubts and fears came flooding back. Humbled, I asked for help. Two professors gave me convincing advice: Dr. Marita Naudé and Dr. Byron Hanson. They explained exactly where I went wrong, what I did right, and what I could do to better my knowledge.

I followed their advice to the letter, undertook bridging courses, and essentially learned to read and write at an academic level. I retook the unit and achieved a distinction — a level I maintained over two master's degrees. Achieving at this level meant the world to me and empowered me to aim even higher. I found myself approaching key people to work alongside, learn from, and help with their research and projects. My newfound sense of self was powerful.

My final projects were spent working with a devoted mother of six, Dr. Fiona Wood (Australian of the Year, 2005), on her legacy project, "The National Education of First Aid and Emergency Survival in Australia." The study was delivered to Parliament and successfully funded. This triumph showed me that with vision and fortitude, anyone can make a difference. As a result, I keep a copy of the Universal Declaration of Human Rights, proclaimed by the United

Nations General Assembly in Paris on 10 December 1948. I regularly reference this important document, and incorporate parts of it into my life, as it serves as a good reminder of what we strive for, especially Article 26, relating to education.

What One Boy Taught Me about the Meaning of Education

In my early coaching days, I had the privilege of training children with multiple abilities to help them achieve their goals through martial arts. In 1995, I was introduced to a fine young man named Daryl who was autistic, wheelchair-bound, and had a strong speech impediment. He absolutely loved martial arts and he, along with his parents, attended every class he could to observe. He adored the greats such as Bruce Lee, Jackie Chan, and Jet Li, and saw me as the embodiment of them.

Over the following weeks, the students and I noticed Daryl had learned all the basics and had memorized the first couple of patterns required for grading, in other words, graduating to the next level. We could see him mimicking us in his wheelchair, and it was obvious that his timing was spot on. After speaking with, and convincing, his parents to allow Daryl to give it a go, he proudly took his place in his wheelchair, front and center, in the line with the other kids. He was in his element. His natural enthusiasm overcame the reluctance of his fellow students until his work ethic earned their collective respect. Now, accepted as one of the team, Daryl excelled. He trained so hard that one day, he simply got out of his chair and continued to train — through sheer faith, belief, and inspiration — a natural progression for him.

His family believed in him and were always incredibly supportive and loving. As his teacher, I merely instructed Daryl, who did all the work — so much so that he graduated to the assistant level in the class. Having earned this responsibility was a huge honor for him and he did not disappoint.

Daryl has always had to work twice as hard as the other kids do because, every single day, he needed to remember to use his muscles efficiently and consciously work on his coordination. One Saturday, he got a bit too excited in class and lost control. Unable to stop his momentum, he ran straight through a glass windowpane, which sliced the length of his arm open. The bleeding was incessant. As martial arts is all about discipline, patience, and nonviolence, the class and I calmly leapt into action and got him to the hospital in time. I was devastated and felt extremely guilty — after all, he was my responsibility; I had failed him and allowed him to hurt himself. I was unsure how he or his family would react to this accident.

However, in no time Daryl was back attending class, again as a spectator, and after his stitches and injuries healed, he returned to training and helping out. The love from all was overwhelming as he was welcomed back with open arms.

Daryl showed me that even though many may not believe a path may be right for you, it is essential to follow that path regardless of where it may take you. The journey is so much more important than the destination. Daryl felt truly free while training, which in turn gave him the confidence to find gainful employment.

Naysayers we encounter in our travels may have a powerful impact upon our thinking — positive and negative — I've learned that no one can make you feel any particular way unless you allow them to. Quality education is so much more than simple didactic rhetoric — it is the embodiment of virtue, the engagement of the spirit, and the empowerment of the soul.

Lead the Way without Getting in the Way

As an owner and operator of schools, it is my belief that we should not dictate to children, "This is what we are going to do today." We all learn differently and at varying paces, we allow the children to "lead the way," with the teachers simply facilitating. "Lead the way without getting in the way." Don't get me wrong; we have established learning goals upheld by knowledgeable teachers in situ. The children are encouraged to embody innovation and creativity in everything they do, putting them "in charge" of their own learning. The teachers then align the children's learnings with time-proven learning goals with positive reinforcement and encouragement. Our children feel empowered and our teachers are engaged in forward-thinking educational outcomes, which we measure consistently through action and happiness; in other words, can they do what is required with a big broad smile?

Staying true to one's beliefs often means not succumbing to popular opinion. For example, when we built and launched our gymnastics center in Kuwait, the government enforced segregation and non-integration by majority opinion — some called it the "law." We disagreed, stating kids do not see age, race, color, creed, gender, ethnicity, nationality or disability. They just want to have fun.

We were inspired to build a center of excellence by Jennifer Bricker, the younger sister of Olympic gymnast Dominique Moceanu. Born without legs, Jennifer's parents placed her up for adoption. With the love and support of her adoptive family, yet without knowledge of her sister, she became the first handicapped high school tumbling champion in the United States. Jennifer idolized Moceanu long before finding out they were sisters and finally being reunited. Our center aims to inspire budding athletes, both those who are able-bodied and those with disabilities, to learn the sport without discrimination. We have integrated gymnastics into a multi-skilled discipline incorporating dance, Pilates, Zumba, ballet, martial arts, Parkour and yoga. Quality education involves placing no limitations.

By running a 100 Kuwaiti fils (US $0.33) campaign every Thursday, we make a huge impact on the initiatives we support. We are extremely proud of this drive because it has taught our staff, parents, and students that a little does go a long way; the coins we disregard can make a difference in others' lives. We have contributed 25,406 days of clean drinking water to countries in Africa and Asia, which equates to over 69 years! We also have:

- Expanded our hydroponics and aquaponics center.
- Provided children with learning opportunities in construction and carpentry.
- Taught gardening and cultivation skills.
- Educated people about crops, seeds, new farming techniques, finance, and entrepreneurship.
- Created an equal, diverse, and inclusive environment for boys and girls, and for children with special needs.

We are proud of our ethics and achievements. They have taught us that individually, we are but one drop; however, together we are an ocean.

THE TRUE PRICE OF EDUCATION
DR. GARY THO

I remember I was around eight years old, sitting on my bed and thinking I wanted to help people. I wanted to encourage, inspire, and empower them to grow, to help them create the lives they deserve. But I didn't know how or what to do. Over time, through education, I learned my knowledge and skill set, which now allows me to influence thousands of lives.

Education is vital to growth, confidence, and purpose in life. It opens the door to opportunity as it equips us with fundamentals like reading, writing, and communication skills. To me, these foundations can change someone's life.

I was fortunate to have an education. My siblings and I received opportunities many others did not, from schooling to music, sports and other activities. This was a result of my parents' determination, for which I'm forever grateful. They truly believed that education is essential for success and a better life. They spent their savings on migrating to Australia so I did not have to suffer the struggles their lack of education and job opportunities created, or the unhappiness they experienced.

I remember a proverb my parents shared with me when I was around 13 years old. It said something like, "Give a man a fish and he can eat for a day. Teach a man to fish and he can eat for a year. Teach a man to farm fish and he can feed his family for life."

To me, education is exactly that. It allows us to create and cultivate the life we desire. It's not just about earning diplomas and degrees. Like learning how to fish, education in one subject can change one person's life. But it's limited — you'll soon run out of fish. Education is more than academia. What if we educate children using growth mindsets? And expand their curiosity and ability to experiment? What if we give them a place to dream, learn skills, and express themselves? If education is given and received with an open mind and open heart, would it unlock our true potential and create endless opportunities? Would these opportunities not only affect one person, but also create a ripple effect, influencing everyone around them?

I was taught to study hard and to get a respectable degree, as this would lead to a well-paid job, money, a house, and therefore a good life. I took education for granted. I was not an "A" student. I had to work my butt off to get good grades. To me, school was just what a kid's life was meant to be: normal and inevitable. From inside the school grounds, I would see my classmates skip school and comment on how lucky they were. If the weather was too hot in the summer and school was canceled, we would celebrate. Not having school was fantastic!

Even when I began university, I viewed it as a normal progression. I was accepted into my top two university programs and didn't think much of it. It never occurred to me that having access to education was a blessing and a luxury.

Since then, I have discovered that education is a gift that not everyone receives. It was only when I joined my friends on charity trips to orphanages around Asia with the Care Givers Group that I began seeing education differently. These kids wanted to learn. They dreamed of studying, of getting a job in the big city to earn money. However, the system often stopped at feeding and clothing all of them. I found out some boys were sent to work on farms when they were physically big enough, between twelve to fifteen years old. Furthermore, the volunteers, mostly foreigners who had made Cambodia their home, told us that we were disrupting the children's learning. Even with our best intentions, our presence made their school days counterproductive. Rather than learning, they spent their time practicing for performances that they showcased for the visitors; their usual classes were canceled. The more people who visited, the more interruptions occurred, and the less they actually learned.

It appeared that it didn't matter if they learned to read or write, because they couldn't advance to the next level. This wasn't their choice or due to their lack of willingness, but rather they were caught in a survival cycle by virtue of a system that may not have the children's best interest at heart.

I remember one moment in particular. In 2013, I was in rural Cambodia, and even with my eyes closed, the morning sun was blinding me. It was a few minutes before five o'clock and I could hear the hustle from the street downstairs. I walked down and was greeted with peak-hour breakfast preparations and motorbikes packed with meats or vegetables to sell at the local market. My friend told me to get a drink from the stall next door.

A young girl, around fourteen or fifteen years old, greeted me. Her eyes lit up when I spoke fluent English. Her dream was to go to university and then help her family and community improve their quality of life. Though she desired an education, she knew it would only happen if her family's food stall could earn enough money. At the time, she went to school only a few days a week. She worked from five to eight in the morning, and then cycled forty-five minutes to school before coming home in the early afternoon to help serve at her parents' stall. The sun goes down around five thirty in Cambodia, and she struggled to read or do her homework in the dim evening light. She read and practiced English as much as she could, taking every opportunity to learn. To say I was inspired by her drive was an understatement.

We kept in touch each time I visited and through Facebook too. I saw her command of English improve drastically. I continued to support and encourage her, as she shared her struggles, including family illnesses, missing school, and her lack of funds. And yet, her conviction kept shining through: "I'm very poor so I must try to study. For my future and my family which I hope I will be success. My future is in my hands."

I met her twin sister and a few of her friends, all of whom shared similar hopes and dreams of helping their families toward a better future. Their "how" was through education.

In 2015, she messaged me:

> When I grow up I want to be a diplomat because I want to help as many people in the country. Cambodia is a poor country. Especially the living area. Some parents are poor and have no education so that they stop their children to study and ask them

to find work to support their families. Today, many students drop out of school. There are many reasons that relate to these issues. I hope that I will be totally successful to become a diplomat so I can communicate with other countries to help more people and help more students receive a scholarship. I am really interested about it. I want to help those who are poor. And I want them to acquire knowledge and education. I need to help my family as well. They always encouraged me to study. I will do my best. Education is the key to better future.

She followed by saying her dad was not supportive of her choice of occupation, preferring she become a doctor.

We still keep in touch. Her mother took out a loan to pay for her education, and she is worried about paying it back. She secured a stable job as a work visa consultant, and is still determined to help improve her family's finances and assist others in rural Cambodia. The true price of education is indeed priceless.

At the Heart of Every Business

I started my business because I wanted to help people. But as time went by, I realized that I want to serve more people than just the person lying on my chiropractic table and their family.

My giving journey began with supporting my friends' aid efforts and joining their charity trips. In addition to donations, I also gave my time. Through a friend's introduction to a monk, I found myself working at a provincial hospital in a small town, Kampong Trabek, a couple hours away from Phnom Penh. I now travel there once or twice a year for four to six days and treat as many people as I can, from post-stroke to chronic pain patients. I am often requested to make house calls to people who can't find transport to the hospital. I saw one man, so amazed that chiropractic treatment had helped his chronic back pain, drive over two hours, picking up everyone he knew that had any inkling of pain on the way. He picked up thirteen people. Locals even show up at my accommodation at five thirty in the morning to see me before I go to the hospital.

After a while, I was concerned with the impact I could make. I could see physical changes on my visits to Cambodia, but I didn't know how my financial donations affected lives. I was thrilled when

I learnt about B1G1, as it makes giving easier to incorporate into my business, and allows me to contribute to various causes and impact people in different countries.

I ask my new clients what is most important to them: education, clean drinking water, or access to healthcare? Based on their response, I create an impact for three projects in that category. So far, we have given over 35,200 days of access to education, over 282,100 days of access to clean drinking water and over 54,730 days of access to health care.

I also participated in the "Joy of Giving" week, where our efforts raised 4,140 days of university education for disadvantaged youths in Cambodia —11.3 years' worth!

On International Women's Day, I wanted to acknowledge the wonderful women in my world, from my wife, daughters, and mother to all my clients and friends who are amazing women. We decided on that day to provide chiropractic treatment to any woman at no charge. My only request was that they would support my efforts to assist women in Bangladesh by giving them access to sewing machines and teaching them how to sew. Through this one-day event, we created 6,900 days of access to sewing machines, allowing women to learn and giving them the ability to generate income for themselves and their community.

Outside of giving, we can also share with our children, family, and friends that we feel blessed to have received an education. It's important to remember to cherish what we do have, from our ability to access learning and knowledge, attend school, or sign up for a course, to typing on our phones and laptops. This collective awareness that we are fortunate to be where we are right now may also awaken a deeper meaning and purpose, and a desire to help others who have little.

EDUCATION NEVER STOPS GIVING
CHRISTOPHER WICK

Education is the breath of transformation.

When people know better, they do better. When people do better, the world does better. When you know *what* to do, *how* to do it, and *why* you do it, you have the ability to effect change.

Our world has more access to information than ever. Within moments, people can search online and find the answer to their questions. For the first time in history, rather than looking to manuals or encyclopedias, we have access to overwhelming amounts of information at any time. However, having access to information is insufficient; we must also know how to apply that information. This is the inherent importance of education: how to apply knowledge toward a specific goal.

While many of us were privileged to grow up going to school, there are many who do not have such a gift. In many societies, it feels normal, even boring, to attend school, learn, pass exams, and progress to the next grade. But if you take a moment, you'll realize that it just seems "normal" because everyone around you is doing the same.

Millions of people don't have this privilege of a "normal" education; they are unable to learn how to read and write, add and subtract, or even socialize. Our "normal" education would be considered a true honor to so many. When you are educated, you have the power to choose. Unfortunately, many around the world lack access to education, and therefore the power to choose, due to their class, gender, income, or societal conditions. Gaining access to education and having the power to choose is deeply impactful.

Imagine how our world would look if those less fortunate had the power to choose, the capacity to change, and the ability to transform.

Growing up in the United States, I was incredibly fortunate to have little choice in the matter; the law required attendance and public schools are free. Many people who inspired and shaped me were extraordinary teachers. It is through the education they gave me that I was granted the power of choice.

When attending college, I was again incredibly fortunate to have earned scholarships that granted me access to a wonderful business education. It was in college that I formulated exactly what I wanted to do and learned the skills to grow powerful businesses.

As I developed my businesses, it gave me great pride to think that I was capable of helping others over the course of their lifetime. One of my companies, a social media marketing agency, has given business owners the ability to understand how to market their brand and connect with people. Something as involved as social media often intimidates people because it is a new technology. Though my agency performs the actual execution for each of our clients, we have the immense privilege of teaching each of them *what* it is that we do and *why* we do it. Often service providers simply secure the contract and perform the work.

It brings me considerable joy to know that every single business I've worked with has learned the *how* and *why* of making these impressive results happen.

Having the ability to advise, consult, and teach is one of the greatest honors of my life. As businesses grow, evolve, and change, it is the fundamentals of what people have learned that shape their future.

When I first began building my businesses, I kept these critical goals in mind:

1. Change the world through the transformation of businesses.
2. Employ people all over the world to create momentum in building others.
3. Give back to those who need it most in a way that could change the trajectory of their path.

Here's how we went about it:

Goal 1. We looked at the bigger picture. We asked questions like:

- If one business could change, how would that affect their family?
- If one business could change, how would that affect their local community?

- If one business could change, how would that affect their society?

As we set out to help hundreds of businesses, we were extremely excited about our impact. Imagine how many families, local communities, and towns or cities could be affected through the ripple effect this would create.

Goal 2. I believe deeply that those from various cultures and backgrounds, and who thus hold differing perspectives, make the best team.

From the first day I began employing people, I sought to hire those different than I. Those who had different backgrounds and upbringings than I did. Those who spoke different languages than I did. Because this affords us — perspective! When looking at a problem or an opportunity, not only are "two heads are better than one," but diverse groups can offer perspectives that produce the ability to see and decide based on deeper experience. Within my first year, our team had worked with people on every continent. Consider the bright minds in our team meetings, all contributing knowledge from their various viewpoints.

Goal 3. I live by the motto, "I can only keep what I have by giving it away." My favorite means of giving has always been offering the privilege of education. Within my first year of my business, I held an entrepreneurship camp for young children in Houston's Third Ward. Hosting this camp in my hometown was such a joy. The camp helped underprivileged children unlock the ability to think of new projects, get inspired by successful entrepreneurs, and receive scholarships.

As we grew, we expanded our local contributions to encompass the globe. Through our partnership with B1G1, we have impacted over 63,384 people within a few short years.

In 2017, I collaborated with an organization called Global Giving and began working with Educating Girls, one of their programs that is committed to educating thousands of young women. Through our recurring partnership, every month we provide scholarships that allow women to learn subjects such as law, coding, and entrepreneurship.

A Small Spark of Belief can Create a Wildfire
Sometimes all people need is a little belief in what they're doing.

One of my favorite memories is of a young boy who wanted to give back and a mother who passionately believed in him.

In the summer of 2016, I sat with my new friend, Urja, on simple, comforting couches in an ashram. An ashram is a place for spiritual retreat, where people go to meditate, take time to reflect, and participate in classes. My favorite ashram is Siddhayatan, located in Windom, on the outskirts of Dallas, Texas. As I was talking with my friend, she told me how much she wanted to help her son, who she adopted from Vietnam, take a group trip with us to India. Her son, Christian, is a passionately energetic young boy with an incredible desire to give back to kids just like him.

As money was going to be a challenge, I asked Urja if she had ever thought about crowdfunding to raise funds to bring Christian along on our pilgrimage to India. As a social media expert, I see trends online and understand worthy causes, and immediately recognized their story as one many people would want to be a part of. Urja asked if I *really* thought people would actually donate to their cause. I said absolutely.

I knew their story would inspire others, due to Christian's background and the story of a mother's love for her son. I encouraged her to take the plunge. Not just the plunge of asking for donations, but also sharing their incredible story with others.

Christian has such a desire to help others and his mom, Urja, has such a deep love for him. I believed in them. I assured Urja that people would be moved by their story, and I would support them throughout the process.

In less than sixty days, Christian's crowdfunding campaign, "Help Christian Dream Big," was shared hundreds of times and had raised over $5,000. Hundreds of people were touched by Christian's story and their efforts allowed him and Urja to attend our pilgrimage in India. Here was a young boy who had started his life in an orphanage in Vietnam, ignited by such big dreams of giving back.

This may sound like the end of this success story, but it's not. We traveled with a group of over twenty people, and Christian was the only kid. His charm, excitement, and eagerness was refreshing to us all. We benefited immensely from experiencing his childlike wonder as we traveled, studied, and grew ourselves.

Christian and Urja took their trip even further due to the amount of donations they raised. They spent an extra week in India after our group trip and visited the slums, donated to communities, and spent time volunteering. Their campaign caught the attention of an Indian music star, and they spent time with him volunteering with children in India. Throughout the entire trip, Christian and Urja took pictures and videos and wrote about their experiences.

When they arrived back in the United States, Christian became the youngest published author I know, publishing his book, *21 Funny, Frantic and Fantastic Facts about My 21 Days in India*, at age ten. It is no surprise that the proceeds from his book go to those in need. Even as I write this, his story continues.

The story of Urja's beautiful family and her son with huge dreams inspires me. To think that it all started with a fun conversation on a couch in an ashram. It shows me the true power of believing in someone's dream and the impact that can create.

WHAT YOU CAN DO TO CREATE A WORLD OF QUALITY EDUCATION

Lifestyle tips:
- Take online courses to improve your knowledge and skills.
- Mentor young people.

Business tips:
- Create training programs for your employees.
- Encourage your team to volunteer.
- Actively share your ideas and success stories with the world.

Giving tips:
- Give to a program to provide free or subsidized uniforms and learning materials to disadvantaged children.
- Help educate children and donate your used books.
- Help fund a school facility.

EVERYONE IS
EQUALLY VALUABLE

---

5 **GENDER EQUALITY**

HOW YOU AND YOUR BUSINESS CAN HELP
ACHIEVE GENDER EQUALITY AND EMPOWER
ALL WOMEN AND GIRLS.

"No country can ever truly flourish if it stifles the potential of its women."

— Michelle Obama

THE CHANGEMAKERS

LEAD FROM THE FRONT
DR. HANAN AL-MUTAWA

Dr. Hanan established innovative curriculum and pedagogical imperatives for Kuwait and the GCC market. Her areas of interest are inclusion, equality, educational diversity, and sustainable "leadership". She serves on various boards of education-related government committees. She speaks on management systems, healthcare, business, government, non-profit, and humanitarian leadership. She is an active member of the Kuwait Red Crescent Society and is a founding member and vice-president of Soroptimist International Club Kuwait.

rb.edu.kw

BE THE EXCEPTION TO THE RULE, A REBEL WITH SOUL
KRISTY CASTLETON

Kristy Castleton is the founder of Rebel & Soul; a socially conscious, multi-award-winning agency that applies a neuroscience methodology to produce highly memorable experiences. Her passion for neuro-marketing and technology, teamed with a love for parties and new experiences, drove her to do things differently. Rebel & Soul works with world-leading brands, including CNN, HSBC, Chanel, Dentsu, and Heineken. Kristy holds a Women Leadership Award from CMO Asia and a Women Leading Change award from Campaign Asia.

rebelandsoul.com

THE ANSWER
HELEN CAMPBELL

Helen has worn many hats: world explorer, director of nursing, counselor, health coach, practice manager, CEO, and mom to three awesome individuals. Helen is the owner of Knox Audiology — "Ears that Give." Knox Audiology is a boutique medical hearing center spanning four locations around Melbourne. It is locally owned and operated by university-trained audiologists and ENT specialists. They are deeply passionate about hearing brilliantly.

knoxaudiology.com.au

EVERYONE IS EQUALLY VALUABLE

Most people have heard of the first man on the moon. But what about the first woman in space? What's her name?

It's Valentina Tereshkova. A Soviet cosmonaut who orbited Earth 48 times in just under three days.

What about Eunice Newton Foote? The first scientist to make the connection between the amount of carbon dioxide in the atmosphere and climate change in 1856.

Or the two futuristic women who built the first solar powerhouse? Do you know the names of physicist Dr. Maria Telkes and architect Eleanor Raymond?

What about Danish seismologist Inge Lehmann who discovered the deeper aspects of Earth's inner core?

The world is full of amazing women and girls. Many are our future leaders, doctors and nurses, activists, Presidents, diplomats, teachers, inventors, entrepreneurs and pioneers. Our daughters, sisters, mothers, and grandmothers.

Despite being half of society, many women and girls remain unrecognized as equal. Invisible. Voiceless. Dismissed.

It seems downright cruel that in a world where there are close to equal amounts of males and females that one could be granted fewer rights than the other simply due to gender. Yet it continues every day. Women and girls all over the world are still denied the same voice and rights as men.

Unbelievably, even in our modern world, we are still stuck with many archaic ideas, prejudices and even laws that suppress and deny the female population.

Warning: what you're about to read is true though it may seem unfathomable to any reasonable human being:

- In 18 countries, husbands can legally prevent their wives from working.
- In 39 countries, daughters and sons do not have equal inheritance rights.

- 49 countries lack laws to protect women from domestic violence.
- Globally, 750 million women and girls were married before the age of 18 and at least 200 million women and girls in 30 countries have undergone Female Genital Mutilation (FGM).
- Only 52% of women married or in a union freely make their own decisions about sexual relations, contraceptive use and health care.
- Globally, women are just 13% of agricultural landholders.
- One in five women and girls, including 19% of women and girls aged 15 to 49, have experienced physical and/or sexual violence by an intimate partner within the last 12 months. Yet still, those 49 countries have no laws that protect women from such violence.

Gender equality is not only a fundamental human right but a necessary foundation for a peaceful, prosperous and sustainable world. Gandhi said, "the future is with woman."

Many people highlight how far we have come with gender equality. There are many hopeful emerging statistics. Facts like:

- Harmful practices such as child marriage and FGM have declined by 30% in the past decade.
- In 46 countries women now hold more than 30% of seats in national parliaments in at least one chamber.
- More than 100 countries have united to track budget allocations for gender equality.

Although these new trends towards equality are encouraging, we must question why they even exist. No human being should have to fight for equality in the first place. Equality is something we should be born with, not fight for. All laws, practices, rules, and behaviors that make one human inferior to another must be abolished. And soon.

Changemaker Dr. Hanan Al-Mutawa is a leader and educator who has been a long-standing pioneer for change. She has taken on individuals, education sectors and even governments to address and change the rights of women. A Kuwaiti born woman, Dr. Hanan has lead the charge at great personal cost. Yet, her fight for the freedom of every girl and woman remains burning in her soul.

Like Dr. Hanan, changemaker Kristy Castleton reminds us that for some people, change is uncomfortable and scary. She encourages women to have courage and stand together. To use business as an opportunity to be socially conscious and to create a new world of equality.

Changemaker Helen Campbell echoes the messages of unity. She has experienced suppression in the workplace and decided to *be the change*. To create a new model that eradicated inequality and suppression. Her message of converting pain to power is paramount in learning how to use the innate power of love and compassion to shift the world towards peace and away from divisive ideologies.

These three authors are strong and powerful women. They have demanded equality. They are living examples of women "leading from the front."

They, like many, demand equality - not just in their lives but everywhere and for everyone. In the world and at home.

Sadly, many girls and women aren't born into an equal home. They grow up automatically labelled as inferior. Change must happen now. The birthright of equality is denied even before females are born.

Equality means many things. It means providing women and girls with equal access to education, health care, decent work, and representation in political and economic decision-making processes. It means changing primitive laws and updating new ones. It means ending violence and harmful practices targeted at women. It means ending child marriages and child trafficking. It means saying no to gender-based inequality everywhere. It means changing things for women and girls denied the right to do it themselves.

It means fairness. It means to be just. It means respect.

To think SDG 5 is a "goal" and not an established, undeniable human right is astonishing. To not act on creating equality is criminal. Let's all "lead from the front" for those who are always pushed to the back.

LEAD FROM THE FRONT
DR. HANAN AL-MUTAWA

Living in the Arab world, it is important for me to be aware of cultural norms, religious inferences, and tribal habits that affect society, the welfare of women, and their economic growth.

I have long been an active campaigner for women's rights and changing perceptions of women. Around the world, women face an uphill battle to enter the top tier of business or take their rightful place in public life. In most countries, women CEOs and directors sadly remain a minority in the male-dominated business community.

I believe, "If you want to lead, you need to lead from the front."

Religion and politics are intertwined in the Arab world of business and the daily management of affairs. Women are often discriminated against when it comes to taking on leadership roles or even being nominated for senior posts. This is why it's so important that I continue to set an outstanding example of a high-achieving female entrepreneur and be a role model who is able to facilitate learning. I have been at the forefront of campaigns for women to play a greater role in public life, and it has come at a tremendous personal cost. But none so costly as the inequality we will continue to face if we don't stand up, be counted, and make ourselves heard.

True to my purpose, and as a way of giving back to the community, I, together with my husband Russell Byrne, co-founded the THRIVE Foundation, a social enterprise designed to support disenfranchised and impoverished women and children who do not have a voice.

Even in our modern society, women's career choices after high school are funneled into selecting careers more suited to conventional stereotyped roles favored by men; discriminatory regulations channel them to be clerks, caregivers for children, and dutiful wives. Compounding this issue, many girls drop out of school due to marriage (at the onset of puberty in some tribes). What about their education and their opportunity to have a career? This happens every day.

To Make a Difference you Have to Get Involved. You Have to Be In It to Win it.

For almost thirty years, I have sought to make a transformational impact on innovative educational provision and empowering gender equality in Kuwait and the wider region. It's not always easy but it is necessary. During the 1990 Iraqi invasion of Kuwait, I was stranded in London. I established an academy for children of fellow Kuwaiti families trapped away from home. Qualified as a teacher, this seemed the best use of my skillset, especially in this desperate time of need. I, together with the Kuwait Embassy in London, negotiated a bilateral agreement with the King Fahad Academy to educate Kuwaiti children formally called "refugees."

The future of Kuwait at this time was desperately unclear and in peril; therefore, my focus was especially devoted to empowering girls to have access to quality education and fighting inequality, thereby helping create qualified future leaders for Kuwait.

His Highness the Amir of the state of Kuwait, Sheikh Sabah Ahmed Jaber Al-Sabah, respectfully stated, "One of the main aspects of democracy in Kuwait is its belief in the freedom of women and their right to expression and to work and to hold leadership positions. Kuwaiti women have surpassed many in the region in achieving political, social, and economic rights and they have cooperated with their countrymen in bearing responsibility in their society."

I actively campaigned for women's rights and for changing the perceptions of women well before SDG 5, "Gender Equality," existed. I was the campaign manager for HE MP Dr. Massouma Al-Mubarak (twice Minister), the first woman to become a Kuwait cabinet minister in 2005, and four years later I was the campaign manager for her successful parliamentary election campaign in which Dr. Massouma became the first woman to enter the Kuwait Parliament in 2009. I was also instrumental in ensuring MP Dr. Rola Dashti, MP Dr. Salwa Al-Jassar, and MP Dr. Aseel Al-Awadhi successfully entered the Kuwait Parliament, setting a never-seen-before precedent and exemplar for all women in Kuwait and the GCC.

The challenges that I and the other campaigners faced were enormous. Not only were we breaking new ground; we were challenging fundamentalist mindsets and ingrained discrimination. It was not until the third election after women were given the right to stand for Parliament that the first female MPs were finally elected.

As campaign manager for Dr. Massouma Al-Mubarak, I played an important role in the historic advancement of women's rights, which was watched closely throughout the entire Gulf region, signaling a major shift in social attitudes by a key Arab state. It took seventy-one years of Kuwaiti parliament elections to see this change. But, finally, change did happen.

How Many Fatimas Are There?

Fatima[1] was a young woman I met who had dropped out of school to marry at a young age. She applied for a job at our kindergarten, looking for any suitable work, not only as a source of income but also as an escape. Fatima had no qualifications, not even a high school diploma; she had no skills on her resume and no self-confidence. I saw a fragile Fabergé egg. She was in her late teens when she got married. Now with four kids and filing for divorce, trying to escape the aggression and abuse of an alcoholic and narcotic-addicted husband, she was a little girl with adult responsibilities and pain she shouldn't need to endure. She didn't have the support mechanisms in place to reach out or any knowledge of who or what to ask for.

She expressed her concerns and anguish with pained hesitation. I myself have had troubles and sadness in my life, but when you listen to the plight of a woman drowning in her grief and turmoil, your issues become insignificant in relation to hers. Why? Because she is in a downward spiral and can't see a way out.

The motto, "Embolden, Engage, Empower," is my *raison d'être*. And here was an opportunity to exercise those values and support a woman whom I believed that, in time, would also support her community. It started with one woman and now our organization is "feminaponics" — lead and grown by women.

Over three years, Fatima has rebuilt her world; she earns a stable income and enjoys her haven at work. She filed for divorce and won a multitude of legal cases awarding her full custody of her children.

---

1   Her name has been changed to protect her privacy.

Her children are safe with her and her mother, who has been her Rosetta Stone throughout. The children are all enrolled in private schools; they have recovered from their violent past.

I am proud of Fatima's efforts to better herself. She has the most amazing personality, positive attitude, and warm demeanor. The parents appreciate her facilitation of learning and her compassionate nature, both of which enrich the lives of children in her care.

We are in the process of launching a project in which Fatima will be a member of the steering group to manage a franchise of the Royal Britannia (RB) Education model, and in turn, she too will lead, manage, and support other women and children in education in Kuwait. This is the power of change in action.

Barriers to Be Broken

Tribal habits are embedded into Arab societal mentality not only in the GCC, but also in the MENA region and Kuwait in particular. A large percentage of tribal families still subjugate their women through violence or bullying. Whatever the percentage, it is unacceptable.

Sadly, numerous female barristers in Kuwait have mentioned that many cases reach out of court settlements, and often the woman's family forfeits their rights to avoid dishonor to the family name. The lawyers I spoke with stated they do not have access to relevant measurable statistics; in most cases, there are no tangible or validated statistics that show the number of women in Kuwait who have been suppressed, abused, or violated by a spouse, elder sibling, male relative, male co-worker, or manager. Disquieting stories reveal that in a number of cases where girls were violated, the family and law enforcement officers force the victim to marry her rapist to save the family honor. If she was at school at the time, Kuwaiti law evicts her from mainstream daytime schooling. These violations are treated as "rumours," and it is generally recommended that business executives act with discretion toward line managers with notorious records.

Unfortunately, these men are promoted or transferred to other departments. As a rule of thumb, spouses or elder male relatives using similar methods of psychosocial tyranny, bullying, harassment, or unnecessary use of force also escape blame rather than cause embarrassment. But the plight and fight for the elimination of all forms of violence and other exploitation of women and girls must be eradicated from all countries. This is a must!

You've Got to Be In It to Win It

Commitment, dedication, and keeping your word are invaluable innate skills in an ever-changing cosmopolitan world.

You've got to be in to win it.

I have a vision of establishing organizations that are purpose-driven and create benefits for all stakeholders, not just shareholders. Through enterprise and volunteering, I fervently believe that we can be the change we seek in the world. I would like to ensure that all businesses are conducted as if people and places matter. Through their products, practices, and profits, businesses should aspire to do no harm and benefit all.

With a mission to "Embolden, Engage, Empower, and Serve the Community," and combining my passion, entrepreneurial spirit, and philanthropy, my ambition is to make inclusive and equitable quality education with life-long learning opportunities accessible to all. This includes the most vulnerable groups such as women, girls, and children with special needs. I ardently believe that entrepreneurs are not born; they're made through the simple philosophy of "learning by doing."

My vision for emboldening disenfranchised women and children involves engagement in education and extracurricular activities. The long-term vision I have is to improve the standards of education within Kuwait and the surrounding region, in both the public and private sectors, to ensure that women graduates will be on par with other students around the world seeking job opportunities. My goal is to lead a non-profit center that offers opportunities for people with a multitude of disabilities. This and many other ventures are currently underway.

There's no time to waste, no opportunity to miss. Be the change, and remember: You have to be in it to win it.

BE THE EXCEPTION TO THE RULE, A REBEL WITH SOUL
KRISTY CASTLETON

From the age of sixteen, I was fiercely independent. I chose the school I wanted to attend and the university where I wanted to learn. At nineteen, I traveled around the world, following my own itinerary, at my own pace, answering to no one but myself. I trekked through dense rainforests and sailed down river rapids in nothing but an inflatable ring. I threw myself out of a plane and even got in a cage with a four-year-old Bengal Tiger — I may have been fiercely independent, but I was also wonderfully naïve.

At twenty-four, I chose the job that I wanted; however, it wasn't a job I loved, so eighteen months later, I took voluntary redundancy and traveled to Asia. I only came home when my bank balance started to feature minus signs. I got a new job that paid more money, bought a sporty car, and was approved for a mortgage to buy a flat.

At thirty-three, I started my first company in London. At thirty-six, I sold my flat to fund my second company in Singapore. My brilliant company team is 75% women and I pay them equally to the 25% that are men.

I decide what I want to do, where I want to go, and when.

I am the exception, not the rule. I am hugely privileged to have been raised in a country that has only two laws that limit a woman's economic opportunities. I don't need my husband's approval to own a passport. I do not live in one of the nineteen countries where women are legally obliged to obey their husband's demands.

I can't imagine a world without the equal opportunities I've had, and I want to help create a world where no one else has to imagine them either.

This philosophy of life was formed very early, at the ripe age of five. My father was a vicar, and living in a vicarage meant there were frequent knocks on the door from those in need. My parents had what I now see as a beautifully generous give-back policy.

Anyone who knocked was given a friendly ear to listen, a cup of tea and sandwiches, a change of clothes if they needed one, and if they did some work around the garden, a bed for the night in the greenhouse or garage.

We had a lot of uptake on the garden work for garage deal, and so my childhood was spent surrounded by people from all walks of life mowing the lawn, digging the vegetable patch, or weeding the flowerbeds. A few homeless individuals became regulars, and they reached the point of being able to play (while supervised) with my brother and me. It didn't matter what their story was or where they were from, at those moments, they needed help, and it felt good to me that my parents were able to assist.

As a five-year-old I thought that everyone did this, so I was quite disappointed when I found out they didn't. It's incredible to find organizations like B1G1, where you can surround yourself with like-minded souls who dedicate their time and resources to making sure everyone has access to tea and sandwiches.

It's Time to Get Equal

I grew up in a household with a strong mother who was the primary breadwinner. My perspective on stereotypes and equality was positively challenged from the outset. Our family didn't operate like others I knew, but it worked. My perspective was that a woman-led household was a successful model.

In male-dominated countries, their view is that their male-led model works and understandably so, as it has been like that for generations. Why change a system that, in their minds, works? Change is uncomfortable, challenging, and produces fear. It's a big leap from fear of the unknown to courage, and from courage to trust; along the way, it requires understanding and acceptance to instigate equality.

The payoff, however, is worth every ounce of courage. First, gender equality encourages global peace. An intriguing study by two women at the University of Uppsala in Sweden found "robust support for a relationship between gender inequality and civil war … countries that display lower levels of gender equality are more likely to become involved in civil conflict, and violence is likely to be even more severe, than in countries where women have a higher status."[2]

Second, improvements in gender equality have been shown to increase the gross domestic product of a country or region. The European Union conducted a study revealing that by 2050, gender equality would produce an increase of two and a half trillion euros and increase the number of jobs by over 10 million.[3]

Third, gender equality can have a positive effect on the family unit. Tremendous pressure is placed on the man in traditional households to bring in the family income. In a gender-equal family, the option exists to have two income-generating parents, reducing pressure and allowing the man the opportunity to spend more quality time with his wife and children. The ripple effects of this are vast, many of which encourage positive memories.

If we can teach countries in which gender inequality exists to focus on the benefits equality brings all people, not just women, and to concentrate on the positive financial and welfare outcomes rather than the change required to get there, we would have more compelling reasons to gain the necessary momentum.

One important note is if you want to try to effect change, speak to people in a language they will understand. If they're numbers people, provide figures on how gender equality can increase global GDP. If they're uncomfortable with change, show them case studies of places where the process has been smooth and outline the steps toward effecting that same change. Always try for a win-win scenario.

Dream On — If You Dare

As children, we believe that anything is possible. Imagine what the world could achieve if we didn't lose that belief? I'm passionate about keeping dreams alive. The more we dream, and believe that our dreams can come true, the more we will be able to make them

2 Louise Olsson and Erika Forsberg, "Gender Inequality and Internal Conflict," in Oxford Research Encyclopedias of Politics (Oxford: Oxford University Press, 2016).
3 "Economic Benefits of Gender Equality in the European Union," European Institute for Gender Equality,
https://eige.europa.eu/gender-mainstreaming/policy-areas/economic-and-financial-affairs/economic-benefits-gender-equality

come true. We can change the world for good, one dream at a time. Dream on and dream big.

Rebel & Soul is a dream to me. It's a socially conscious business. For every memorable experience we create for brands, we generate life-enhancing experiences for those who need them the most. The team chooses the charities that they feel strongly about, and when we finish a project, we generate a gift to that charity. We also trigger donations when our clients connect with us on social media and via our website.

As a company with a neuroscience methodology that seeks to create the most impactful memories, it's imperative that we have positive memories associated with everything we do. Having this as one of our values allows us to have a positive "better business and better world" proposition that unifies the team.

The team also dedicates their time and skills to our partner charities. We help organize and run charity events, create event technology to help people connect at these events, and help our partners create and pitch marketing strategies to larger, world-renowned organizations to win charitable grants. This allows more trust to be built between our clients and our team. We offer our clients genuine, heartfelt business for good value, and they have the opportunity to feel like they have helped generate purposeful results.

When a business has a purpose more powerful than generating more business or more funds, the business can also feed your soul. Now that's a business worth creating.

THE ANSWER
HELEN CAMPBELL

The answer was right there … on a train in Japan.

I was shocked and saddened when I heard the words, "Your brother Julian has been accepted at a boarding school." As an eleven-year-old girl about to start at the local secondary school, I knew I would miss my younger brother. But something else was going on deep inside me too. Why was his education and career prioritized above his two sisters, Ally and I?

I felt indignant, wondering how society could favor boys/men like this!

This, of course, was long ago. Yet still there is a need to take action on gender inequality. It's like a *disease* — if not stopped it grows and gnaws away at the very fabric of our society. SDG 5, "Gender Equality," is something our world needs more than ever before.

As I write this, I'm on a train in Japan. For a number of reasons, Japan is not the country in which you might expect to see SDG 5 in action. Yet you do. Everywhere. And I saw it just now, in the most gracious way.

As the train conductor walked through the carriage, he stopped and gently yet purposefully bowed to all the occupants. He turned and proceeded to the next carriage to repeat the process. Each respecting the other — the conductor respects the occupants and vice versa.

Gender equality is founded on respect. And respect is founded on love — love both for ourselves, and for others.

Sometimes this is difficult. My life story bears witness to these challenges. And thankfully, it lets us see the way forward too.

I grew up in a remote part of South Wales, Great Britain. I chose a career that took me around the world and later settled in Melbourne, Australia.

When I travel, I'm always in awe of women around the globe as they go about their everyday lives, carrying out multi-dimensional tasks that are often overlooked and unappreciated. Women's work spans such a wide range — caring for families, running a home, becoming leaders and business directors. Anything and everything seems to be possible for us when opportunities are equally available.

Yet inequality is still ingrained in our psyche by our collective consciousness of time gone by. And it's this inequality that has fueled my thirst to end it.

When, as Steve Jobs famously described, I connect the dots backward, I see that it's actually become a life purpose for me. And now I see positive movement (like SDG 5) helping diminish inequality.

I have been involved in B1G1 study tours to Cambodia, India, Indonesia, and Kenya. These tours enable participants to see the difference giving can make, and how it directly affects those in need.

I've experienced the impact that microloans have when given to women to learn a skill and gain independence. I've helped build playgrounds in Cambodia to encourage girls and boys to go to school. And I've seen incredible things in rural India, where boys and girls go to special solar-driven e-learning schools. The difference in the children is so profound that their parents now go to school in the evening. And the children become their teachers.

There are now women who label themselves as "Professors of Goatology." They run complex goat-breeding programs and implement systems to make sure each family that receives a goat gives its progeny to another family, beautifully nurturing the community. It's respect and care in action every day.

But it's not always success stories; being a woman in business is tough. It is not for the faint-hearted, and you certainly have to believe in your abilities and be resourceful and determined. On numerous occasions, men have forcefully attempted to undermine me, talk over my ideas, intimidate me with their strength, or ignore my presence.

I have even been told, "We have got this. You just go home and have a glass of wine or don't worry your pretty head. This is men's business!"

Well, on that occasion, they were manipulating the system, and if I had stepped away at that time, they would have gotten away with a sub-par job and charged me megabucks too!

I was determined to take business a different way, prioritizing compassion and respect. I was determined not to run our business using a hard-nosed, head-driven, profit-first approach but rather from the perspective of serving our patients and supporting our team and our community. We start and move through each day with a greater sense of sustainable purpose. A purpose that I believe doesn't stop when your workday does.

Turning Care into Action and Pain into Power

My determination to conduct business differently, prioritizing compassion and respect, didn't stop at the workplace. In fact, my life has become a testament to finding a more heart-centered approach in all areas, and many people feel the same.

My favorite evenings are spent sitting around a table with delicious morsels of food and drink, and conversing with my family and friends. The conversations I hear over and over again prove to me that most people deeply care about our world. The topics include health, equality, the government, the environment, refugee camps, world hunger, and much more. But we also seem frozen by the pain of global atrocities, although we all really want to help. We just do not know where to begin and who to trust. Perhaps the best place is moving our care and compassion into *action*.

I've found that the words from Arion Light, of Melbourne's "Warrior of Love" program, can help us all take action. Here's Arion:

I'm just one human. Can I really make a difference?

I read through the 17 SDG goals of the UN and my heart breaks. The size of the problems and the complexities of the solutions are beyond me. I am just one human.

I have a son to raise, bills to pay, and my own life to manage — can I really make a difference? I am not wildly wealthy, a politician, doctor, or technical expert. I have but one thing I am truly passionate about. People.

Looking at the SDGs, I was paralyzed by my own lack of ability to answer any one of the seventeen major problems. But I realized there was an eighteenth goal hidden in the other seventeen. The gap between caring and action.

So many people care but so few have time to express their care in action. How do we cause care and love to become action?

Without millions of people across the globe rising to support solutions for these seventeen problems, we have no chance. The size of the problems require a rising of love in action across the globe.

Yet I have a vision. Warriors of love rising across the globe to make a difference in millions of little and big ways. People willing to put in their time, money, and resources to make the solutions happen.

Each of us is so small and can offer so little, but if many of us offer a little, it can build momentum and become a wave of love.

So, I ask what is needed to cause those millions of little people to become a wave of love. An army of love? What will cause them to put their phones down and get involved in what matters?

I don't know. I am but just one human.

At the heart of this apathy, I see pain. A frozen mass of people across the globe too paralyzed by the global pain, and their pain, to have any power to do anything about it.

I say we have to learn how to turn our pain into power.

We are inundated with images of war, famine, global catastrophes, and too much abuse to comprehend. Many of us have become numb, reaching for our phones and reality TV to cope. We need tools to transform this numbness. We have to turn our pain into power. I know many are not ready or willing to do this yet, but I also hope and believe there are many who are.

I discovered this too. A week or two after my wife had passed from her sixteen-month cancer journey I was left with our two-year-old son and an immense amount of pain. I was broken open by grief, love, and loss.

I was lucky enough to be supported by all the core men in my world. One day, these twenty-five men gathered our men's circle by the Yarra River, where we shared our stories of love, loss, and what my late wife, Mirabai, meant to us.

My story of love, pain, conflict, numbness, resentment, grief, healing, hope, family, death, rebirth, and so much more poured out of me. Men's tears fell to the earth with mine. As they carried me into the Yarra River, it became a moment of deep healing and surrender.

This story speaks of the power we have, as a community, to move through numbness and welcome the pain and grief that having a caring heart will bring. And while this is a very personal story, I believe the same response is required on a global level, especially for any of us truly called to look at and feel the pain of the world.

Three Steps to Move from Pain to Power
- *Look.* Notice your emotions and do not waver. Notice grief, powerlessness, and any other emotions.
- *Feel* and express all emotions until they move fully through you.
- *Take action.* By sustaining the first two, your pain will transmute into the possibility of power. You claim this power by taking action. When you take action, you crack the powerlessness story and build momentum to truly being someone who has the power to change these things. Actions are your power.

— Arion Light

Love-Inspired Action
As I sit here, reflecting on Arion's words and paying homage to my own experiences, the Japanese countryside whisks past me.

I stepped onto the train not knowing how to write this story. I took action. I found my voice, and I wrote what mattered. Every one of us needs a clear voice, a new story of respect for and acceptance of who we are.

And as the train conductor walks through the carriage again, he stops again and gently, purposely bows to all of us.

All we all need to do is that. Respect and accept. And, of course, to take love-inspired *action.*

I have a global vision for humanity. I believe that as we each reconnect to our hearts, we will move into action and create powerfully. As we share our care and compassion, it will flow like a tsunami of loving action all over the globe.

WHAT YOU CAN DO TO
CREATE A WORLD OF
GENDER EQUALITY

Lifestyle tips:
- Share the workload at home.
- Find female mentors and leaders.
- Be aware of gender stereotypes. Recognize them, avoid them and educate others about them.

Business tips:
- Make your decisions based on ability not on a stereotype.
- Offer equal pay for equal work.
- Set gender equality goals in your business.
- Encourage dialogue to support female workers.

Giving tips:
- Fund programs that support education of young girls.
- Support awareness-raising programs that educate communities on the importance of gender equalities.
- Support programs that provide sanitary items to adolecent girls so they can continue their education uninterrupted.

WATER AND SANITATION FOR ALL

6 CLEAN WATER AND SANITATION

HOW YOU AND YOUR BUSINESS CAN ENSURE AVAILABLE AND SUSTAINABLE MANAGEMENT OF WATER AND SANITATION FOR ALL.

"Pure water is the world's first and foremost medicine."

— Slovakian Proverb

THE CHANGEMAKERS

WATER IS LIFE
PETER FOWLER AND DAVID KEITH

Peter Fowler and David Keith help transform local, national, and international businesses with astute commercial advice, and offer growth and innovation initiatives that help them to thrive.

The multi-award-winning duo help fast-track business success and personally mentor altruistic business owners and board members. They are recognized as two of Australia's business leaders, having been awarded multiple national and international business excellence awards.

collinshume.com.au

THE ONE VITAL THING
SHANNON BURFORD

Shannon Burford is a vibrant health practitioner dedicated to wellness and health. He faced many health challenges through his teenage years and early twenties, which led him to herbal medicine. He embarked on his second bachelor's degree in health science in Melbourne. He graduated as a clinical naturopath and medical herbalist and opened his clinic, Cura Integrative Medicine, in Perth. He now runs his busy wellness center, helping patients heal naturally.

curamedicine.com.au, superkidsdetox.com

INSPIRE "FREEDOM DAYS" FOR ALL
BEN WALKER

Ben Walker founded Inspire at age twenty-three with nothing but a laptop, a borrowed printer, and a simple idea — what if, instead of just doing taxes and reporting on history, accountants could give game-changing advice to help people write a better future for themselves? Six years on, Inspire has been showcased as a global example of what an accounting firm should be. Thanks to Ben's disruptive approach to the traditional "old school" accounting model, accountants can now single-handedly change lives — every day.

benwalker.com, inspire.business

WATER AND SANITATION FOR ALL

You could be forgiven to think that water is a free-flowing resource we can indulge in at whim.

Just looking around bustling cities you see water flowing everywhere. There are ornamental fountains, drinking fountains and a choice of sparkling or still in every café. There are public toilets, waterparks, swimming pools, car and pet washes as well as rivers and canals streaming with action.

Take a look in many homes and you'll often see more than one bathroom, lots of water outlets, spas, swimming pools, ponds and people watering their lush gardens and lawns.

You'd be forgiven for not knowing that we are currently in a global water crisis.

And it's a crisis so big that in 2016 the UN General Assembly followed up the launch of SDG 6 with the "Water Action Decade" — that is, they dedicated an entire decade to seeking global solutions. And they did that quite simply because without this goal, no other goal is possible.

We, as a species, do not survive without fresh water. It's that simple. But the practical solutions are a little more complex.

The reality is that there is sufficient fresh water on the planet to give fresh water to everyone. However, due to things such as poor infrastructure or poverty-stricken economies, millions of people die every year from diseases associated with inadequate water supply, sanitation and hygiene.

Currently, 844 million people live without access to safe water. And 159 million depend on surface water. Think of it this way — a staggering six times the population of the US lives without a household water connection.

And worse, every year 3,575,000 people die from water related diseases. This is equivalent to a jumbo jet crashing every hour. And 2.2 million of these people are children. 2.2 million!

All of this is preventable. And that means we can change it. But it's not just *we can*, it's *we must*. Not only can we save millions of people's lives but we can enrich millions of others' lives too.

And that's because just like with all of the other Sustainable Development Goals, there's a ripple effect. Water scarcity, poor water quality and inadequate sanitation also impacts other vital areas – like growing food, children going to school, people living a healthy, happy life. Drought also impacts some of the world's poorest countries, increasing hunger and malnutrition and decreasing food production and health. It's a vicious cycle that we must change.

Fortunately, inspiring progress has been made in the past decade. Over 90% of the world's population now has access to *improved sources* of drinking water. But water scarcity still affects more than 40% of the global population.

The UN has released some facts to show us the areas where we need improvement.

- 1 in 4 health care facilities lacks basic water services.
- 3 in 10 people lack access to safely managed drinking water services and 6 in 10 people lack access to safely managed sanitation facilities.
- At least 892 million people continue to practice open defecation.
- Women and girls are responsible for water collection in 80% of households without access to water on premises.
- Over 1.7 billion people are currently living in river basins where water use exceeds recharge.
- 2.4 billion people lack access to basic sanitation services, such as toilets or latrines.
- More than 80% of wastewater resulting from human activities is discharged into rivers or sea without any pollution removal.
- Approximately 70% of all water abstracted from rivers, lakes, and aquifers is used for irrigation.

There's still much to be done. Every drop counts.

What's more promising is that businesses are replying to the urgent cries for action in unprecedented ways.

Global businesses, including those involved in the production of food, energy, chemicals, metals, and medicines play a huge role in turning this crisis around. In fact, just like every drop counts – every single person counts too. So too, every business.

Changemaker Ben Walker is an accountant. And his accountancy business is a valued contributor to this and many other goals. More than just 'contributors' though, Ben and his team have built their entire business model around giving back. For every dollar in tax they save their clients, they give to global initiatives aligned with the SDGs. Ben's business not only gives to meaningful initiatives, he personally visits such places to see first hand how other people live and the difference a conscious business can make.

Changemaker Shannon Burford is another conscious business leader. His clinical health practice is driven by his knowledge and passion to keep people healthy and well. His poignant message simplifies this goal for everyone. He said, "I wondered about what one thing could improve our health. It's hard to refine it down to one thing, but out of food, supplements, shelter, clothing, etc, I had to choose clean water. I believe that the number one thing that is essential for better health would have to be clean, accessible water."

Changemakers Peter Fowler and David Keith have already contributed over 11 million impacts in this area and are on a mission to achieve more. They see this goal as the foundation to achieve all the others. They said "real sustainability comes from the sense of giving and caring. We believe that everyone, regardless of who they are or where they live should have access to clean water. They should also have access to acceptable sanitation and hygiene practices. These two goals are pivotal to achieving any of the other SDG goals."

It really is that simple. Clean water and sanitation must be more than a goal to achieve. It *must* be achieved to make all the other goals possible. Poet, H. Auden wrote, "Thousands have lived without love, not one without water."

Maybe we can live with both.

WATER IS LIFE
PETER FOWLER AND DAVID KEITH

Water is life.

We need water for drinking, cooking, cleaning, and sanitation. Our livestock need water to survive. Our food crops need water to grow. Our forests and environments need water to thrive and produce oxygen.

Without water, there is no life.

The UN estimates that over 40% of the world's population suffers from water scarcity. This number is projected to rise with increasing global temperatures due to climate change. In the next 30 years, it is estimated that 1 in 4 people will be affected by increased droughts, desertification, and recurring water shortages.

Further, over 4 billion people lack access to basic sanitation such as toilets. Each day, over 1,000 children die due to preventable water and sanitation related diseases. 1,000 children ... each and every day!

In our travels, we have witnessed children and families bathing and drinking from dirty livestock dams and potholes on the side of the road, and children struggling in school due to lack of water, food, and basic sanitation.

We know we can make a difference by building wells, investing in adequate infrastructure, and providing sanitation facilities for better hygiene, which will ultimately reduce illness and disease, improve agricultural production, and provide a better life for those who experience water scarcity. With improved health, children can grow strong, further their studies, break the cycle of poverty, and provide a better future for their families.

In Australia, we are so lucky. We have clean water, toilets, and sanitation, as well as medical support. We also know the effect droughts have on the livelihood and mental welfare of our farmers. Water scarcity is a current issue in rural Australia. The majority of our population lives in cities or suburban areas where although water scarcity remains a problem, water is generally taken for granted.

Nearly every household in Australia owns a motor vehicle and washing the car is a weekly ritual. Thousands of liters of fresh, clean water go down the drain each week, just to keep our cars clean.

We also use fresh, clean water on our lawns and gardens, not necessarily irrigating fruit trees or vegetable patches for food, but usually so that we can lay claim to having the greenest lawn or the prettiest flowerbeds on the street.

The Australian governments have built desalination plants to keep up with demand for water in urban areas and charge for each liter of water that we use. However, this does not seem to have curbed the amount of water that we use or change our attitude toward the way we use water.

It wasn't until we started traveling overseas that we began to understand the scale and severity of people around the world living on a daily basis without access to clean water. Traveling through developing countries, we were able to see the effects first-hand.

Coming from an affluent country, the first time we saw people defecating in the same river they bathed in and drank from left us with a lasting impression. We immediately put ourselves in the situation and asked how they could do this. But for many people around the world, they have no other option.

In our travels to Africa, in particular Tanzania, we witnessed the crises facing the people living (or merely surviving) there. Seeing children wash and drink from dirty potholes on the side of the road. Visiting a school of twelve hundred students in Karatu that had no toilets or running water, and had dirt floors in the classrooms. Watching children and women walking six kilometers roundtrip every morning and evening to the nearest well so they could drink clean water. It left us with a far greater understanding of how important clean water and sanitation are. For these people, it's survival.

We went to Tanzania for the holiday of a lifetime, to see the amazing wildlife of the Serengeti Plains and the Ngorongoro Crater. We loved every moment of it, but most importantly, we left with a deeper appreciation of how important clean water is for those who don't have it. It created a lasting imprint on our lives and is something we remember daily.

Together we have the capacity, technology, and resources to help these people build wells, put an end to open defecation, and provide them with access to sanitation.

We fully understand the severity of not having enough water and sanitation and the ramifications it can have on one's life. Knowing this, we are now massive advocates of organizations supporting these causes.

We believe real sustainability comes from a sense of giving and caring. Everyone, regardless of who they are or where they live, should have access to clean water. They should also have access to acceptable sanitation and hygiene practices. These two goals are pivotal to achieving any of the other SDGs.

We are privileged to be able to live, work, and play in one of the most beautiful and prosperous regions in Australia and the world. On our doorstep, we can choose to partake in any number of lifestyle choices; we thrive in our locale and our kids are healthy and strong. Given this, it would be remiss of us not to play a small part in bringing basics such as clean drinking water, sanitation, and hope to people around the world.

When Collins Hume began in 1980, our mission was simply to deliver the best value tax services in our region. But the world has changed and so have we. Today, we've added to our mission; our overriding purpose is to inspire business owners to achieve business and lifestyle success in powerful and meaningful ways. We believe there has never been a more exciting time to be in business and it is clear that successful, profitable businesses are the lifeblood of the communities in which we live. By partnering with and inspiring business owners to achieve extraordinary results, collectively we build stronger communities, change lives, and build a better world.

Clean water and sanitation have always been at the forefront of our giving activities; to date, through our partnership with B1G1, we have created over 11 million giving impacts in this area.

As business advisers, we are passionate about connecting with and helping altruistic business owners that want to not only create a legacy but to live a legacy. We know that it will be business owners and their teams that will change the world. This is why we love embracing the SDGs.

By connecting with, educating, and helping other business owners create purposeful business strategies and environmentally sustainable businesses, we can build stronger, more purposeful companies with minimal impact on our environment and create a better world for all.

It is through our experience and our advice to others we are helping change the world, one impact and one smile at a time, and that's what drives us each and every day.

Change the World One Smile at a Time

One time, in Bali, after visiting the mobile clinic set up by the John Fawcett Foundation, we headed to Canggu to visit clients. Our driver was a man called Wayan. We had never met Wayan before this day, but his brother-in-law, Kadek, had been a great friend of Peter's for many years. Usually, Kadek would drive us around Bali, but on this occasion, he had to attend a friend's wedding. Instead, Kadek arranged for Wayan to drive us.

Kadek and Wayan were both born and bred in a remote rural village of Bali called Balian. Upon returning to the car after catching up with our clients, Wayan indicated that he had read the John Fawcett Foundation brochure we had left on the front seat. He asked us if we supported and donated to the Foundation. When we told him that we did, he was so very thankful to us.

He proceeded to show us his glasses from the eye clinic and proudly shared his story about how he and his family had visited the eye center and received glasses to help them read better, which enabled him to drive and earn a living. More importantly, he told us his mother-in-law (Kadek's mother) had received life-changing cataract surgery from the clinic. Something that Kadek had never previously mentioned.

We went on to learn that up until Kadek's mother received cataract surgery, she required constant care from her daughter, as she was almost completely blind. This was a burden on her family as her daughter could not work nor support her family adequately. After the surgery, she no longer required constant care and her daughter opened a small convenience store on the main road near their village.

They were not only able to create a better life for themselves and their family, but also could provide quality schooling for their son, who went on to finish high school and university and become a teacher. He has since returned to the village and is now teaching local children. It was fantastic to hear about the ripple effect of how a simple and relatively inexpensive surgery not only changed one person's life, but flowed on to their family and the community where they live.

Without this surgery, Kadek's mother would have spent the rest of her life blind. It's hard to put into words how thankful they are to us and other donors. It was a touching moment and something we will remember for the rest of our lives. The most ironic thing about this story is that if Wayan had never visited the eye clinic, he would never have been able to read the brochure, share his family's story, and tell us how grateful he was for our support.

This is only one story among many. There are incredible people changing lives every day. But we need more. We need more smiles. Water equals health and happiness. Water and care equal smiles. One impact creates one smile. One smile at a time, we can collectively make the world a better place. Always give more than you receive. If everyone did the same, no one would ever go without and the world would be full of smiles. ☺

THE ONE VITAL THING
SHANNON BURFORD

I believe health is the most important thing we have. No matter who you are or what you are doing, you absolutely need health to do it.

You can do more, achieve more, enjoy more, laugh more, and live more with better health. Has anyone ever hungered for more sickness, or chosen to keep their cold or flu?

When patients come to me for healthcare, I prepare a herbal medicine mix, design an individualized diet plan, and prescribe an extra boost of nutritional supplements.

My family and I are truly blessed to have an abundance of food choices, as well as access to the best integrative medicine in the world. There is no doubt the same applies to almost all families in my hometown of Perth, Western Australia.

I wondered about the one thing that could improve our health. It's hard to narrow it down, but out of food, supplements, clothing, shelter and clean water, I had to choose the last. I believe that water is the number one thing needed for better health — clean, accessible water.

Water is the most important health-sustaining ingredient for every living thing on earth. Healthy people, healthy plants, healthy animals, and even healthy little insects need water to sustain life. And yet so many on the planet struggle to have access to clean water.

For this reason, supporting projects around the globe to help supply access to clean, accessible water is central to my own and the Cura Integrative Medicine core mission.

I graduated from university and dived into working in a goldmine laboratory. Something didn't feel quite right and I had a yearning to learn more. I lasted only six months at this job and left it knowing that I had to learn more.

In 1999, I left Perth to travel for a year. I returned seven years later, a little more aware of the gifts we have living in Perth such as the luxury of clean tap water, hot showers, and an abundance of comforts to sustain our lives easily.

I started my learning first in Indonesia, then throughout India. I traveled as a backpacker on a budget of around $2–3 a day, so I ate simple food and unfortunately sometimes experienced bedbugs. Along the way, I spent some time in an Indian hospital due to sickness, where I hit a deep low and my health dropped considerably.

After India, I retreated to the United Kingdom for one year to rebuild my funds and health. I was still hungry to learn more about the world. My school friends lived around the world and were meeting at a beach party in Thailand for a reunion. I thought it was a great idea and jumped on a plane. The journey continued to Cambodia, where I stayed for eighteen months teaching English to airport staff and government workers.

Although I had already learned a great deal about disparities between cultures, it was in Cambodia that I truly understood the need for clean water and better health throughout the world. After those eighteen months, I had to leave because I just could not cope with the reality that the changes needed to shift the levels of poverty would take decades. I was mentally exhausted by the insanely disproportionate levels of healthcare allocated to the global population.

My time and experience in Cambodia left me with bigger questions about how I could get the ball rolling to help make changes in the world. How could I be part of the change to bring clean water to everyone? This is where business enters.

Business Can Save People and Create Dreams

Growing a better, conscious business is a joy and gives everyone a bigger reason to wake up in the morning. I'm hungry to drive my business into a future that will help all children (including my own) and their children live in a better world.

I also can't dream of doing anything else. I get a huge buzz from guiding patients to better health and seeing big smiles. Can you think of a time when your day passed incredibly slowly because you found yourself in a peaceful zone, created by the absolute joy of what you were doing? Maybe your job is the same. Or maybe you feel that way when you play with your children. Well, if I keep my eye on the bigger picture, thinking not only of the patients sitting in front of me, but the greater ripple extending out to help a wider sphere of people, I live in that zone every second.

Whatever you believe or trust in, you most likely enjoy helping others through your business and daily interactions. How can you do that more — how can you magnify your difference — while also running a successful business? Start right now, through micro-giving on a daily basis. A little each day or week can help projects around the planet.

As a bonus, the magic of the universe will surprise you and you will see the ripple reflected in the growth of your business, too. It's a win-win, because you are able to create even more of an impact while watching your business grow.

Simple mathematics demonstrates that if every single small, medium, and large business contributed to projects that align with their values, we could overcome global inequalities. It all starts with the first steps as individuals, which are then are magnified into much bigger things.

I'm assuming you are reading this book because you have an understanding that there is something more to this life. We're spinning around on a big rock in an expansive universe with many questions regarding what it's all about. At this point in time, we all have the power to improve the planet and all of its inhabitants. Even if I'm wrong, I feel that it will not do any harm if we do attempt to dream big.

As John Lennon said, "Love is the answer and you know that for sure, love is a flower you got to let it grow."

I have two beautiful children and an amazing wife to share my life with. They bring meaning to my world and remind me of how lucky I am. Throughout our day, we drink from a tap and use a water filter. We have an abundance of food and comfortable shelter. We drive cars and live in safety. Life is good (for us)!

There are, however, many stories that bring tears to my eyes — it is just so hard to understand the suffering of so many in the world. I can still smell the putrid water of the slums in multiple countries that turned my stomach. Seeing families collecting this water for drinking was crippling.

Although the families boil the water before drinking it, I know there are still unsafe levels of heavy metals and environmental chemical contaminants, that are not removed by this method alone.

While I have seen an endless stream of desperate people begging for food, water, and money, the most difficult to forget is one little baby. I still have a clear image of a woman, carrying a baby in her arms, begging for food in Cambodia. She was frantic for milk formula for her baby, who only had one eye. I could only pray for a better basic level of medical care for those beautiful people.

I still have a dream of basic medical care being available to all humans and I want to be part of the change to make it happen.

My ultimate legacy is for the Cura clinics to help children around the world grow up healthy, with access to everything they need to thrive and shine as brightly as they desire.

I've helped many different people in my clinic and the most rewarding are children. They bounce back the fastest and I know that if I can get them on a healthy path, it will ripple through their whole lives. I'm passionate about healthy children, and if I can help them flourish early, then they have a better chance of helping people as well.

INSPIRE "FREEDOM DAYS" FOR ALL
BEN WALKER

Water is such a basic human need that it really should be available to everyone.

Being an accountant, I was surprised, shocked, and compelled when I researched the basic numbers regarding water.

It's baffling that in Australia, we get cranky when we pay over $1.50 per liter for petrol, but we're happy to pay over $6 per liter from the same service station for a bottle of water. Meanwhile, you can give one person in Malawi water for their *entire life* for around the same price — just five US dollars.

And here's a promising statistic from the World Health Organization: For every $1 invested in water and toilets, it returns $4 in reduced healthcare costs for individuals and society. The more we focus on this goal, the better it will be for the local economies where help is most needed.

The Clean Water and Sanitation SDG is one of the most achievable and sustainable, given the price per impact, and the flow-on effect solving this problem would have on communities.

I recognized the importance of this goal when I first heard Paul Dunn speak. It was April 2013, and I was at a "Power of Small" event he was hosting in Brisbane. It was toward the start of the event when Paul asked the audience, "Who loves coffee?" I jumped up and put both hands in the air.

Then he asked, "Who's a bit grumpy if they haven't had a coffee by 10 a.m.?" I think I inherited this from my mom, but yes — my hands remained up.

"Well, what if you weren't able to have water until 10 a.m., or if you had to go a whole day without water?"

I thought that would be rough. Maybe I could do it — but not without headaches, tiredness, and dehydration.

Paul went on to tell us that almost a third of the world doesn't have access to clean drinking water. Now, I know that this may seem super obvious today, but back then, it hit me like a ton of bricks.

I'd known nothing but abundance growing up, especially an abundance of food as my dad is a chef. To imagine families without access to something as free flowing (in Australia) as water was absolutely heartbreaking.

Hearing Paul speak at this event was a major turning point in my business life. Originally, I'd started Inspire as a tool to help clients achieve much greater than the industry standard. That day, however, I saw my business as a tool for a much greater purpose. Needless to say, we have never looked back.

Inspire now contributes to clean water as one of our primary giving projects in our Day-for-a-Dollar campaign. Day-for-a-Dollar is where we give a day's worth of access to food, water, health, or sanitation to a family in need for each dollar of tax savings we create for a client.

At Inspire, we also help other business owners to "live the good life." Most believe that wealth is measured in dollars, but we believe wealth should be measured in days, or what we call "Freedom Days." Freedom Days are calculated as net wealth divided by cost of living per day.

Let's take two business owners, both worth $10,000 on paper.

Person 1 is living the "high life" — has the latest Mercedes, owns a massive mansion on the Brisbane River, and goes to expensive restaurants. This person's cost of living per day is $1,000.

Person 1's Freedom Days are 10. ($10,000 net wealth divided by $1,000 per day.)

Person 2 lives a modest life — drives a nice car, has a nice house, but nothing so flashy as to accrue debt. Person 2 goes on date nights, enjoys a nice holiday, and lives within a healthy family budget. Their cost of living is $100 per day.

Person 2's Freedom Days are 100. ($10,000 net wealth divided by $100 per day.)

In our eyes, Person 2 is wealthier. Ten times wealthier, in fact.

Our goal is to increase our clients' Freedom Days by doing one of two things:

- Helping them increase their net wealth (e.g., wise investment decisions, asset protection).

- Helping them decrease their cost of living (e.g., reduced debt, living within a budget).

We believe helping someone increase their Freedom Days gives them the ability to have more, so that they can live more and give more.

I want to help people create businesses that give them the freedom to put their family first and make a difference in the world.

I was inspired by my grandfather, who started an international removal business in the early 1980s. When I was young, my grandmother was diagnosed with cancer and my grandfather was able to effectively "retire" from his business — stepping back to solely focus on being there for her, while still being able to provide financially.

Having that sort of flexibility from your business doesn't come without hard work, structure, and great people. But the rewards are incredible.

I want to help people use their business to create that ability to put their family first — not just when a family member gets sick, but when they want to attend a netball or soccer game, take their family on a holiday, go out for a nice meal, or simply enjoy time spent together.

If One Goat Can Make a Difference — So Can You

My wife Stevie and I went on the 2018 B1G1 study tour to Kenya. One of the places we stayed in was the village of Odede.

We met with the chief and visited the place where the women walked every day to get water for their families. After walking thirty minutes down a hill, we finally got to the lake where the women filled up their drums of water.

Some people organized a race — a water carrying race. It was the visitors against the locals. They filled twenty-liter drums with water from the lake and put them on our heads. Not only was it bulky, heavy, and awkward to position on our heads, but we then had to race about one hundred meters in a straight line while keeping it there.

It was a bit of fun for us; we had plenty of laughs and talked with the locals. But what really hit home was the fact these women walk thirty minutes downhill, then back up again with twenty liters of water on their heads — multiple times a day. This is their only drinking water, and while it suited them, it wasn't anywhere near as clean as we would see in a developed country.

A water pump and filter could do amazing things for this village. The hours involved in organizing water could be redirected to other outcomes for the village.

While in Kenya, we also met with a family who had received a goat many, many years ago. The mother bred the goats and used the income to put her children and foster children through school and then university. We meet the mother and one of the daughters and talked with them about the impact the goat had on their lives.

It got me thinking, if the gift of a single goat can change a family's life, then surely I could too.

WHAT YOU CAN DO TO CREATE A WORLD OF CLEAN WATER AND SANITATION

Lifestyle tips:
- Be mindful. Turn off running water.
- Organize a clean up project for waterways, rivers and oceans.
- Raise awareness about the hygiene issues in your community.

Business tips:
- Learn about the program WASH (water, sanitation and hygiene) and implement it as the workplace pledge.
- Educate your team on conscious saving of water.
- Install water saving taps at your business facilities.

Giving tips:
- Support programs that build wells and provide water filters.
- Support programs that provide sanitation to rural communities.

NATURAL ENERGY TO IGNITE OUR LIVES

7 AFFORDABLE AND CLEAN ENERGY

HOW YOU AND YOUR BUSINESS CAN ENSURE ACCESS TO AFFORDABLE, RELIABLE, SUSTAINABLE, AND MODERN ENERGY FOR ALL.

> *"The shift to a cleaner energy economy won't happen overnight, and it will require tough choices along the way. But the debate is settled. Climate change is a fact."*
>
> — Barack Obama

THE CHANGEMAKERS

HOW BUSINESS LEADERS CAN SPEARHEAD CLIMATE ACTION
JEREMY BENTHAM

Jeremy Bentham has been in the energy business for more than 35 years. A graduate of Oxford University, he joined Shell in 1980 following postgraduate study at the California Institute of Technology. He also holds a Master's degree in management from MIT, where he was a Sloan Fellow.

Jeremy has held many different positions during his career at Shell – including technology process design, manufacturing economics and commercial information technology. Since 2006, he has been on the leadership team for Shell's overall corporate strategy. In this capacity, Jeremy leads the Global Business Environment team, which is best known for developing forward-looking scenarios to support the company's strategic thinking.

shell.com/scenarios, #shellscenarios

LIGHTING UP LIVES THROUGH SUSTAINABLE COMMUNITIES
DR. MADHAV SATHE

Dr. Madhav Sathe is an anesthesiologist working at Bombay Hospital, Breach Candy Hospital, and Sportsmed Hospital. He has presented award-winning research papers at various conferences and has served as the joint honorary secretary of the Bombay Mothers and Children Welfare Society (BMCWS) since 1985. Dr. Sathe uses his entrepreneurial skills to transform dying organizations into sustainable social enterprises. The BMCWS run three ultra-modern, low-cost hospitals in urban and rural areas and provide shelter to one hundred cancer patients to help them complete their treatment with a smile. Dr. Sathe initiated low-cost and innovative rural development programs in ninety-one villages. He is a visiting faculty member at the School of Social Entrepreneurship at the TATA Institute of Social Sciences in Mumbai.

thebmcws.com

NATURAL ENERGY TO IGNITE OUR LIVES

Ever heard of Perovskite? You soon will — it might become as common as the word "meteorite."

It's one of those recently discovered easily synthesized naturally occurring structures that has similar efficiencies as the current photo-voltaic cells yet it can be produced at dramatically less cost. So, the outlook looks bright. But it needs to.

Consider these startling facts:
- 13% of the global population still lacks access to modern electricity.
- 3 billion people (that's nearly half of us) rely on wood, coal, charcoal or animal waste for cooking and heating.
- Energy is the dominant contributor to climate change, accounting for around 60% of total global greenhouse gas emissions.
- Indoor air pollution from using combustible fuels for household energy caused 4.3 million deaths in 2012, with women and girls accounting for 6 out of every 10 of these.
- The share of renewable energy in total energy consumption reached 17.5% in 2015.

And whilst we're on facts, consider this huge one: there is 5,000 times more solar energy hitting the surface of the Earth than the human species uses in a year. Or to put it another way: every 5 days, the sun provides us with an energy supply exceeding all proven reserves of oil, coal, and natural gas. Capturing just 1 part in 8,000 of this available solar energy would allow us to meet 100% of our energy needs.

The good news is we're doing better at "harvesting" it too. Peter Diamandis at Abundance 360 illustrates that with this chart:

And consider those photo-voltaic (PV) cells we spoke about earlier. They're now pushing close to 20% efficiency (as opposed to 6% when they were first used) and they're pumping out power at close

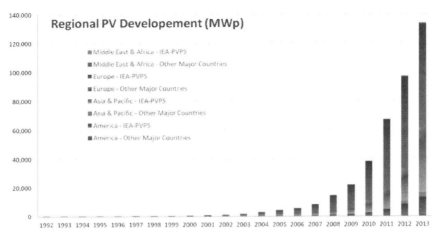

Source: 'Evidence of Abundance' - Peter Diamandis

to $3 per watt (compared with $300 per watt in 1956).

That relatively new material, Perovskite, is already at a 20% efficiency and growing rapidly. And currently, there are other issues to be solved until its widespread introduction. But Perovskite now has "friends" in the EU with EU's Solliance solar cell research organization birthing a new consortium called EPKI, the European Perovskite Initiative, and tasked it with facilitating "joint-research programs and synergies among universities, institutes and companies" to advance the cause of perovskite solar cells.

And as exciting as these new developments are, solar energy currently only accounts for 0.4% of electricity generated in the U.S. That is though expected to grow 30% year on year. That means in 20 years, we'll be at 98% if that growth rate continues.

Maybe we don't have that long.

And that's something that deeply concerns changemaker Jeremy Bentham. He is, as he puts it: looking deeply at the global energy system and considering how the world can provide more energy to meet the demands of growing populations seeking a decent quality of life, while also reducing greenhouse gas emissions.

You'll see the delicate balances at play.

Right now in the US nearly 63% of energy is sourced from fossil fuels. But consider this, in 2018 twice as much power was generated from wind than from coal. And that enabled the UK to go completely coal free for an entire week.

These kind of changes are totally disruptive in a positive way. Consider for a moment the changes that can come in our massively energy-dependant transport systems by using drones.

Google's, or more correctly Alphabet's, drone delivery start-up called "Wing" is now doing un-manned deliveries in Canberra, Australia and across Virginia, northern California and Helsinki in Finland.

Interestingly, Wing stresses the impact on communities like this on its website[1]:

With Wing, we help bring neighborhoods closer together. We're partnering with local businesses to help them deliver goods to community members within minutes. We strive to partner with community members, through in-person engagement in cities where we fly, to understand the needs of each person.

And that "impact on communities" drives changemaker Dr. Madhav Sathe.

Read on to discover how he realized the importance of uninterrupted energy supply and its role in improving the delivery of education in neglected rural schools. And his story beautifully illustrates the ripple effect and interactivity and alignment of the Global Goals — students in rural India — effectively powered by solar — outperforming their confreres in fossil-powered city schools.

It's stories like this that empower all of us to get involved with the Goals — not necessarily as scientists and researchers looking into Perovskite, but as connected human beings looking at how each one of us can support the other and our planet.

It brings home this truth. B1G1 used to say that the Goals are a pathway for business, but now they say they're a pathway for humanity.

---

1 https://wing.com

HOW BUSINESS LEADERS CAN SPEARHEAD CLIMATE ACTION
JEREMY BENTHAM

As a young man, I held a naïve and jaundiced view about business, thinking that the underlying morality was inevitably exploitative. I joined a business out of necessity, to support my family, but expected it wouldn't be long before I returned to the purer lands of academia. However, early in my career, I visited a former Shell refinery in Venezuela that had been nationalized in the 1970s. While I was there, a mature operator in the refinery went out of his way to track me down because he wanted to tell me something.

What he wanted was to shake my hand and thank me, as a representative of Shell, for all that refinery had meant in the community. He said that before the refinery was built, before that investment had been made, there had been little but misery and unemployment in the area. The presence of that refinery not only brought employment and jobs, it instilled pride, purpose, and disciplined norms of behavior that helped the community thrive in deeper and better ways.

I was a young man, and this older man wanted to thank me for something that I'd had nothing to do with. I felt seriously humbled and out of place but — for the first time — it really, really struck me that my concept of the nature of business was completely wrong or, at least, massively incomplete. Good investment brings jobs and hope and order and inspiration, as well as providing desired goods and services. At its best, the commercial engine innovates and builds things that wouldn't otherwise be built. At its best, as much public good is created as private transactional benefit, an idea sometimes referred to as "shared value."

Later, I came to appreciate how much of the common good derives from, and is sustained by, the social constructs we create together, whether security or education or healthcare or legal systems. In fact, one of the most powerful constructs is the public limited company, which enables investment risk to be pooled and partly socialized. This unleashed the commercial engine in ways that hadn't been possible before, and today brings us many of the benefits we associate with a decent quality of life.

Now, it's not my argument that business is always good — it clearly sometimes isn't — but the insight was that my internal narrative was immature. Realizing this led me not only to a deeper understanding, but also to a stronger sense of purpose and direction in my life.

This affected many of the choices I made over the subsequent decades. I became a quiet promoter of the commercial engine and well-directed investment as one means of improving the quality of life of people beyond the privileged minority. Of course, additional social constructs are also needed to enable these to be effective, such as restraints on corruption and the protection of property rights. But there can be a broader purpose to business than enriching the already privileged, as significant a motivator as that might be.

Throughout my first decade in the energy business, I grew increasingly aware of how central energy is to almost everything people do or make. It seems obvious now, but we need energy all the time, and access to modern forms of cleaner energy makes a huge difference to people's life possibilities. This was brought home to me viscerally when I first started visiting less-privileged parts of the world and saw people struggling to use peat, wood, or dung as their primary energy source. Then, as a former physicist, I remember suddenly grasping the significance of climate challenges following the Rio de Janeiro Earth Summit in 1992.

At Shell, we have long recognized the importance of climate challenges — along with the ongoing critical role energy plays in enabling a decent quality of life for people across the world. The global energy system is changing, both in response to greater demand as growing populations seek better lives, and in reaction to environmental stresses. Simply put, the major challenge for society is to provide much more energy with much less carbon dioxide. The Paris Agreement was a constructive milestone in this journey, and attention is now turning to its implementation.

Shell aims to play a role in meeting these challenges by exploring solutions in our areas of technical expertise, including natural gas production, efficient future fuels such as biofuels and hydrogen, carbon capture use and storage, and emerging energy-system technologies. We know our long-term success as a company depends on our ability to anticipate the types of energy our customers will need in the future in a way that is both commercially competitive and environmentally sound.

The overarching goal of my professional life is working toward a decent quality of life for the majority of people, and a healthy environment that enables this to be sustainable. This has translated into understanding how much energy is required to ensure people have a decent quality of life, and working toward a world in which net-zero carbon emissions are possible.

I look at the global energy system and consider how the world can provide more energy to meet the demands of growing populations seeking a decent quality of life, while also reducing greenhouse gas emissions. That is what SDG 7 is all about. I also see it as strongly connected to achieving SDG 1 ("No Poverty"), SDG 8 ("Decent Work and Economic Growth"), and SDG 13 ("Climate Action").

If we are to avoid the worst effects of climate change while at the same time providing a better life for all, the global economy and its underlying energy system must undergo a major transition. Everything is up for grabs: how we use energy, how we produce it, how we distribute it, and how we pay for it.

Shell's own "Sky" scenario is a technically possible but challenging pathway for a rapid energy transition that enables worldwide net-zero emissions before 2070 and meets the primary goal of the Paris Agreement to limit warming to well below 2°C, with a stretch ambition of 1.5°C.

This transition has already begun. The cost of solar and wind technology continues to fall, and the amount both contribute to the grid rises every year. Hybrid cars are more common in the developed world, while more battery-electric vehicles are expected on the world's roads in the years ahead.

That doesn't mean the job is done. Electrification of the economy will grow, and those electrons increasingly can be generated in low-carbon ways, but electrons alone cannot supply all the energy needs for development in the coming decades. Cement, steel, glass, plastics, trucking, shipping, and aviation — several of the main building blocks of development — all rely on hydrocarbons to provide extremely high furnace temperatures, chemical reactions, or dense energy storage. Reducing emissions in these sectors is technically possible but will be difficult. It requires new technological approaches to be developed, tested, and deployed at scale.

SDG 7, "Affordable and Clean Energy," is brilliantly simple in its ambition. But it will take an enormous effort to get there, with extraordinary and unprecedented coordination, collaboration, and leadership across all sectors of society. I'm delighted to be able to make even a small contribution to charting the path forward. Ultimately, I want to have contributed to developing a better life for people and preserving a healthy planet.

The Power of Personal and Collective Action

One of the best things that ever happened to me was not being offered a job I thought was mine by rights. Hurt as I was, I spent a day sitting on a bridge in the sunshine, writing a new personal mission statement. The disappointment of not getting the job triggered a deep self-assessment of my values and what I wanted to achieve. The conclusion I came to that day — and the principle to which I have tried to stay true — is this: "Who we are is more important than what we do, though that is important too."

Making a difference is not easy. But the more it flows from who a person really is at their core, the more likely it is to succeed. That brings grit, persistence, and resilience. We all have a personal and collective power, and there is both an individual and shared dimension to these efforts.

To achieve the goals of the Paris Agreement and reach net-zero emissions requires the widespread transformation of the energy system. This includes not only the volume and proportion of different primary energies consumed (e.g., oil, gas, coal, solar, wind, nuclear) and the energy carriers they produce (e.g., electricity, liquid fuels), but also how consumers—including businesses—use energy in homes, offices, industries, and transport systems. How quickly and how far society can decarbonize depends on how much historic patterns of energy use and material demand can change.

On an individual level, consumers will need to choose lighter cars with more efficient drives. They will need to employ heat pumps, LED lighting, and other energy-efficient appliances, and to increase recycling. Collectively, they can insist on structural efficiencies in their cities such as public transport; integrated waste, water, power, and heat management; and efficient construction and quality building standards. Once built, such major infrastructures stay in place — and shape our energy needs — for decades. Therefore, it is critical they are designed and implemented as efficiently as possible from the outset. By choosing to live in compact cities, for instance, consumers lower their demand for energy because they don't need to travel as far.

Businesses can act in multiple ways to enable the SDGs to be realized. Business is the engine for commercial innovation and extending energy access, mass deployment and integration of new technologies and providing customers with new possibilities. Business also has a voice in encouraging the development of smart government policy frameworks that can promote critical new pre-commercial technologies, develop key infrastructures and frame new market structures (e.g. emissions pricing) that are seen as fair by society.

I am passionate about the need for different forms of collective action to solve the challenge of delivering the cleaner energy that the world needs. This may span the spectrum from explicit collaboration between unlikely partners through to empowering markets to function effectively. This requires the emerging and established components of the global energy system to evolve and grow together. It entails the large-scale implementation of alternative technologies. Above all, it needs the active involvement of millions of consumers, policymakers, civil society leaders and businesses across the planet.

It can all be done. But it is a massive job. We have to get to work now. We must not allow more decades to drift by with only half-hearted progress. The direction is clear and the tools and technologies are available or close at hand, but how long it takes depends on our collective choices.

Mahatma Gandhi said, "The future depends on what we do in the present." In other words, each of us has a role to play in helping the world to achieve affordable and clean energy. For instance, policymakers can help create the conditions for change. The academic community can provide the research necessary for decision-making. NGOs can shed light on the many economy-wide sets of challenges. Businesspeople also have an important contribution to make — as consumers, innovators, and enablers of the mass scaling of sustainable solutions.

The most significant challenge is whether there is the political will, and underlying this, the societal will, to implement and maintain the frameworks necessary to address this awe-inspiring task: re-wiring the entire global economy in just fifty years. A net-zero emissions future is possible if we can build common understanding and action across the public–private divide and nurture transformative collaborations across different sectors.

LIGHTING UP LIVES THROUGH SUSTAINABLE COMMUNITIES
DR. MADHAV SATHE

We all depend on governments to do everything. Governments are handling too many things due to peer pressure and ever-increasing demands. Governments unfortunately cater to the needs of city people more, and every investment is made in consideration of the outcome measured in terms of return on investment.

We live in a modern and progressive world but often forget the less fortunate. Essentially, a country's development is measured by its cities' development and the opinions of the upwardly mobile middle class. In order to reach the most remote, deprived communities whose voices never influence the administration, we must develop new methods to measure the impact. For example, a remote primary school with twenty-five students will never receive funding that will allow it to progress, as return on investment is bound to be poor compared to a school with one hundred students. Unfortunately, funding organizations are trapped by this calculation. Often, impersonal governments do not reach grassroots organizations. We calculate our impact by the depth of our reach and therefore deprive certain levels of community. Reaching impoverished communities needs to become a reality, not a false promise. As an educated person, I have invested my thought processes in a charity to create an approach to strategic sustainable philanthropy.

I have invested my time and effort in the Bombay Mothers and Children Welfare Society (BMCWS) for the last thirty-three years. It is my innovative way of getting involved in social upliftment. When I began, I was aware that I had the good fortune to receive a quality education, an opportunity few receive. I was convinced I needed to give back to society. There are many avenues to help underprivileged communities. A few common questions on everyone's mind are: How can I help? Where is the money coming from, and going to? Will my contribution reach the target and make an impact? How will I know the outcome?

We at BMCWS are aware of these questions and have developed programs to suit every avenue. Credibility, transparency, accountability, and impact assessments are standard in every program. We have broken down our program needs so anyone can participate.

We, as Mumbai city residents, are comfortable as we have everything abundantly provided. As long as it is available, we are not concerned. Problems are read about in papers and forgotten. We are people who are used to staying within themselves (I, me, and myself) and never look outward. I was one of them. I wasn't persuaded by solar energy as a solution to societal lighting needs. To get residents to shell out money was impossible as the government was providing electricity without fail.

But as I started working in rural areas, I realized the importance of an uninterrupted energy supply and its role in improving the delivery of education in neglected rural schools. In India, all villages have electricity; however, continuous supply and high costs remain a daunting problem. The majority of the population living in rural India suffer from unmet basic needs due to underdeveloped infrastructure. High electricity bills for lighting are quite taxing. Rural schools devoid of continuous electricity and without the budget to pay the bills cannot use modern teaching aids to improve delivery of education.

In rural India, the quality of education can be poor. Inferior infrastructure, lack of teaching aids and demotivated teachers are often at fault. Tribal villages can be dark and gloomy. Electricity connections are provided, but the costs are unaffordable to most laborers. For many, an immediate change in infrastructure is unlikely. Rising energy bills with no guarantee of continuous supply is a constant problem.

On the outskirts of Mumbai, everyone was living in the dark, distressed, and their future was uncertain. Providing them with solar power was a brilliant idea. It changed the landscape immediately.

We decided to tackle the problem holistically. Working in ninety-one villages with a total population of four hundred thousand, we decided to improve rural education first. Poor rural education is a major cause of poverty.

Adequate teaching aids and continual power supply were our main problems. We launched a program to strengthen existing government schools with e-learning and solar energy to enhance the delivery of education with no internet required. This system provided an animated and digitized curriculum to make education interesting and attract children to school, thereby reducing the dropout rate. Soon we realized the utilization of e-learning was not up to standard. After talking with teachers, we discovered this was due to frequent power cuts.

Solar energy emerged as a solution.

We proposed the use of solar energy to the teachers and villagers and they immediately responded positively. They were ready to participate. Participation and support from the villagers encouraged us, and inspired our team. This year, one hundred and forty schools will use e-learning supported by solar energy. Rural houses can receive light from solar panels, and their water supply schemes can be completed with solar pumps. We found that use of solar energy could solve many problems faced by poor villages.

When Communities Unite, Everything Changes and Everyone Benefits

Tribal villages are quite remote and lack basic facilities like roads, electricity, and a water supply. Supporting them with solar power is a community program. We developed a new person, public, and philanthropy (PPP) model in which one individual supports one school or many schools, or many come together to help one school.

All successful entrepreneurs want to give back, yet they often do not know where to give. No accreditation system exists to indicate the quality of organizations or that contributions will reach their target group. We reached out to friends and relatives to present our credentials and ask for donations. Organizations like B1G1 accredited us after visiting and scrutinizing our inner operations. After seeing they were indeed adequate, they approached small businesses to ask for support. They broke down the investment total into small amounts to make it affordable for everyone. I am happy to say that all our schools are digital and solar today thanks to the support of small businesses and entrepreneurs with social concerns.

Next came the corporate social responsibility (CSR) and now they are ready to take on big projects with vision. I feel that this partnership is a step forward in developing disadvantaged communities. Strategic philanthropy is the key to structured, participatory programs.

To create confidence in the minds of investors, philanthropy organizations must transform into professionally managed social enterprises.

As an organization, we decided to use our CSR money to provide solar power and a water scheme to the village of Kanhewadi. Kanhewadi is a remote hamlet situated in the hills of the Sahyadri mountain range, about ten kilometers from the main road. The last five kilometers are extremely steep and difficult to climb. Dusty roads can only be traveled by four-wheel drive vehicles. Electricity connections were provided but paying the bills was a problem. The village was in the dark. Water sources were two kilometers away and the villagers had to walk there every day, which took a toll on their energy, health and time.

We announced our program to give the entire village solar energy and a water scheme to increase the capacity of their village well by increasing its depth. The villagers were on board; they contributed and laid down the pipeline provided by us. We were ready with a pump, but the three-phase power supply was not available and the bill payment was a perpetual problem.

Power connection was never in sight. Implementing solar energy for each house required plenty of counseling and education regarding its zero energy bill.

After a while, thirty-two families contributed three thousand rupees each toward 15% of the total system cost. Sixteen families were extremely poor and could not afford to give anything. One local resident, a businessman, decided to pay for them. Themis Medical paid 85% of the total cost. We collected one hundred fifty thousand rupees as the villagers' contribution.

Tired of waiting for an electricity connection, and having realized the difficulties in paying the bills, we decided to use the funds collected for a solar pump. Now, the village is entirely reliant on solar energy. We have a plan in place to provide solar power to all tribal villages and schools in Rajgurunagar during the coming financial year.

This is a story of so-called "uneducated" but learned villagers. After the completion of the water scheme, they had access to water in close proximity to their homes. This created a significant change in their lifestyle and saved them from extremely strenuous efforts.

On my regular visit, I saw many walking to get water. I stopped and asked why. My first impression was that the solar pump had failed. They said that everyone in the village meeting decided against using the water pump until the necessary season; they had endured poor rain in previous seasons and feared water scarcity in summer. In fact, the villagers' decision to avoid using the easy supply of water stems from seventy years of suffering from low water supplies. Their long-term vision is based on deep knowledge of their environment and appropriate use of limited resources.

They were being wise in their use. Preparing for scarcity in summer. They also asked the schoolteacher to use the pump to fill the school tank so the children would not suffer. I was shocked and aghast with this learned decision. At the same time, I was ashamed of the blatant misuse of the same facilities in the city. We could learn a lot from these villagers. Many urban citizens have a great deal to learn from them.

Innovate and Dream

We have developed many technologies to support energy requirements, but have now realized that 60% of greenhouse gases are generated by energy producers. This is a major contributor to climate change, considering one in seven people have no access to electricity and 40% of people use alternative polluting fuels for cooking.

Social entrepreneurs are individuals with innovative solutions to society's most pressing problems. They are ambitious and persistent, tackling major social issues and offering new and innovative ideas to effect far-reaching change.

Perpetual fundraising is not the solution to sustain an organization. Organizations require more than the minimum to sustain themselves; they must also maintain the projects they create. It is imperative for organizations to achieve this goal sooner than later and start working on it as a long-term goal.

The hybrid model, an exercise in profitability, should be implemented when investors for change are plenty but transparent takers are few. Investors are in perpetual search of organizations who can deliver effectively to targets. This hybrid model works on the principle of a solution economy, which requires a new means of solving entrenched societal problems.

The profit earned is pumped back into the organization for other operations. This not only makes the organization sustainable but also gives it room to initiate other small projects. This, in turn, creates positive energy among stakeholders. Investments for change (donations) become easier as investors (donors) are happy to know that 100% of their money will reach the target group.

I believe in developing new models to change the world. To think, innovate and dream.

Very few Indians have the chance to receive a good education. Those lucky few should use their education and skills to draft a plan for organizations. The onus is on the educated to help these organizations improve their functioning by developing strategies. We need to help rural communities and those with fewer opportunities blossom.

WHAT YOU CAN DO TO
CREATE A WORLD OF
AFFORDABLE AND CLEAN ENERGY

Lifestyle tips:
- Support and invest in businesses that are working on clean energy.
- Switch off your appliances at the socket. Turn off the lights when you're not using them.
- Turn off your air conditioning, especially for sleeping – open a window or use a fan.

Business tips:
- Improve the energy efficiency of your business. Reduce your energy needs by implementing energy-saving devices and guidelines.
- Understand where your energy is currently coming from and plan to make changes to support clearn energy.
- Create awareness for the effort your company is making by sharing ideas with your team.

Giving tips:
- Give to programs that provide solar-powered devices to rural families.
- Support social entrepreneurs that are working on developing clean energy solutions.
- Support crowd funding projects that aim to develop new clean energy solutions.

GROWING TOGETHER

---

8 DECENT WORK AND ECONOMIC GROWTH

HOW YOU AND YOUR BUSINESS CAN PROMOTE SUSTAINED, INCLUSIVE, AND SUSTAINABLE ECONOMIC GROWTH, FULL AND PRODUCTIVE EMPLOYMENT, AND DECENT WORK FOR ALL.

> *"Sustainable development is the pathway to the future we want for all. It offers a framework to generate economic growth, achieve social justice, exercise environmental stewardship and strengthen governance."*
>
> — Ban Ki-Moon

THE CHANGEMAKERS

WHEN GOOD, THEN GOOD
STEVE PIPE

Steve Pipe is a chartered accountant, researcher, bestselling author, speaker, former UK Entrepreneur of The Year, and founder of the Get and Give a Million initiative. His books include *The World's Most Inspiring Accountants*, *The UK's Best Accountancy Practices*, *How to Build a Better Business and Make More Money*, and *Stress Proof Your Business and Your Life*. He has a master's degree in economics and is the driving force behind the annual B1G1x Northern Hemisphere conference.

stevepipe.com

HUMANITY: THE FOURTH INDUSTRIAL REVOLUTION
JEANNIE AND PAUL MCGILLIVRAY

Jeannie and Paul McGillivray co-founded Remote, a custom online software development company. They are also co-founders of Code Assembly, most notable for the Incoder SaaS platform.
Jeannie is a speaker, writer, and podcaster, her upcoming book is *Changemaker Mindset*. Paul is a TEDx speaker, writer, podcaster and music producer. His upcoming book is Purpose First. They are proud parents of a twenty-one-year-old daughter, Ella Joy, a music producer and entrepreneur.

remote.online, codeassembly.io, paulmcgillivray.com, jeannie.online

LOOKING FOR EQUALITY
STELLA PETROU CONCHA

Stella Petrou Concha is the co-founder and CEO of management consultancy and recruitment agency, Reo Group. Her mission is to elevate human potential by working with organizations in leadership, strategy, and vision. Reo has won many industry awards and has been included on the BRW Fast 100 list, Stella was recognized as one of Australia's Top Ten Women Entrepreneurs by *My Entrepreneur Magazine*. Her mantra is "When you succeed, I succeed."

reogroup.com.au, stellapetrouconcha.com.au

GROWING TOGETHER

When we look around at "work" we see massive changes. We see "digital nomads," usually young entrepreneurs choosing to work in whatever country they like and doing it as and when they like, blending travel with work seamlessly and harmoniously.

We see people operating brand-new, highly scalable enterprises quite literally from their bedrooms, out-performing long-standing brick and mortar stalwarts.

We see high-growth enterprises like Upwork where those enterprising bedroom dwellers and their digital nomad traveling "colleagues" can sell their services to the highest bidder and move from project to project as opposed to being employed statically by one company. It's growing so fast, it even has a name — the so-called 'gig' economy.

We see the growth of co-working spaces, where start-ups (and more frequently now, long-standing businesses) are sharing usually funky office surroundings and facilities with many businesses.

These are all examples of what is frequently described as *the future of work.*

Yet for some, that future is bleak in spite of some major gains that sometimes mask the opportunities we now have to do what SDG 8 focuses us on: in short, Decent Work for All.

Let's begin our *Legacy* exploration here by looking at some stats — as always they bring things into sharper focus. On the bright side, there have been some dramatic and positive shifts.

For example, over the past 25 years, the number of workers living in extreme poverty has declined dramatically. And that's happened despite the significant and still-lasting impact of the 2008 economic crisis and global recession.

In developing countries, the middle-class now make up more than 34% of total employment – a number that has almost tripled since 1994.

However, as the global economy recovers, we are seeing slower growth and most significantly, widening inequalities.

Equally, the number of available jobs is not keeping pace with people wanting jobs.

According to the International Labour Organization (ILO), more than 204 million people were unemployed in 2015. More significantly in a 2018 update to that research, the ILO says, "Significant progress achieved in the past in reducing vulnerable employment has essentially stalled since 2012. This means that almost 1.4 billion workers are estimated to be in vulnerable employment in 2017, and that an additional 35 million are expected to join them by 2019. In developing countries, vulnerable employment affects three out of four workers.

Changemaker, Steve Pipe makes the point directly when he says: "Economic growth is good. When more people earn more in this way, it also has an indirect effect on others. They and their families have more money to spend. And, of course, one person's increased spending is another person's increased sales. So that increased spending means other businesses also grow, and they too employ more people, pay better wages and generate bigger profits. And this cycle, which economists call the "multiplier effect," keeps repeating.

But according to the World Bank[1], most of this extra money is spent at home and very little of it "trickles down" to the developing world. As a result, we see the lives of some people, mostly in the already richer nations, getting much better, much faster. Which is unfair, dangerous and wrong on so many levels."

These stats bear witness to Steve's point;

- Some 700 million workers lived in extreme or moderate poverty in 2018, earning less than US $3.20 per day.
- Women's participation in the labour force stood at 48 per cent in 2018, compared with 75% for men. Around 3 in 5 of the 3.5 billion people in the labour force in 2018 were men.
- Overall, 2 billion workers were in informal employment in 2016, accounting for 61% of the world's workforce.
- Many more women than men are underutilized in the labour force — 85 million compared to 55 million.

1   https://data.worldbank.org/indicator/NE.IMP.GNFS.ZS?view

Another changemaker, Stella Petrou Concha further emphasizes this point.

"Working mothers do not have equal opportunities to have a sustainable income simply because they can't give 60-70 hours of their life per week to their job. They have to balance work with their commitment to their family. I didn't see a future so I resigned and started Reo Group. I wanted Reo Group to be a place that provided men and women alike the same opportunity to thrive and grow. Regardless of age or gender, I wanted to run a company that gave everyone a fair and even platform for work satisfaction and growth."

And you'll see in this chapter of *Legacy* how Stella has not only done that but leveraged it in inspiring ways. She has also developed a giving initiative inside her company called 'Elevate a Nation' which has far-reaching implications.

The SDGs themselves promote sustained economic growth, higher levels of productivity and technological innovation. Encouraging entrepreneurship and job creation are key to this, as are effective measures to eradicate forced labor, slavery, and human trafficking.

With these targets, the goal is to achieve full and productive employment, and decent work, for all women and men by 2030.

In reflection, perhaps the term "decent work for all" could evolve to "meaningful work for all." Changemakers, Jeannie and Paul McGillivray share this view and educate others how to seamlessly integrate work, passion and purpose.

"No matter where we live or who we are, we all have at least one thing in common. When we feel our work is meaningless, it seems pointless. We feel unseen and undervalued. We experience a lack of self-worth that leads to disengagement and even depression. Conversely, when we feel we're working for or towards something bigger than ourselves — something important — we feel engaged; part of something great. Our work has meaning. We feel valued and happy. Our lives feel full."

SDG 8 is an important goal. Taking action on all the insights you receive will help you promote inclusive and sustainable economic growth, full and productive employment and decent work for all.

WHEN GOOD, THEN GOOD
STEVE PIPE

Economic growth can make life better for everyone.

And that's true for people who work in growing businesses, their suppliers and customers, and their families and communities.

And economic growth can make life better for people who have nothing to do with growing businesses too.

Economic growth makes life better in three ways. One is obvious. One is often overemphasized. And one has the, as yet, largely untapped potential to make a truly profound difference in our world.

Obvious Direct Benefits

Many benefits of economic growth are, of course, direct.

As businesses and economies grow, they can employ more people, pay better wages, provide better working conditions, and treat people more fairly. The entrepreneurs behind that growth benefit as well, by earning bigger profits.

Overemphasized Indirect Benefits

When more people earn more, it has an indirect effect on others.

They and their families have more money to spend. And one individual's increased spending is another's increased sales. This increased spending means other businesses grow, and they too employ more people, pay better wages, and generate bigger profits. This cycle, which economists call the "multiplier effect," keeps repeating.

But according to the World Bank, most of this extra money is spent at home.[1] For example, in the United States, approximately 15% of GDP is spent on imports, 20% in Australia, and 30% in the United Kingdom. These low percentages leaving our countries mean that most of the indirect benefits are felt at home, and very little "trickles down" to the developing world.

---

1   https://data.worldbank.org/indicator/NE.IMP.GNFS.ZS?view

As a result, we see the lives of some (mostly in the richer nations) getting much better, much faster. Which is unfair, dangerous, and wrong on so many levels.

The Truly Profound "When Good, Then Good" Benefits

Happily though, a small, influential group of growing businesses is showing us a third way.

These groundbreakers are proving how easy, quick, affordable, and rewarding it is to help the world achieve the Global Goals (or the SDGs) by making a small change to their business models.

That simple change is to ensure that *when* something good happens in your business, *then* something good automatically happens in the world.

When something good happens in your business — such as receiving a referral, winning a customer, making a sale, delivering a service, getting paid on time, or receiving a testimonial…

Then something good automatically happens in the world — for example, you make it possible for a child to have access to food, water, sanitation, or education.

Interestingly, many of the businesses pioneering the "When Good, Then Good" approach are accounting firms:

- Tayabali Tomlin in Cheltenham, England: *When* they win a client, *then* the new client can choose whether a Kenyan family receives a sheep or a goat to provide milk for their family and a sustainable income through the sale of surplus production, or whether someone blinded by cataracts is given surgery to renew their gift of sight.
- Mordfin Group in New York, USA: *When* they complete a tax return, *then* they provide an underprivileged child with an improved learning environment for one year.
- Wood & Disney in Colchester, England: *When* they finish a meeting, *then* they ask the client which SDG they would like the firm to contribute to on their behalf. Manchester-based Brackman Wolf does something similar.
- Inspire CA in Brisbane, Australia: *When* they proactively save a client a dollar in tax, *then* they provide a family in need with a day's access to life-changing food, water, hygiene,

or sanitation.

- James, Stanley & Co. in Birmingham, England: *When* they produce a set of accounts, *then* they give a chicken to a family; its eggs provide a sustainable source of food and income.
- BUSINESS *buddy* in Auckland, New Zealand: *When* they run a "Get and Give a Million" meeting with a client, *then* they take another step toward their target of creating a million micro-impacts (which they call "smiles") for those in need.

Extraordinary Impact and Potential

Using the "When Good, Then Good" approach, these seven accountancy firms have collectively created:

- 2,534 days of shelter (Goal 1: "No Poverty")
- 13,139 days of food (Goal 2: "Zero Hunger")
- 51,875 days of vitamin supplements (Goal 3: "Good Health and Well-Being")
- 9,308 days of education and 29,075 days of access to library books (Goal 4: "Quality Education")
- 14,163,348 days of access to clean water (Goal 6: "Clean water and Sanitation")
- 3,437 days of business training (Goal 8: "Decent Work and Economic Growth")
- 41,400 trees with annual maintenance (Goal 13: "Climate Action")
- 1,313,099 other micro-impacts (most falling under another SDGs).

This adds up to a staggering 15,627,215 impacts to the SDGs. All from just 7 groundbreaking accountancy businesses that created an average of over 2 million micro-impacts each. Just imagine the difference that is already making to the world.

And imagine the extraordinary potential if every single business used the "When Good, Then Good" approach. In conjunction with the direct and indirect benefits discussed earlier, that really would change the world, wouldn't it!

People in every corner of our world would earn more, find better jobs, and live in a happier, healthier, safer, fairer, and more caring world.

Good for Business

Groundbreaking businesses like the ones above are using the "When Good, Then Good" approach to support the SDGs because it is the right thing to do. Because they care. Because they want to make a difference. Because it makes them happy. Because it makes their families proud.

A wonderful side effect of doing good in this way is that our businesses receive very real commercial benefits in return. And the payback can be enormous.

For example, recent research by leading academics Nielsen, Cone, and Havas into many types of business behavior that can collectively be labeled as "doing good" suggest the payback includes:

- Faster growth — because on average, businesses doing good grow four times faster than others.
- Competitive advantage — because 89% of people are likely to switch from a business that isn't doing good to one that is.
- Improved loyalty — because 88% of customers are more loyal to businesses doing good.
- Word of mouth advertising — because 81% of customers will tell others about businesses doing good.
- Higher prices — because 66% of people are willing to pay more for products and services from businesses doing good (several studies indicate this could be as much as 12-20% more).
- Higher productivity — because, as one study found, salespeople make 143% more sales when working for a business doing good.
- Future proofing — because 79% of consumers expect businesses to do more good in the future than they have in the past.
- Millennial appeal — because doing good is even more important to millennials, who will be your customers for longer than any other group.

As Sir Richard Branson often says, "Doing good really is good for business."

Quick, Easy, and Affordable

Thanks to technology, adopting the "When Good, Then Good" approach is remarkably quick and easy. For example, the B1G1 giving platform allows you to find and fund projects that align with your values, interests, and priorities in just a few seconds.

Technology also makes the approach affordable. For example, it costs as little as:

- USD 0.01 to provide a day's worth of e-learning, pesticides, or rabies protection
- USD 0.10 to provide a week's worth of vitamin supplements, library books, or sanitation
- USD 1.00 to provide a child with a year of clean water
- USD 1.28 to irrigate an entire village for a month
- USD 1.85 to provide grain seeds that will grow into a year's worth of food
- USD 5.00 to save a square meter of rainforest or provide a mosquito net

The cost and effort involved in using the "When Good, Then Good" approach is tiny. And that tiny cost can easily be funded out of the much larger amounts of money and other benefits generated when more of the good things (such as more new clients, more sales, and more on-time payments) happen in the business.

So there really is nothing to stop every single business getting on board!

An Unstoppable Force for Good

As business leaders, we face a perfect storm of five factors:

1. The world needs businesses to adopt a leadership role in ensuring the SDGs are met.
2. We are good people who want to do the right thing.
3. Doing good also helps our businesses become more successful.
4. The "When Good, Then Good" approach shows us exactly how to do it.
5. Technology now makes it quick, easy and affordable

Over the next few years, this perfect storm will lead all genuinely forward-thinking and caring entrepreneurs to:

- Become a "Businesses for Good" by using the "When Good, Then Good" approach, placing contributing to the advancement of SDGs at the heart of their business strategy.
- Choose which SDGs to focus on — some will choose to support just one goal, while others will support many, driven by their values, interests, and priorities.
- Measure, manage, increase, and be accountable for their impact on their chosen SDGs.
- Go public with what they are doing, why they are doing it, and the quantified and verified impact they make.
- Inspire and encourage other businesses to get involved.

The technology and methodologies currently used by a small number of groundbreaking businesses will make doing all of this easy, quick, joyful, affordable, profoundly effective and profitable too.

As such, all good business leaders will see this makes sense. And all good business leaders will get on board making the movement unstoppable. And, as a result, we will be making things better for ourselves, our customers, our teams, our families, our communities, our economies, and people in need — at home and around the world.

It's now incredibly easy and affordable for any business to have an extraordinary impact on our world. This approach enables us to eradicate poverty, address inequality, protect the environment, and so much more. And all for as little as a dollar a day, and less than five minutes of effort a month. There are no obstacles, and no excuses. Every single business *can* make a difference. And every single business that really cares *must*.

HUMANITY: THE FOURTH INDUSTRIAL REVOLUTION
JEANNIE AND PAUL MCGILLIVRAY

The average person has just under eighty years to make their impact on this earth. We spend about one-third of that precious life working. That's twenty-five to thirty years of our life, and a solid thirteen years and two months spent in the workplace. If we put in overtime often, we can add another one year and two months to that total. That's over one hundred thousand hours.

Regardless of whether we experience our work as a daily grind or feel we've found our dream job, our working life takes up a lot of our time. When we look at just how much of our lives we spend working, we can appreciate that if we feel stuck in an unfulfilling job, our days can feel empty and worthless, and that can influence our happiness, both at work and at home.

So, what could it be that gives us the most fulfillment in our careers? Is it power? Is it recognition? Is it a high salary? Is it finally finding our "dream job"? We would argue it isn't any of these things. We would argue that happiness and fulfillment aren't found in money, power, or that one-in-a-million role, but in finding meaning in whatever we spend our time doing.

No matter where we live or who we are, we all have at least one thing in common. When we feel our work is meaningless, it seems pointless. We feel unseen and undervalued. We experience a lack of self-worth that leads to disengagement and even depression. Conversely, when we feel we're working for or toward something bigger than ourselves — something important — we feel engaged, part of something great. Our work has meaning. We feel valued and happy. Our lives feel full.

In addition, we've found that most people are kinder; more supportive, creative, and thoughtful; contribute more, and are more productive when they feel they are part of a greater purpose and mission. Our workplaces, the places in which we spend so much of our lives, can become the central point for that greater purpose and mission, making them much more enjoyable places to be, and — as we've discovered — this is essential to the quality of our lives as a whole.

Meaningful work, with purpose at its core is also demonstrably more profitable, because more people want to do business with and be part of a company that works for the good of the people and the planet.

This is an incredibly simple and incredibly powerful about-face that we can all make for ourselves, the people we work with, and the planet as a whole.

Redesign Your Life, Your Business, and Our World

About three years ago, we realized we had lost our zest for the company we'd spent seventeen years of our life creating.

We were working in a nice office, on interesting projects, for great clients, and yet the work somehow felt hollow. No matter how hard we tried to bridge the gap, there was a top-down hierarchy and a division between the leadership team and the staff that felt tricky to navigate. No matter how hard we tried to make work more enjoyable, we were mainly working to pay the bills, and the work was often stressful and unfulfilling. There was no celebration when we completed projects, no indication that we were making a difference, and no feeling that what we were doing was worthwhile.

We knew we needed to make a change — to "reboot" our business — but we didn't yet know why it felt "wrong," or what to do about it. We began to look hard at why we felt the way we did, and why there was such a disconnect between our inner lives, our home lives, and our work lives. We knew that our workplace and team had untapped potential. We wanted to turn our work into something that made everyone feel good, that provided fulfillment and a sense of depth to us, our team, and our clients.

As we explored these ideas, we came across a book by Daniel Pink called *Drive*. In his book, Daniel proposes that money only motivates employees to a certain level of work. Beyond that, what really drives people in the workplace is *autonomy*, *mastery*, and *purpose*.

This led to a series of experiments within our company, Remote. We spent focused time with each team member to help them articulate their individual talents and strengths. We actively encouraged knowledge sharing and learning, nurturing an aspiration for mastery within our team. We introduced robust systems and project management processes, softening the top-down hierarchy and adding the structure necessary for autonomy to flourish.

We then decided to focus our efforts on working with organizations that are doing good in the world, so that the reason for our work would be more aligned with our personal values.

The idea was that work would become more meaningful for each member of the team, because it would matter whether we all brought our best self to work and our best work to a project. If it made a difference in someone else's life when we improved a feature or automated a system, then we would feel far more motivated.

We soon discovered that putting purpose at the core of our work meant that we were always working for something bigger than ourselves, and that felt wonderful because it gave our days greater meaning.

We imagined the impact it would have if everyone had the chance to experience the power of this simple change in perspective.

It became our mission to carry this message to every workplace we touched, so that everyone could begin to appreciate that if they made their work about creating a better world, no matter what they do, it would make every job worthwhile and meaningful. It would generate economic growth in every locality and every industry in a way that would help us all to thrive.

This shift in perspective expanded. We saw that we could actively work toward a vision for a world of business and economics where higher purpose drives sustainable global transformation, putting our skills and resources to the best use possible by empowering those making a real difference in the world.

Our values became clear, and we now encapsulate them with the phrase, "The Power of Purpose." This phrase has four underlying values, which are embedded in the heart of our company and which guide and influence how we work:

- *Support:* We are in it together and have the good of the company, our clients, and the wider community at heart.
- *Mastery:* We aim to reach the highest standards, personally and professionally, and share knowledge to create an environment of learning and growth.
- *Purpose:* We celebrate purpose; it makes us stronger and gives work meaning and direction for us as individuals and as an organization.
- *Impact:* We are committed to groundbreaking work that makes a meaningful contribution to the world.

Our ultimate legacy? Harnessing the power of technology to help solve the world's most meaningful problems.

Put Your Superpowers to Work for the Greater Good

As we redesigned our organization, we began to transform our lives in a similar way.

We began by looking at who we are as people. As we did this, we looked back at the seemingly disparate hobbies, interests, activities, and projects we had taken part in.

We started to ask ourselves "What did we really enjoy?", "Why did we love doing that?", and "What was it about that project that lit us up?" We began to see common threads, a theme emerging — the same "reason" was the foundation of everything, time and time again.

We deepened the one-on-one sessions with our staff. We looked at what parts of their job they enjoyed the most and why they loved doing certain things, and then investigated the why beneath that, and the why beneath that, and so on.

In doing so, we discovered a driving force behind everything we personally care about; a unique theme for each of us that stems from something deep within and informs all aspects of our lives. A fire — our *why*.

We discovered that when our work bursts forth from our *why*, it gives us each a unique sense of purpose. When we work within our purpose, we can find our "superpowers" — the things that we find so enjoyable and so natural that we assume everyone else finds them natural and enjoyable too; the things that make time disappear when we're doing them — and unleash a powerful force for good.

In the context of Simon Sinek's brilliant book, *Start with Why*, your purpose is your *why* and your superpower is your *how*. Once you are clear on those, your *what* can be multiple, varied, and ambitious.

You can do this too, no matter what you do in your business. Simply by looking deeply, at the strands that weave the fabric of your life — your different careers, hobbies and activities — and encouraging your team members to do the same, you will each discover your purpose and individual talents — your superpowers.

You can then make a conscious effort to implement a supportive culture where you and your team can use your purpose and superpowers for the good in your organization, community, society, and ultimately the planet.

This is where the transformation begins, because when you do this, your days will be more fulfilled and your work will have meaning.

Life bursts open! So many possibilities present themselves when you work with purpose at your core and within your superpower. It liberates innovation. Days became full of energy and excitement and growth and connection. Everything feels new and full of potential.

As business leaders, you can also join thousands of others who have aligned their businesses with one or more SDGs, and you will become part of a global community making an enormous positive impact in the world.

As we enter a new age of industry, powered by exponential technologies in which repetitive and time-consuming tasks are automated by software systems using artificial intelligence and machine learning, we will enter the fourth industrial revolution.

We believe the businesses that will not only survive, but thrive, in this new age will be those that are truly driven by the power of purpose. The businesses doing meaningful work for the good of the whole. The ones that realize the impact of human attributes that cannot be automated — creativity, compassion, empathy, connection, and love.

Imagine the legacy that will leave.

LOOKING FOR EQUALITY
STELLA PETROU CONCHA

Before I founded Reo Group, I worked for two global multinationals; my experience at neither was great. I was unable to see how a woman could progress equally alongside men. At one of the organizations, I reported to a woman, who also reported to a woman. We had gender diversity and gender balance. However, after the global financial crisis in 2009, the landscape changed. People were forced to work long hours to keep their job. I witnessed first hand the inequality between men and women and the true lack of support for working moms. Slowly but surely, each of my female colleagues resigned. Before long, I was the last woman at the Sydney branch. I felt isolated and scared. The gender balance was inadequate and as a result, I couldn't see a future. The behavior of the organization supported KPIs and profit over the sustainability of people. The drive to keep the business afloat affected whom they chose to keep and whom they let go. I immediately realized that when a business is under pressure, working mothers do not have equal opportunities to maintain a sustainable income, simply because they are unable to commit sixty to seventy hours of their life per week to their job. They must balance work with their commitment to their family. I didn't see a future so I resigned and started Reo Group. I wanted Reo Group to be a place that provided men and women the same opportunities to grow and thrive. Regardless of age or gender, I wanted to run a company that gave everyone a fair and even platform for work satisfaction.

As a young ambitious woman, I felt very isolated at my previous company. I didn't feel I was granted the same opportunities due to my personal values and beliefs. I remember one instance where the "star performer" within the organization behaved toward me in a way that would be characterized as workplace harassment. Drunk, he indecently and sexually assaulted me in front of my colleagues and manager. Although there were witnesses and a human resources claim, because this individual was such a high sales performer, he received a mere warning and life continued as normal. In any other organization, this individual would have been dismissed immediately. This made me realize that not having a clear view on what constitutes workplace decency can compromise individual and company culture. I promised myself that I would run a company with zero tolerance for disrespect and a strong focus on inclusiveness for all genders and cultures.

Design a Blueprint for Workplace Equality

When my husband, Marcelo, and I founded Reo Group, we immediately sat and wrote the blueprint for the type of organization we wanted to run. Our first mission was to build a workplace where men and women had equal opportunity for growth. There would be no tolerance for bullies. Our framework was based on family values; we would create a place where fairness, job satisfaction, and growth wasn't the exception, but the rule. We knew it was up to us to rid the workplace of outdated practices and be leaders in equality and harmony. Our blueprint also included encouraging our clients toward a "recruit without prejudice" culture.

SDG 8, "Decent Work and Economic Growth," inspires me because our industry has a direct route into the heart of the matter, as we can ensure our recruitment practices embrace this necessary global endeavor.

Currently, men earn 12.5% more than women in forty out of forty-five countries. The gender pay gap stands at 23% — globally! According to the statistics, it will take sixty-eight years to achieve equal pay.

As a woman, that's a difficult pill to swallow. In fact, it's one I refuse to swallow. I have two daughters, and I will do everything that I can to ensure they are equipped with the tools they need, and cognizant of the issues they face, to be a woman in corporate society. Every person, every business, every organization can chip away at achieving this goal. All it takes is an attitude of equality and actions congruent with it.

Equal pay: We have a pay matrix contingent on the level of the employee's role. Pay is linked to output, never to gender. This pay matrix means employees are paid for the work they do and the experience they bring to their role. This eliminates pay gaps between genders and is vital to instill as a normal work practice

Flexibility: We have complete workplace flexibility. If an employee needs to work from home for a day, they can. If they have a sick child, they can work from home and not feel judged. Work–life flexibility allows for a workforce where men and women make decisions to either work in the office or out of the office in a mature fashion. Of course, we have a framework in place and we keep each other accountable to the deliverables of the organization. But this policy means that parents can attend school functions or do school drop-offs and pickups occasionally or at various times during the week.

Encouraging equality in others: We encourage other businesses to provide an equal workplace. For example, if a client gives us a long list of requirements that we believe edge toward racism or sexism, we challenge them to adopt a more inclusive view. We also include a "wild card" candidate in the mix — someone we know can do the job (and will probably get the job) but doesn't fit the initial criteria. We know it's important to break down barriers and show that equality is both an action and an attitude.

Linking winning to giving: Reo Group are a B1G1 partner and we have linked our winning to our giving! One of the inequalities we see regularly in the workplace is discrimination against those without a tertiary education. If an individual doesn't have this level of education, businesses in Australia simply won't consider them for a corporate job. We decided we needed to bridge this gap. In remote Australian communities, only 24% of children have access to a school that goes to year ten. These children will never have the opportunities that other children have. Therefore, each time a candidate placement happens (someone gets a job), Reo Group gives fifty days of technology education to children in these communities. A lack of education is the root of many problems; access will eventually lead to accomplishing SDG 8, "Decent Work and Economic Growth." They go hand-in-hand.

The Three Questions Every Business Owner Should Ask

My motivation to create equal workplace environments started early. My best friend from the age of five was a girl called Kelly; she had spina bifida. Kelly passed when she was thirty-one. As we grew up, it became more and more apparent that it would be near impossible for her to have a decent job. She couldn't walk, so she was dependent on her travel arrangements. Although she had no mental disabilities, her physical disability severely limited her in all areas of life, especially in finding employment. I did what I could to help Kelly, but sadly, I couldn't change the system.

I can see now why recruitment suits me so effortlessly. It can change the system. I can advocate for those that need opportunity, equality, and a voice.

I believe we all have the ability to contribute to SDG 8, "Decent Work and Economic Growth," simply by putting the well-being of our employees first. I see it all the time in corporations that people's personal lives become compromised when their employment is not harmonious. People are looking for a sense of belonging and contribution. This starts by building a work environment that is fair, equal, and inclusive. I realized that as CEO of a recruitment agency, I had the opportunity to create change.

I asked myself three powerful and important questions:

- Are you the type of leader you wish you could have?
- Is your organization the type of organization you wish you could work for?
- Does your organization promote decent work?

This led to ensuring our workplace practices and culture allow people to flourish.

People Are Looking for More Than a Job

After interviewing over 5,000 people seeking employment, I realized something profound. Many people looking for a job are "sick and dying": sick of their boss and dying to get out of their company. People don't want just a job anymore; they want a job with purpose and meaning. An organization that makes a difference, not just a profit.

Business owners need to recognize that the world is changing rapidly and people will only want to work in their organization if it is one that's good for society.

No longer are individuals interested in just working for a big brand that can give them excellent remuneration and an opportunity to succeed. People are looking for organizations that have a specific focus on elevating the world as a whole.

Thinking about SDG 8, "Decent Work and Economic Growth," it's an immense goal. As business leaders, we have a prime opportunity to link our business to something bigger than profit and performance. Become a social purpose business, and attract and retain high performing talent as a result. Create an environment that closes the equality gap and make decent work practices a strategic focus. We all deserve it. Don't we?

Be the leader you wish you could have.

WHAT YOU CAN DO TO
CREATE A WORLD OF DECENT WORK AND ECONOMIC GROWTH

Lifestyle tips:
- Be a conscious consumer – if something is very cheap it's likely to be hurting people or the planet in some way.
- Read about workers in other countries and businesses.
- Buy from local producers.

Business tips:
- Identify employment challenges in your supply chain.
- Promote responsible recruitment practices.
- Employ people with disadvantages and provide specialized training. Create an empathetic work environment.

Giving tips:
- Provide tools for people who to start their own business.
- Help provide training programs for skills development.
- Provide micro-financing through well-managed programs.

"Let's you and I explore this next great frontier where the boundaries between work and higher purpose are merging into one; where doing good really is good for business."

— Sir Richard Branson

This new and great frontier has arrived. And almost halfway through this book, we encourage you to join the movement between work and higher purpose.

To help you do this, we have made *Legacy* an interactive book.

This includes additional content, videos and links to useful information. You can see firsthand how small changes can lead to global impact.

It's a way of adding additional experiences for your fuller enjoyment of *Legacy*.

For your interactive copy go to:

b1g1.com/legacy-interactive

INNOVATING FOR A BETTER TOMORROW

---

9 INDUSTRY, INNOVATION AND INFRASTRUCTURE

HOW YOU AND YOUR BUSINESS CAN BUILD
RESILIENT INFRASTRUCTURE, PROMOTE
INCLUSIVE AND SUSTAINABLE
INDUSTRIALIZATION, AND FOSTER INNOVATION.

> *"Learning and innovation go hand in hand.*
> *The arrogance of success is to think that what you*
> *did yesterday will be sufficient for tomorrow."*
>
> **— William Pollard**

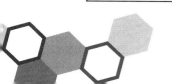

THE CHANGEMAKERS

INCLUSIVE INNOVATION FOR SUSTAINABLE GROWTH IN THE NEW AGE
NATALIE JAMESON

Natalie Jameson is the founder of the Heroworx Institute, a training, software, and service design company. They solve complex business and social problems with design thinking and technology. Natalie has steered a multidisciplinary portfolio career and education across five countries and four industries, including acquisitions finance, sustainable interior architecture, and start-up healthcare, while raising two children. She is passionate about reimagining business education as the lever to advance diversity, women's empowerment, and sustainable digital innovation. She believes if business practitioners think like human-centered designers, our approach to work and life will be purposefully diverse, creative, and connected to humanity and the planet.

theheroworx.com

BECOMING BETTER, LIVING SMARTER
PAM FEATHERSTONE

Business coach, Pam Featherstone has over 36 years of experience in entrepreneurship, management and business planning. Before her coaching career, Pam ran multiple businesses: a boutique clothing chain, hair salons and a gymnasium. In her 40s, Pam suffered a serious illness which forced to grow her team rather than do it all herself. In four years, Pam transformed the company, sold it and retired at age 46. This experience motivated her to help others do the same. Pam is the World #1 Business Coach in the largest coaching franchise in the world, growing her business to over £1 million revenue in less than three years.

ibusinesscoach.co.uk

INNOVATING FOR A
BETTER TOMORROW

Sometimes, we forget. Need light? We flick a switch and voilà – we have light. Thirsty? Turn on a tap and our most precious resource flows to quench our thirst. Need to go to work? Jump on the train, take a car, tram or taxi. Want to chat to a friend? Pick up your cell phone and press a button. Need to travel overseas for work? Just book a ticket and you're on a plane.

Yet somewhere along the journey to development, we forgot where it all began. We "forgot" that pioneers, inventors, companies, entrepreneurs, engineers, architects, technicians, innovators, business leaders, companies and governments worked tirelessly to change the landscape of what's possible.

The road from invention to mainstream has been well-worn by countless brave pioneers before us. What we take for granted in our own cities and private homes was once someone's idealistic thought taken seriously. And these ideas, inventions, industrial innovations and developments created a new world for many of us. But not for all of us … yet.

For many, it's not until we lose what we have that we begin to value it. What happens when your Wi-Fi connection goes down? Or it's ultra-slow. How grateful do you feel? More likely you feel annoyed. You suddenly remember how important it is. How reliant you are on its accessibility.

Still, more than 4 billion people do not have access to the internet, and 90% of them are from the developing world.[1] Approximately 1.2 billion people do not have access to reliable phone services. Around 2.6 billion people face difficulties in accessing electricity full time.

And all of a sudden, that slow internet connection seems bearable, doesn't it?

Ever had a problem with your water supply? Perhaps a blocked

---

1 Undp.org

toilet or burst pipe? Major "first-world" headache, right? Calling a plumber is the obvious solution, however, most of us complain about the cost.

But what about the cost of not having it? Like the 2.3 billion people worldwide who lack access to basic sanitation, and the near 700 million[2] who lack access to water. The cost for them is often their health, maybe even their lives. And that's a price that no-one should ever pay.

Despite the way it looks on Google Maps, basic infrastructure like roads, communication technologies, sanitation, electrical power and water remain scarce in many developing countries.

How can this be possible in a world where our watches can be our phones and our phones can monitor our sleep, footsteps, calendars and lives? They can even pay our bills and turn our lights on. How can some people be dripping in technology, innovation and industry whilst others can't access a phone or a clean toilet?

Once again, it's not that we don't have the means. It's that we have to make the means available to everyone. And we need those in privileged positions to help those less fortunate.

Over half the world's population now live in cities. This makes mass transport, renewable energy sources and the growth of new industries and communication technologies more important than ever.[3]

As the United Nations point out: *"Technological progress is the foundation of efforts to achieve environmental objectives, such as increased resource and energy-efficiency. Without technology and innovation, industrialization will not happen, and without industrialization, development will not happen."*

Let's put that more simply: the lack of technological progress and innovation equals increased poverty. Lack of industry equals lack of development, equals less jobs, equals less skills, equals more poverty.

According to the UN, manufacturing jobs have a 2.2 multiplier effect. This means that for every single job created in manufacturing

2 Undp.org
3 Undp.org

another 2.2 more jobs are created in other industries. This creates such a positive ripple effect on job creation, wealth generation, and then combating other goals like poverty and hunger.

Of course, SDG 9 does not stand alone. It weaves into all the other goals and is a contributing factor to the SDGs like decent work, economic growth, sustainable cities and communities, clean energy, responsible consumption and production, gender equality, climate action, education for all, clean water and sanitation.[4]

Low-income countries who lack in the areas of Infrastructure, Industry and Innovation experience a loss of productivity of around 40% — a devastatingly huge economic loss to a country in need.

So how do we fix the problem? We need to start thinking differently. We can begin by investigating deeper questions such as — what does infrastructure mean? Can we support sustainable industrialization? Can we support equal innovation in a world where counties are constrained by inequality? If so, how?

These questions ignite awareness and awareness is vital.

Being aware of the intertwined nature of infrastructure, industry and innovation is the first step. The second step is understanding. Helping people truly understand that **infrastructure** is what provides basic physical facilities, or foundations, essential to business and society; that **industrialization** is what drives economic growth and job creation, which in turn, reduces income inequality; and that **innovation** within business or industry expands the technological capabilities of sectors and leads to the development of new skills.[5]

It's a perpetual cycle. Developing these sectors will help develop a responsible, socially inclusive and environmentally sustainable future. It will provide those in need with what we take for granted. Countries, government and businesses alike need to:

INVEST in building resilient infrastructure

PROMOTE inclusive and sustainable industrialization

FOSTER innovation.[6]

---

4 Undp.org
5 https://unstats.un.org/sdgs/report/2016/goal-09/
6 Ibid

As changemaker Pam Featherstone rightfully points out, innovation and effective business systems are at the heart of a truly sustainable business.

Leveraging off what is known, what has been proven by research, is critical. The following statistics reveal where potential exists and indicates future investment opportunities:[7]

- Small and medium-sized enterprise who engage in industrial processing and manufacturing make up over 90% of business worldwide and account for between 50-60% of employment.
- Least developed countries have immense potential for industrialization in food and beverages (agro-industry), and textiles and garments, with good prospects for sustained employment generation and higher productivity.
- Middle-income countries can benefit from entering the basic and fabricated metals industries, which offer a range of products facing rapidly growing international demand.
- In developing countries, barely 30% of agricultural production undergoes industrial processing. In high-income countries, 98% is processed. This suggests there are great opportunities for developing countries in agribusiness.

We know that a functioning and resilient infrastructure is the foundation of every successful community. Changemaker Natalie Jameson adds to that by suggesting that we need highly-skilled talent to achieve sustainable economic development. She's right. Educating, empowering and elevating people across markets and geographies are vital components to creating our tomorrow. Our future. Our future is just that: ours. We build it together. We create it together. Now, what type of future shall we build?

---

7   https://www.undp.org/content/undp/en/home/sustainable-development-goals/goal-9-industry-innovation-and-infrastructure.html

INCLUSIVE INNOVATION FOR SUSTAINABLE GROWTH IN THE NEW AGE

NATALIE JAMESON

Diversity, evolution, and global citizenship are   ., DNA. I am the daughter of a rebellious, white, middle-class English rose who married a young African American/Cherokee Indian US Air Force officer in the late 1960s. I grew up in a melting pot of races and cultures, which meant I learned how to embrace differences and overcome ignorance and intolerance at an early age.

As a little world traveler, we moved every two years to foreign lands and experienced a plethora of diverse people, foods, spices, architectures, and cultures. I created bonds with wonderful multicultural families from across the globe. This helped me hone what I now call the three "superpowers" to success: empathy, resilience, and gratitude.

It is widely agreed that military kids, referred to as brats, are brought up to value honesty, loyalty, idealism, antiracism and patriotism. These values, coupled with a multicultural outlook on life, have developed my deep-rooted belief that everyone has the power to act and influence the world.

This unquestioning call of duty, to fight for freedom and the rights of others, is what business leaders must respond to today. SDG 9 provides clear guidance and targets for creating a vibrant, inclusive, and sustainable growth economy. This is inspiring because the global business community faces so many challenges to creating and maintaining a flourishing private sector. Not least because of a looming global talent crisis, we are going to face significant unrealized output, experience increased ransom costs, and be ill placed to leverage the productivity promise of robotics, digitalization, and machine learning. It is thought that the shortage of skilled laborers will hit 85.2 million workers by 2030.[1]

---

1   *Future of Work:* The Talent Shift. 2018. Korn Ferry

ucture, industry, and innovation all require highly skilled pipelines. Educating, empowering, and elevating diverse ople across markets and geographies is vital to the production of jobs. Work not only provides the financial means for basic human needs, but is central to friendship, socialization, human connection, and our own personal identity. These factors are essential to achieving a happy, thriving population and planet.

Unfortunately, there is an immense disparity of access to work and diverse talent due to patchy infrastructure in many countries, and not just in those considered "developing" economies. For example, when comparing the infrastructure in the North of England with the South, it is evident that discrepancy and fragmentation exists.[2] The North has:

- Higher unemployment, lower wages, and slower productivity; the five lowest male employment rates are in the North and reach as low as 67%.
- 4.4% lower graduate numbers and fewer medium grade workers.
- 17% fewer businesses and 34% fewer patents per head than the UK average.
- 66% less foreign direct investment (FDI) projects per head.

Ultimately, these types of figures result in endemic and structural health inequalities and deprivations being passed on from generation to generation. It is worth noting that life expectancy in the North is as much as 8.2 years less.[3] If inequality in England poses such severe risks to life, then developing countries must also receive our urgent aid and attention.

The Impact of Industry

Until 2009, I was a financial services professional working in acquisition finance. Most financial and business services professionals lead with, and are measured by, their successes

---

2 *Northern Powerhouse strategy.* 2016. HM Treasury, U.K
   https://assets.publishing.service.gov.uk/government/uploads/system/uploads/attachment_
   data/file/571562/NPH_strategy_web.pdf
3 "Study Finds North-South Divide in UK Life Expectancy," National Health Service, 2015,
   https://www.nhs.uk/news/lifestyle-and-exercise/study-finds-north-south-divide-in-uk-life-
   expectancy/

and failures on organizational-level key performance indicators, such as income or complaints. Hence, I had little concept of the impact our organization had on infrastructure, industry, and innovation in relation to the wider environment, ecology, or society.

After the birth of my second child, I left the financial services industry and moved from the South to the North of England to support my husband in starting Britain's first dental network in a supermarket, Sainsbury's. This gave me the opportunity to retrain. I had always wanted to be an artist, designer, or architect. So, following my dream, I studied interior design for three years in pursuit of a bachelor of arts. The school head was heavily influenced by the sympathetic redevelopment of historic areas from the Industrial Revolution, such as Castlefield and Ancoats in North West England. As a result, I learned about retrofitting sustainable technologies on heritage buildings, as well as humanities subjects including ethnography, behavioral economics, environmental psychology, and human-centered design.

Sustainable infrastructure design is not just about new infrastructure. Becoming aware of the impact of the industry and the built environment on humanity and the planet was a real eye-opener.

My belief is that sustainable industrialization and a circular approach to business can force a hotbed of innovation and growth, lift communities out of poverty, and arrest further irreversible damage to people and planet.

Did you know that around 33% of UK carbon emissions come from the built environment, while 10% of emissions derive from heating buildings alone?[4] Green buildings present an opportunity to save energy, reduce water and carbon emissions, lower crime, educate the population, increase productivity, create jobs, inspire creativity, strengthen communities, and improve health and well-being. Green design and sustainable business practices really can be a true catalyst for addressing some of the world's most pressing issues.

---

4   "Climate Change: UKGBC's Vision for a Sustainable Built Environment is one that Mitigates and Adapts to Climate Change," UK Green Building Council, 2019, https://www.ukgbc.org/climate-change/

Sustainable ethical practice is not only the right thing to do; it's better for business. By pushing ourselves to create empathy-driven innovation, to design responses to the deeper needs of people, planet, and to carefully consider the use of resources, beyond the cost to P&L or effect on the balance sheet, we will achieve authenticity and longevity. With fewer resources, people tend to view issues more expansively than where abundance occurs, at which point people have fewer incentives to use what's available to them in novel ways.

Creating a Better World

In today's world, creating a business that matters is about creating art/work/interventions that leave life and land better than when you started. At Heroworx, we believe that the future of work and the Fourth Industrial Revolution is also underpinned by a four-dimensional evolution in which a quadruple bottom line approach can create a legacy. A Four Ps business leadership model will make every effort to serve people, align to purpose, steward the planet, and make a profit.

Issues such as pollution, climate change, and the displacement of people are seemingly defeating governments, global agencies, and other organizations meant to find solutions. Design, at its core, is about identifying and defining the big, unsolved problems. There is a genuine expectation that business can and should take the lead in driving social and environmental change where government regulation is absent or inadequate. To collect on our human potential and tackle new and unrecognizable challenges in volatile and complex circumstances, we must have tech-savvy professionals and greater participation of women and underrepresented groups in positions of influence in the digital economy. We must retrain our workforce with the skills to approach a new way of problem solving for the future of work. For equal and inclusive development we must involve women and underrepresented groups in entrepreneurship and the growth of digital technologies. The development of technology must also create wealth, interventions, and knowledge for the 99%, not only the 1%.

Unfortunately, equal participation is far from the case. Women face a threat of technological displacement, as they will account for as much as 57% of the 1.4 million jobs to be replaced by 2026. The real potential for long-term unemployability also lessens their ability to contribute to the sustainable development of industry infrastructure and society. We believe that by empowering women, underrepresented groups, and people in business with design, digital innovation, and science, technology, engineering, arts, and mathematics (STEAM) skills, we can step up to the challenge. Investing in inclusive technology and innovation will unlock the unlimited knowledge and connective potential of the internet for everyone, and create more jobs in, and across, developed and developing countries alike.

Be a go-giver in business rather than a go-getter for effortless success, focus, and peace.

A better business should focus on making the world a better place, by creating positive change and making an impact. I encourage businesses to look at ways to improve — whether it is through process, or through culture.

Embrace Diversity and Adversity as the Path to Innovation

Businesses can tackle diversity issues by addressing biases and blind spots in executive boards, thus improving innovation. Augmenting boards through non-executive directors (NEDs) is a feasible and easily implemented solution to increase diverse thinking regarding innovation. We could fast-forward more inventive thinking on boards by equipping women and people from underrepresented groups as NEDs. This would lead to fewer unconscious, biased-based faux pas. Boards would have a system of checks and balances in place that includes and embrace a wider range of perspectives from persons of various ages, races, genders, religions, physical and neural abilities, and socioeconomic levels. With a greater field of view, they would reduce risk from bias blind spots or missed growth opportunities in response to the evolution of markets, customers, ideas, and talent.

Equality is the presence of opportunity plus ability, not just the absence of discrimination.

Create Your Higher Order Thinking Statement

As a leader of a start-up in times of constant, accelerating, substantial change, what could be the one constant we could anchor ourselves to? Many of us have read and loved Simon Sinek's *Start with Why*. I read it years ago as a senior exec. I loved it then; however, now I need it. Never before had I felt like I needed to cling onto a fundamental and powerful leading central question that guides me through the "imposter syndrome" infested seas. Yet the why needs the what, which is the tricky bit in today's choppy "changey" seas. This is where the higher order statements and central questions come in such as #theheroworx higher order statement, "Equality is the presence of opportunity plus ability, not just the absence of discrimination."

Find your Central Question

Our central question is, "What if women and underrepresented groups were empowered, aligned to purpose and educated to innovate, how much quicker could we reach the #GlobalGoals?"

Embrace the Power of Collective Intelligence to Multiply Your Resources and Impact

Accomplishing the start of my mission to empower women to progress the SDGs seemed so out of reach, but it forced me to fundamentally change my beliefs about who I am. And to me, that is a huge part of the power of not doing it alone: you become more agile and able than you ever believed possible. The B1G1 team has helped me to keep progressing forward, guiding me with the power of purpose.

I truly believe that when you are working with a community of like-minded people, the wisdom of the crowd is considerably greater than any one person working alone. Collectiveness is the way to achieve and increase the power of impact. Together, we will all make a difference.

BECOMING BETTER, LIVING SMARTER
PAM FEATHERSTONE

Building resilient infrastructure and promoting inclusive and sustainable industrialization relies on education. Good health and education should be available for everyone throughout the world, no matter where they come from or how much money they have. Unfortunately, this isn't the case. To create a more even playing field around the world, it is vital for underdeveloped countries to receive the education and knowledge they need to improve their infrastructure and their health.

The SDGs set out the importance of building sustainable infrastructure that supports economies. The solution is all about innovation. This includes education and marketing; you must ensure that people know you exist in order to have a sustainable business. I believe that the answer to how we can have a more sustainable business is simple. Businesses just need to focus on the two key areas. The first is innovation and marketing. The second is system investment. Developing and growing a business must be done alongside robust systems. This will guarantee the business is resilient, no matter what happens.

We need to ensure people have enough food and water to survive, and then teach them how to grow their own food. We need to create a health system that works and put systems in place to ensure that it will grow and develop. Similarly, we need to educate people on how to set up a business, teaching them that robust systems safeguard stability and long-term profitability for the good of the owners and those they will eventually employ. This is something I am passionate about teaching my clients. It is vital to run a business on systems and let people run the systems. The more systemized you can be, the more consistent you will be. Systems eradicate mistakes, which leads to cost savings. People like to have a clear direction, to know what is expected of them, and to have a definite structure in place.

Build a Cathedral and Become a Visionary

Until I was made aware of SDG 9, "Industry, Innovation, and Infrastructure," I didn't know about the global effort being made by world leaders. However, we all need to take ownership, and should all be looking at what we can do. As individuals, we need to accept ownership of the global problem, take responsibility for what needs to be done, and hold ourselves accountable. There's no point making excuses, thinking that we can't possibly do anything or that it should be something that governments and big corporations deal with. No, we can't put our heads in the sand about this and pretend it's not happening. Thousands of small steps by each of us around the world can have an enormous effect collectively.

I truly believe that everyone on this planet can do something to help, no matter how small. Every little step and every tiny action creates a huge impact. However, developed countries need to take ownership of the global issue and help poorer countries build the infrastructure they need to have a great health and education system. This is where becoming a "better business" is important.

A business that matters is sustainable, has a sense of purpose and a long-term vision, and will leave a lasting impact on the world. The people who work in this type of business have a greater sense of purpose because they are working toward something much bigger than just having a job. It's like the analogy of the stonemasons: Two stonemasons chipping away at a huge rock were asked what they were doing. The first said, "I am cutting this stone into blocks." The second replied, "I'm in a team building a cathedral!"

It's important for people to understand what the vision is and to know that what they are doing matters in the grand scheme of things. When you are working toward a bigger vision, you feel so much more valued. Part of delivering this purpose involves the culture of the company. The culture is what people do when no one is looking! One of the most overlooked resources of the company is the discretionary effort of the team — when people do over and above what is expected of them because they are engaged in what they are doing and because they want to, not because they have to.

In order to deliver the vision, it's important as a business to set out your mission, and how you are going to achieve it. It's essential to have written goals and a written plan. Break your work down into bite-sized pieces and have robust, clear systems in place to deliver the plan as efficiently as possible — and on time. It's also very important that everyone is engaged and involved in the plan and understands their contribution to it.

Businesses with a clear plan and vision achieve great results and prosperity. When I talk about prosperity, I don't mean simply having more money and profit. I mean a holistic approach to developing and scaling your business and creating an environment that is not only financially secure but encourages people in their own personal development. This gives people an increased sense of health, mindfulness, well-being and balance in life. Prosperity leads to sustainability, including people accepting more social responsibility, and ultimately a fulfilled life.

Businesses I work with don't just take but give back. They help others become more successful, too. It's a chain reaction. Lots of small acts over time have a monumental impact. I encourage other businesses to be part of this chain reaction.

The Day Everything Changed

In the year 2000, I was running a very successful laser clinic in Hull, England. However, it was more than a full-time job and I had taken long working days to a whole new level. All for no other reason than I hadn't figured out how to do things differently. I didn't have a quality business education and therefore had no systems in place to support the business, simply unbridled enthusiasm and a strong work ethic. Convinced that I could not take a day off, I had inadvertently created a business which drained all my time and energy. Over the years I sacrificed quality time with my son. I didn't know how to balance home and work, so I felt guilty all the time. Unfortunately, I didn't know how to change things, and I was blind to the fact that before the business could become better, I had to be better.

---

2 Louise Olsson and Erika Forsberg, "Gender Inequality and Internal Conflict," in Oxford Research Encyclopedias of Politics (Oxford: Oxford University Press, 2016).

3 "Economic Benefits of Gender Equality in the European Union," European Institute for Gender Equality, https://eige.europa.eu/gender-mainstreaming/policy-areas/economic-and-financial-affairs/economic-benefits-gender-equality

In starting the business, I was looking for freedom and personal choice, but I ended up with the absolute opposite — trapped and without any alternative but to work hard.

Disastrously, the pressure that I was putting myself under finally brought the house down around me. On New Year's Day 2000, I succumbed to a virus that left me paralyzed and in the hospital. The three years in which I was not able to work, however, proved to be the major turning point of my life. I could do nothing else, so I invested my time and energy in learning — mostly about business. It was during this time that a horrible realization hit me. In all those hard-working years, I didn't realize how little I had known. I had been so "in the business" that I could not really see beyond it.

I had worked 95 hours a week for 20 years because I had no education in how to run a business. The self-improvement and business books I read showed me that my best, previously, could have been so much better — if I had had the right education and knowledge. I felt an enormous sense of sadness and regret, believing that if I had had the right education, I would have had systems in place that would have meant I could have spent more quality time with my son. I can't have that time back, so now I am on a mission: to inspire and educate people to have the life and the business they deserve, and to enable them to see that they too can get to where they want to be. I want all business owners to understand that they can run a great company and still have the experiences that are really important to them.

Over the last 30 years, I have learned the importance of working harder on yourself, rather than the business. In order to achieve personal and business success, it's a must. I absolutely love inspiring my clients to become the best version of themselves, both personally and in their business.

By gaining this knowledge and putting systems in place, I was able to sell up and retire at the age of 46 — all because of the right education! I now have more time to do the things I enjoy and more time to spend with my son. That is why I am so passionate about teaching others and sharing that knowledge — so we can all have a happy, fulfilled, and sustainable future.

I am most passionate about making sure people have a great education. That includes me as well as others. Everything starts with education. To do this, everyone needs to take ownership of their development so that they live proactively, purposefully, and in accordance with their own agenda. The problem with having no clear plan is that you end up living life according to everyone else's agenda. My approach is about people living peaceful, tranquil, fulfilled lives, and having the financial freedom to make their own choices in life and to spend quality time with the people they love.

Becoming a "better business" and a better person involves having a sense of purpose, clarity of vision, and a written plan that you put into action. These all come from acquiring a great education, staying curious, having gratitude, and living life proactively. The reality is, life happens *for* you, not to you.

Key tips I recommend:

- Think about what you want to achieve. What purpose do you want to have? What gets you out of bed in the morning?
- Be clear on what you want to do.
- Find a source of inspiration. It can be anything or anyone. For me, it's my son Zander, who continues to inspire me daily.
- Create a written plan, putting in step-by-step tasks to achieve each goal. Make it as simple as possible. Break each goal down.
- Take ownership of what needs to happen to have the vision you want to see. Be the change you want to see.
- Think about what values are important to you, because when you are true to your values, it's much easier to take action.
- Consider how best to serve others. It's important that while we try to make the world a better place, we always maintain humility and respect for others.
- Become great at your own self-management. We all need to optimize our time and manage our energy levels because no matter how great your plan is, if you don't manage your time or your energy levels, you won't be able to action your plan.

The quality of life ladder is another tool I encourage everyone to use. It's a wonderful way to reassess our current state, including the direction we are heading for, or the direction we want to go.

Each step affects the quality of the next level up:

6. Quality of life you want
5. Quality of results you get
4. Quality of actions you take
3. Quality of decisions you make
2. Quality of questions you ask
1. Quality of education/your coach/your mentor

When we are successful, it's important to find out how we can make an even greater impact; to find a deeper sense of purpose in what we do. I am passionate about helping others create better versions of themselves.

WHAT YOU CAN DO TO
CREATE A WORLD OF INDUSTRY, INNOVATION AND INFRASTRUCTURE

Lifestyle tips:
- Purchase products that promote fair trade.
- Invest in innovations and new technologies to help make them affordable for all.

Business tips:
- Establish standards and promote regulations that ensure sustainable management of your company's initiatives.
- Collaborate with NGOs and the public sector to help promote sustainable growth within developing countries.
- Use social media to push policymakers to prioritize the SDGs.
- Actively provide internship and apprenticeship opportunities.

Giving tips:
- Help fund projects that build roads, schools, businesses, clean water and sanitation systems.
- Sponsor Social Entrepreneurs by giving coaching, mentoring and funding support.

CLOSING THE INEQUALITY GAP

10 REDUCED INEQUALITIES

HOW YOU AND YOUR BUSINESS CAN REDUCE INEQUALITY WITHIN AND AMONG COUNTRIES.

> "As long as poverty, injustice and gross inequality persist in our world, none of us can truly exist."
>
> — Nelson Mandela

THE CHANGEMAKERS

THE FULL EXPRESSION OF EACH PERSON
HEATHER YELLAND

Heather Yelland is a leading authority in values-based leadership and a respected voice in the international arena of business and corporate innovation, consulting, and coaching. Having worked with over ninety thousand individuals and businesses worldwide, Heather specializes in growing people. She is also the founder and director of the internationally acclaimed Green SuperCamp® Australia, which provides personal leadership, academic acceleration, environmental awareness, and social contribution programs for children aged ten to eighteen.

greensupercamp.com.au, theelevationcompany.com

RECOGNIZING THE DEPTHS OF INEQUALITY
STACEY KEHOE

Stacey Kehoe is the founder of Brandlective, a digital marketing agency. Since establishing Brandlective in 2012, Stacey has built over 500 websites, brands, and marketing campaigns, and gained media recognition and award nominations. Stacey's vision is to help those with an entrepreneurial spirit find the resources to rise above the noise, stand out from the crowd, and show their audience who they really are. Stacey is leading a movement called #1MillionDays that aims to reduce inequality through social, economic, and political inclusion of all people.

brandlective.com

SMILES ARE THE IMPACTS WE MAKE
DR. CATHERINE YANG

Dr. Catherine Yang is a happy dentist and the founder of Chats Dental. Since being awarded an Alumni Scholarship at the University of Sydney in 1995 and receiving the First Prize GC Australia Research Award in 1999, Dr. Yang has served many communities in Sydney. Dr. Yang is also a speaker at the ADA Congress. Her first book, *S.T.E.P.* on Fear, will be released soon.

chatsdental.com.au

CLOSING THE
INEQUALITY GAP

A Lebanese proverb says: "If you think life is hard, go live in a city."

But for many, a city is the epitome of wealth – in some areas, tourists even take bus tours to see how the rich live. Fifth Avenue in New York, New Bond Street in London, Causeway Bay in Hong Kong and L'Avenue des Champs Elysées in Paris are just a handful of the world's most expensive streets to live.

Interestingly though, only a stone's throw away from where the rich live, you find the homeless or people living in cramped apartments struggling to make ends meet.

In fact, the gap between rich and poor has become so visibly obvious that international photographer John Miller has an entire portfolio, aptly named "unequal scenes" (unequalscenes.com). These drone-captured shots show us that in some countries simply crossing the street can mean the difference between rich and poor. That one side can be luxury mansions with swimming pools while the other side can be makeshift tin housing, and shanty town-like structures.

But what about the differences that can't be seen? The differences that hold more weight than manicured lawns and flashy cars. The deeper differences, like lack of opportunity, suppression of rights, feelings of despair and struggle, limitations on health, education and career opportunity.

How can it be, in a world characterized by globalization, a world where advances in technology and groundbreaking innovations are increasing that inequality still exists? Worse still, it doesn't just "exist" — it is flourishing.

How can we be so advanced yet so behind?

Today, the richest 10% of the population earn up to 40% of the total global income. The poorest 10% earn between 2-7% of the total global income. It's mind-blowing to think that in our "progressive" world, inequality has increased by 11% in developing countries.[1]

The following statistics present a portrait of insight into factors that contribute to this rise:[2]

- Over 75% of the population in developing countries are living in societies where income is more unequally distributed than it was in the 1990s.
- Evidence from developing countries shows that children in the poorest 20% of the populations are still up to three times more likely to die before their fifth birthday than children in the richest quintiles.
- In developing countries, rural women are up to three times more likely to die in childbirth than women living in urban centres.

Staggering. Yet inequality isn't isolated to developing countries. As changemaker Stacey Kehoe points out, inequality shows itself in many forms — the country of our birth, the color of our skin, social position, gender, religion, sexual preference and even disability.

It's perhaps because inequality isn't always seen in obvious ways that it's still increasingly prevalent. It's often a silent insidious culture that runs like a toxic weed through society. Think income gaps. Gender inequalities. Racial discrimination. Suppression of rights. Archaic laws that aren't updated.

Inequality harms the growth of countries and prevents poverty reduction. It also affects the quality of relations in the public and political spheres and individuals' sense of fulfillment and self-worth.[3]

In a global survey conducted by a UN Development Programme, policy makers from around the world acknowledged that inequality in their countries is generally high and potentially a threat to long-term social and economic development.[4]

---

1 http://www.undp.org/content/undp/en/home/sustainable-development-goals/goal-10-reduced-inequalities.html
2 As measured by the Gini coefficient. The Gini coefficient is calculated by comparing cumulative proportions of the population against cumulative proportions of the income they receive. The score ranges between 0 and 1; 0 indicating perfect equality and 1 indicating perfect inequality.
3 http://www.undp.org/content/undp/en/home/sustainable-development-goals/goal-10-reduced-inequalities.html
4 Ibid

The good news is efforts are now being made in many countries to reduce inequality.[5]

Countries, organizations, businesses and individuals are pro-actively looking for ways they can make a difference. Be it zero-tariff access to exports for developing countries, regulation and monitoring of financial markets and institutions, policies to empower the bottom percentile of income earners or campaigning for economic inclusion of all regardless of sex, race or ethnicity[6] — initiatives are taking place. This is encouraging. Business leaders pay a major role here.

Changemaker Heather Yelland is one such leader; a woman who also encourages others to reduce the inequality bias. Heather takes the stand that reducing inequality can be achieved through education and empowering people to realize their full potential. She's right, we can all lift another to help everyone achieve their full potential; to not limit another based on prior ideas or prejudices.

We can lift up people, communities and entire countries to help them achieve their full potential.

That's where *you* come in. That's where *you* make a difference. We need to see ourselves as part of the world, not just our own backyard, our own city, our own nation.

As changemaker Dr. Catherine Yang reminds us, it's the power of the collective that makes the difference. We must act on behalf of our fellow citizens, not only the ones we see in our neighborhood but acting as if all citizens are in our neighborhood. We need to know that more than ever before, we all are one.

Join these three changemakers as they carve the way for change.

---

5   https://sustainabledevelopment.un.org/sdg10
6   Ibid

THE FULL EXPRESSION OF EACH PERSON
HEATHER YELLAND

Every person deserves the opportunity to live their best life. Many of us feel that living in the Western world affords us many opportunities to create a life of our own choosing, and in many ways, it does. There's no doubt that access to education, higher standards of living, greater financial security, and even the absence of war are great blessings that allow us to live comfortably in our Western lives. However, I don't believe this necessarily means we are happier.

For our business, reducing inequality is all about increasing empowerment. Be it providing international assistance to children who do not have access to education, rescuing young people condemned to forced labor, or supporting people who feel they are not able to be their best, we respond to inequality, as it constrains the human spirit. Each of us experiences some level of inequality in our lives. However, the more we feel a sense of personal empowerment, the greater our ability to take risks, experience new things, and step out into the world in a way that shows who we are and the difference we were born to make. The greater our sense of personal insight and awareness, the more we can exercise our right to choose who we want to be and how we want to live.

There is something incredibly inspiring about seeing people in a joyous state that is born out of full self-expression.

For our team, addressing inequalities takes into account social, cultural, economic and emotional barriers that occur at multiple levels. Whether it be enabling young people in India to access education, engaging young women in Cambodia in community education to keep them out of sexual slavery, or assisting young people in Australia to glean the best from their education, we are reducing inequalities and increasing empowerment at every level. Doing so allows a stronger and fuller expression of each person's unique and wonderful soul.

Love is Power

There was once a time when I thought the only way to address inequality was to do something grand and wonderful, to solve every issue. I felt uncertain about what else I could do to make an impact. However, I came to realize that the one thing we can all do is to ensure we better understand ourselves — our own unique gifts, talents, skills and abilities — and how we can use these to make the greatest possible impact in the world, even if only on the people in our immediate circle of influence.

In many ways, world peace begins with our own inner peace and the fullest expression of our capacity for love.

Our team directly affects the lives of over 25,000 people each year. This positive impact doesn't take into account the ripple effects of other people reached. I have noticed that the wider our reach and impact on issues of inequality and promoting empowerment, the more we focus on expanding that reach to others. This is the uplift created when our internal empowerment is strong, and we feel inspired to share that joy.

Understanding the *Why* of Business

My business life has taught me that "good business" means good for *everyone* — if it's not, then it's not good business. Over the last thirty years, I have worked to refine and improve the ways in which my business makes a difference and fulfills the legacy I want to leave behind.

For me, it started with understanding the *why* behind what I do. I asked myself questions: Why am I here? Why do I want to share the gifts I have? Why does finding and living the difference I was born to make really matter? These are crucial questions that need answering if you want to build a "better business" that is good for everyone. Over the last ten years, the team and I have developed a range of services built on the foundation of a clear why, an alignment of values and a shared commitment to create a better business that addresses the issue of inequality and works to empower as many people as possible.

My *why* is all about connection; connecting people to their own truth, connecting people to what I believe are universal truths, and most importantly in this fast-paced, electronic age, deeply connecting people to each other. When I reflect on my life, I realize I have been doing this for as long as I can remember, even before I realized that's what I was doing!

Upon discovering this capacity, I then asked the question, "Why is this important and what can I do to share this gift to benefit others?"

This led to the birth of my business, and over the last thirty years, I have worked to refine and improve the ways in which my team and I make a difference. This question has also resulted in me making the occasional choice to join other businesses and learn from other people along the way. A clear *why* creates an alignment of values and a shared commitment to form a "better business" that addresses the issue of inequality and works to empower as many people as possible every day.

Fundamentally, our team believes that all anyone really wants is to love and be loved, and to be known, seen, and "got" for who we really are. A business that is imbued with this philosophy and develops services in alignment with this belief will always be a "better business" that can make a greater impact on people's lives.

The Gift of Who We Really Are

For me, the cornerstone of addressing inequality is education. No matter what the struggle, education is the key that opens the door to new possibilities. Every aspect of what we do — our support, participation, and consulting and the programs we run — focuses on educating people.

It's for this reason that our business offers a range of services and programs that support children and those in their world — parents, families, schools, and the like. The best known is our Green SuperCamp® Australia program, which supports young people aged ten to eighteen. This program is built on four pillars: personal leadership, academic acceleration, environmental awareness, and social contribution. We have been running this program for about seven years and over thirteen hundred young people from all over Australia and eleven other countries around the world are graduates.

In 2013, I was contacted by a woman wanting to send her fourteen-year-old girl, who had been told by her school that she had a learning disability, to camp. The mother wanted to ensure our team had the capacity to "deal with someone with this kind of disability." What a great mother to want to create this opportunity for her daughter. I confess, I'm not a big fan of labels, as they often end up defining the expectations people have of the person laboring under their weight, robbing them of the opportunity to simply be who they are at that point in time.

I commended the mother for her courage; we discussed her daughter's needs and agreed that she would benefit from the Green SuperCamp® Australia program. After four weeks, the young woman had made significant improvements in her reading. Her confidence increased, her social skills improved, and her leadership abilities blossomed. She had transformed simply because she began to experience self-belief. In her own words, she "discovered who she really is."

Two days later I had a call from the young woman's principal. He was rather aggressive in expressing his displeasure for the fact I had encouraged her to come to an "academic camp, when we only just got her comfortable with the fact that she has a disability." That caused me to reflect on our current education system's inability to cater to unique individuals. Don't get me started!

Fast forward four weeks to the camp's quantum reading (speed-reading) session. The young woman's first session indicated she was reading at about a grade three level, when she was in year nine, so the picture wasn't great.

By the end of the second session, her words per minute reading score went from 169 to 786, without any loss of comprehension — the highest increase we had experienced in the program at the time. But this is not the highlight of her story. That came when watching what happened during the remainder of the program. This young woman began to experience self-belief. She started to speak up, she led team activities without being prompted, she made new friends on other teams, she represented her team and spoke in front of the entire camp, and best of all, she called her mother and told her she had "discovered who she really is." Then she told me that too and we both cried.

Six months later, she emailed me telling me she achieved three As in her end of year marks. She wanted us to know that one A was for her, for applying herself so well. One was for her mom for supporting her and believing in her. And the other one was for our Green SuperCamp® Australia team for showing her who she really was.

That young woman went on to be the school captain in her final year at school. Meanwhile, I resisted the temptation to call the principal and suggest he alter his leadership methods and his limiting influence on young people's development.

When introduced to the truth of who we are as unique individuals, we understand every one of us has gifts to give and a difference to make in the world. This young woman inspired me to constantly seek to challenge all manner of inequalities in every aspect of how I run my business and live my life.

Every Journey Begins with a Single Step

If we each take one step a day, we could eradicate world hunger, educate the world's children, create world peace, and use our businesses as a vehicle to create equality.

I encourage you to find the difference you were born to make and make it boldly. Be a changemaker and exert a positive influence on the people you love, those you lead, and the world.

RECOGNIZING THE DEPTHS OF INEQUALITY
STACEY KEHOE

The country of our birth, the color of our skin, our social position, or our gender should not dictate what we can achieve in this world. But it does. Despite raising awareness, inequality still exists — both socially and economically. The launch of the 2030 SDGs provide hope. They have helped me understand the facts around why inequality occurs — something I have witnessed firsthand — and what steps need to be taken to reduce it.

I was born and raised in New Zealand. At the age of 22, I left to travel the world. During this time, I visited more than 50 countries where I witnessed poverty, young children forgoing education, and a lack of access to basic living requirements such as food, water and shelter.

Yet in each of these places, I observed extreme wealth too.

I remember thinking I was lucky to be from New Zealand, where we don't seem to have such an extreme imbalance in wealth distribution.

Naturally, I tried to immerse myself and learn about the culture, beliefs and politics in each country. But that didn't help me see what I could do to leave any lasting impact. After all, I was just one person and the problems seemed so overwhelming.

Like many of us, I assumed that local governments and international bodies had it under control; that they had plans and were doing everything possible to eliminate these obvious inequalities. And again, I couldn't see how I would be able to do anything that would make a difference.

I had also seen the negative in my own life, being made redundant three times as the world moved toward the global financial crisis of 2007–2008.

I decided then that I needed to take action to be more in control of my own destiny first. I did that by setting up my first business.

And that wasn't easy, either.

I experienced judgement due to my lack of formal education. I was repeatedly told how difficult it was for women-led businesses to succeed. But this focus on what others felt I "lacked" prompted me to focus on what I could do to help or support others and promote equality. SDG 10, "Reduced Inequalities" stood out to me immediately because it aims to empower and promote the social, economic, and political inclusion of all: improving income growth, developing social protection policies, regulating the global financial markets, and increasing the proportion of voting rights of developing counties in international organizations.

Goal 10 has provided me with a roadmap, highlighting the things that can be done to achieve the targets set out. I understand I can make micro-changes in my life to contribute to the 2030 targets. By using the tools available to me — public forums, social media, and linking business activities — I can influence others to begin making small changes and steps toward these same goals.

Reaching one person at a time may seem like a slow approach. But when we work on things collaboratively, over time, our own small "ripple" turns into waves, and the momentum created ensures that we really can tackle inequality.

And adopting the SDGs adds even more to our own sense of purpose.

Purpose-Led Business

Running a purpose-led business has never been more important. A business that looks beyond its financial objectives is one that makes a real impact. Every business has a footprint — meaning everything we do has a social, economic, and/or environmental impact. And like an ever-increasing number of business owners, I want my business' footprint to be a positive one.

I discovered there are steps to making this happen. The first is to create a business rooted in core values; these values become what might be described as your own "North Star."

Our values are: Be bold. Ooze credibility. Empower others. Cultivate adventure. License success.

As a digital marketing agency, these core values underpin

our purpose: to give visibility to those who think differently. We want to be known for our enthusiasm for entrepreneurship and disruption. We strongly believe that every individual, product, brand, and business should make a positive impact, and when doing so should be given their time in the spotlight.

By keeping our purpose and core values at the heart of everything we do, we are driven to create positive results for ourselves and the businesses we're privileged to serve.

In 2017, Brandlective committed to support SDG 10, "Reduced Inequalities." It was a collaborative decision by the team, who were key to helping embed this goal as an essential part of our business. Together, we decided how to contribute to the targets; our methods include financial donations, raising awareness via social media, pro-bono work for charities contributing to this goal, and educating our clients, families and friends.

The partnership we established with B1G1 has inspired us further and led to the launch of our #1MillionDays initiative. We plan to give one million days of human rights wages, access to education, and basic living requirements by 2030.

Aligning these micro-giving goals with our everyday business activities means that our donations are sustainable and consistent. For example, when we take on a new client, we give one day of social workers' wages to enforce human rights. Each website development project enables a woman in Malawi to receive two days of business training. Each request we receive from a client allows a disadvantaged girl in Cambodia to go to school for a day. For every thirty-day marketing contract we complete, we give an entire month of access to clean, lifesaving water to families in need.

Being a purpose-led business allows the culture of our company to thrive. As each team member works through their daily tasks, we become a powerful unit, contributing to the crucial cause of reducing inequality within and among countries.

It's a far cry now from what I observed on the travels I mentioned earlier. Yet those experiences still play a part in driving us to make a difference.

There are things you can never forget.

For example, as I write this, my mind goes back to meeting a woman called Fatima living on the streets of Sucre in Bolivia with her twin babies. Her friend, who spoke a little English, explained her husband had kicked her out so that his mistress — who was pregnant — could move in with him. I was sickened at the thought.

A few days later, I was mugged. It was a common occurrence and tourists were warned about it by the police and local accommodations. It dawned on me that this was due to the desperation felt by individuals living on the streets in Sucre, just like Fatima — it was their way of surviving.

A few weeks later in Cusco, Peru, I met groups of children aged five to nine selling tissues, cigarettes, and chewing gum on the streets after 11 p.m. to try to make enough money for their families to eat. Their parents had only seasonal jobs and no steady income.

Our guide told us that their parents knew tourists were more likely to buy from young children than an adult hawker, so they sent their children out late at night to earn a living. At the time, I was angered by this; upon reflection, I realized it was coming from a place of desperation — the only way they knew how to earn money for their family.

I can remember many other awful situations and atrocities I observed while traveling. Though I spent the first ten years of my career refusing to acknowledge that inequality existed in the "developed" countries where I lived and worked, I now know that things need to change. Over these last few years, I have stopped burying my head in the sand and decided not only to acknowledge it, but act on it.

And that realization now drives what we do.

As a woman who runs her own business, I am passionate about helping others that haven't had the same opportunities I've had.

Recognizing Inequality and Refusing to Accept it Allows Us to Begin to Change

There are many ways to make a difference in the world. The simplest, and what I encourage others to do, is to learn about inequality and the effect it has on our world. The more knowledge you have, the more equipped you are to make a change.

Other key tips I recommend for businesses wanting to become more focused, more purposeful, and more able to make a difference include:

- Spend more time listening to what is important to your family, your friends, and your staff.
- Talk about inequality. Raise awareness. Tell three people what you learned and why it is important.
- Write an article or share a post on social media detailing how you are making changes in your life or your business. Explain why these things are essential and what you hope to achieve.
- Be successful. When you reach a certain level of success, people around you are interested in what you do and how you have achieved it. In this way, you can raise awareness of how reducing inequality contributes to your success.
- Use technology. I encourage small businesses to embrace technology and social media, and to promote themselves online. In the past, corporations monopolized every industry; today, technology and social media allow small businesses to compete. The playing field is becoming more level. The rise of podcasts, video content, and social media allows businesses of any size to communicate their message to their ideal demographic at very little expense.
- Connect with the B1G1 Movement. Everyone in B1G1 believes in "the power of small" and can help transform the way we do business. No matter how busy you are or the size of your business, B1G1 can help you achieve your goals by automating giving on behalf of your business.

It is so simple. Don't wait another day.

My ultimate legacy is to create a ripple effect that turns into a wave by supporting people and doing good for others. If I can change the course of one person's life for the better, and they can do that for one other person, then each of us leaves this world having made an impact worth celebrating.

All of us really can make a difference.

SMILES ARE THE IMPACTS WE MAKE
DR. CATHERINE YANG

Have you ever stopped to ask why there is so much tension, suffering, and struggle in life? I often wonder this.

In today's world, it is often not fierce competition that puts people off trying, but the encountered inequalities that leave people in a state of hopeless despair. Although we are unique individuals who are special in our own ways, we all want to be treated equally. A sense of fairness leads us to expect the freedom to make decisions and access education. It is here that we can equip ourselves for the journey of learning, gaining skills and knowledge for a better life, a better future, and a better world.

Many people prefer getting to giving. But as Masami Sato, the founder of B1G1 says, by creating a "sufficient cycle of abundance," and giving what we have, we will attract more in return. The more we have, the more we are driven to give. This self-sustaining cycle will never deplete, because it keeps growing through the power of giving.

By empowering all and promoting their inclusion in social, political, economic, and environmental decisions, we can reduce inequality as set out in SDG 10. The world will be a better place when all are provided equal access to health, education, and opportunity.

Living Proof that Wild Dreams do Come True

I was born and raised in Taipei, Taiwan. As a child, my family moved frequently. I lived in various areas and interacted with people from all walks of life. Irrespective of their age, gender, or ethnicity, I could see how many struggled, even if they worked hard. The cost of living in Taiwan made money an issue, with services like education and healthcare considered luxuries before the 1990s. I remember the time my thinking changed and the seed to be a changemaker was first planted. I was eating my favorite beef noodle soup on a cold winter day at a local food stall, watching the news of a flu outbreak. The owner said to me, "Poor people like us cannot afford to be sick.

Expensive medical treatment is for the rich people." On my way home, I thought to myself, "Wouldn't it be nice to make healthcare accessible to all people?"

Fast forward to 1994, when I was in my last year of high school and considering career options. We took turns seeing our school career advisor to chat about our future career paths. It was hard enough for me to study all the subjects in English as a second language learner, not to mention how awkward it felt to talk about my wild dream to become a dentist. Surprisingly, Ms. D., my advisor, told me with a smile, "Go for it, Catherine, go and make this world a better place with more smiles!"

Because of her encouragement and belief in me, I applied to the University of Sydney; after an interview, they offered me the Faculty of Dentistry Alumni Scholarship. Here I am today, practicing dentistry since 1999, and still loving it! It is deeply rewarding to help people enjoy life with their healthy smile.

Embed a Giving Model into Your Business

As Simon Sinek put it so well in a 2009 TED Talk, "People don't buy what you do, they buy why you do it." More so than ever before, people like to engage with a business that cares. With readily accessible information available on the internet, people seek more than just product details, services provided, or price comparisons when making a decision on what to purchase.

Chats Dental is a "better business" as it creates a meaningful impact around the world. We have been able to contribute to many SDGs, but SDG 10, "Reducing Inequality," is the one the business supports the most.

Our giving model is simple and exemplifies how any business can integrate actions that make a difference into their corporate ethos. We feel privileged to offer the following as part of our contribution to SDG 10:

- When a new patient appointment is made, we provide one daily dose of vitamin A supplements to a child in Turkana, Kenya.
- When a client accepts a cup of tea or coffee at reception, we provide one day's worth of grain to nourish a child in Malawi.
- When we see a client for emergency care, we plant a tree to

support reforestation in Borneo.

- When we provide painless dentistry using IV sedation, we give a meal to a rescued animal through Edgar's Mission in Victoria, Australia.
- When a new child sits in the dental chair, happily counting teeth with us, we provide one day of education support to a disadvantaged child in New Zealand.
- When a client laughs in the dental chair and thanks us for an enjoyable dental experience, we provide one day of access to personal hygiene to a girl in Kenya or Nepal.
- When a client returns for their six-month dental check-up, we provide one day of access to dental hygiene to a child in El Jebha, Morocco.
- When a client's smile is transformed by functional aesthetics, four rainforest trees are planted and protected to help the survival of the southern cassowary at Mission Beach in Queensland, Australia.
- When we perform the Chats Dental Puppet Show to educate preschoolers and schoolchildren, we give one special learning tool to a child in Buffalo City, South Africa.
- When we give out a "Certificate of Gratitude" to a valued client, we give one day of access to reading materials to a girl in Cambodia.

We believe that giving is not just about what it does for others. Giving is also about what it does for us.

By working together to reduce inequalities in the world, we can fight inequality in education, access to healthcare and opportunities for employment. By equipping disadvantaged children with necessities, improving access to healthcare, and providing better opportunities, we can help open doors to good health, quality education, decent work, and improved well-being.

Be a Voice — No Matter How Small

Even in the twenty-first century, many around the world still suffer from inequality. I had always assumed that charity work, especially in the international arena, was the responsibility of governments and large or multinational corporations. This misconception may be shared by many people. One day, that changed.

I attended an event with hundreds of people. The presentations were both informative and resourceful, but what stirred my heart was a video showing how one company had changed the life of hundreds of disadvantaged children in Thailand by helping a charity supply them with food, education, and medical supplies.

That meaningful fundraising initiative required a membership fee for participation. One that I couldn't afford at the time. Suddenly, I fell into despair, thinking I was not good enough, feeling like a failure, watching so many other people put their hands up to join. I felt awful and wanted to leave. I couldn't make a difference. During the break, I met a friend, Mark Williams, the managing director of Imagine Accounting. Mark asked me to stay for the last speaker at the conference. He promised me that it would be worth it.

That was the first time I met Paul Dunn, co-founder and chair of B1G1. When Paul talked about the joy of giving, I didn't really understand at first. He never used the word "donate" and we never saw photos of him presenting an oversized check to anyone. Instead, he demonstrated how "giving impacts" (smiles of people) can be achieved through the power of giving small amounts, collectively. With every transaction made by a small business partnered with B1G1, something great happens in the world as a result.

As Paul spoke, he happened to mention that a dental discomfort had disturbed his sleep the night before. Of the hundreds of people attending the conference, I was the only dentist. Being so inspired by the power of small, I plucked up my courage, went up to Mr. Dunn, and asked him if I could have the privilege of serving him. Looking back now, I think he was the courageous one, taking up an offer of treatment from an unknown dentist.

Paul visiting Chats Dental and telling us more about the B1G1 projects was the pivotal moment for me. We felt privileged to serve Mr. Dunn, who opened our eyes to a new perspective on deep and meaningful human connection. By 2018, Chats Dental had grown from two to eight employees, serving both local communities and overseas visitors. As B1G1 thinks of each impact as a smile, it truly makes our hearts sing when more smiles are created in the world.

That day, I had the courage to speak up, and it changed my life.

Don't think that your voice doesn't count, or you can't make a difference. Nothing will change if we silence ourselves; inequalities will continue. The internet and social media have created a platform where we can have our voice heard far and wide, almost instantly and free of charge. If you see or hear something unfair or unjust, have the courage to stand up for what is right. Never underestimate the power of small.

Collectively we can get our message across, influence people, and make this world a better place for all.

WHAT YOU CAN DO TO CREATE A WORLD OF REDUCED INEQUALITIES

Lifestyle tips:
- Speak up against any type of discrimination.
- Make sure everyone's voice counts in policy making.
- Be kind and empathic.

Business tips:
- Create commercially viable and sustainable solutions.
- Be transparent about the progress you are making and experiment with new approaches to create equality.

Giving tips:
- Contribute to programs that support people with disadvantages.
- Support migrants and refugees in your communities.
- Visit local shelters, orphanages or minority community centers and organize a conversation space.

A GOOD LIFE IN OUR CITIES

11 SUSTAINABLE CITIES AND COMMUNITIES

HOW YOU AND YOUR BUSINESS CAN MAKE CITIES AND HUMAN SETTLEMENTS INCLUSIVE, SAFE, RESILIENT, AND SUSTAINABLE.

> "The chief function of the city is to convert power into form, energy into culture, dead matter into the living symbols of art, biological reproduction into social creativity."
>
> — Lewis Mumford

THE CHANGEMAKERS

CREATIVE COMMUNITIES | THE CITY OF THE FUTURE
ALEXANDER INCHBALD

Alexander Inchbald paints in extreme locations all over the world. Each experience, whether it be Mont Blanc, Mount Fuji, or the Russian Caucasus, leads to a feeling of oneness with nature. Alexander published his first book, *#Balance*, in 2018, which explains how leaders and their organizations can situate purpose at the heart of everything they do. He is the founder of The (artist) inside, a partner of Ashoka, and a master trainer at the Entrepreneur's Institute, and he is currently working with the Presencing Institute's S-Lab, United Smart Cities, a UN partnership to use art to reconnect communities. He lives in France with his beautiful wife and two children, Sasha and Daniel.

alexander-inchbald.com

GIVE AND GROW – NEW BUSINESS SOLUTIONS
DEBORAH HARRIS

Deborah Harris is a passionate philanthropist, speaker, and entrepreneur. She is the founder of The Grow CFO Co., a company specializing in growing the financial capabilities of businesses. Grow Events delivers education to business owners to enable their businesses to thrive by developing the skills and knowledge for success. Deborah is a mother to five young adults and shares her business journey with her husband, Jeremy. Together, they travel the world.

growcfoco.com, groweventsglobal.com

THE CITY KID AND THE COUNTRY KID
JAMIE SELBY

Jamie Selby is a proud dad, husband, international bestselling co-author, pricing consultant, chartered accountant, owner of an award-winning accountancy practice, entrepreneur, Blockchain enthusiast, investor, qualified marketing specialist, speaker, NED, and continual giver. He is driven to make a difference in the world through the use of technology and B1G1's Business for Good Movement.

cloud-pricing-software.com, jamieselby.co.uk

A GOOD LIFE IN
OUR CITIES

Not everyone is born into "the good life." In fact, if you are, you've won the lottery of life. You've been given one massive advantage.

Life is unpredictable. We don't get to choose where we are born or who our parents are. We aren't given the birthright of "living the good life." But we are given the ability to make decisions, to choose new paths, to think, to innovate and to develop our innate gifts and use them.

This means we can do a lot. We can deliberately create the good life for everyone.

We can build good cities, safe communities and sustainable futures for all. A city that cares and supports its citizens. A city that is healthy, vibrant and inclusive. A city with great facilities and resources. A city that is a home, not just a place to reside.

Singapore is one such example. A city that started a mere 54 years ago with very little and was built into a thriving, growing and innovative country. A country with a clear focus on Sustainability and the Goals in general and a model for so many other countries.

One shining citizen of this wonderful country is Goh Swee Chen. Swee Chen wasn't born into a privileged background, but she is dedicated to creating thriving cities.

Most people in Singapore know Swee Chen for her incredible career and her role as the president of the Global Compact Network Singapore. Her active contributions to this leading-edge city is the perfect example of how people really are the backbone to creating great communities.

Swee Chen has a diverse professional background, having led significant businesses in the oil and gas, consumer goods, and IT sectors. She joined Shell in 2003 and retired as the chairman of Shell Companies in Singapore in January 2019. Swee Chen is on the boards of CapitaLand and Singapore Airlines. She chairs the Institute of HR Professionals and the Global Compact Network Singapore. She also sits on public service boards, including the Legal Service Commission and National Arts Council. Swee Chen has previously chaired/sat on the boards of Shell Joint Ventures in China, Korea, and Saudi Arabia. She graduated with a B.Sc. from Victoria University and an MBA from Chicago Booth, University of Chicago. She received a Distinguished Alumni Award from Chicago Booth in 2018. She is also a wife and mother with three children.

These credentials represent far more than a well-educated woman. They reveal an involved and dedicated citizen passionate about her role in the community.

Many people may not know that Swee Chen came from a small town in Malaysia, with a population of 75,000. Her father was a mechanic and her mother a seamstress. The values of working hard and seeking strengths in a community were instilled from a very young age. She grew up with a deep sense of social responsibility and a drive to help others thrive.

Swee Chen's personal experiences and professional success had led her to believe in the power of legacy.

Enjoy the wisdom of leading changemaker, Goh Swee Chen…

Building a New Way of Life Together - Goh Swee Chen

The world's population is constantly increasing and we must all learn to live together. To accommodate everyone, we need to build modern, sustainable cities. For all of us to survive and prosper, we need new, intelligent urban planning that creates safe, affordable, and resilient cities featuring green and culturally inspiring living conditions. Can we leave such a legacy?

When one talks about legacy, the issue of inheritance comes to mind. As each individual contemplates the legacy that he or she commits to leaving behind, a question arises: What inheritance do we desire for the next generation?

Never has the topic of sustainability been more widely discussed than now. Amongst both nations and corporations, there is a growing sense of urgency. This urgency is brought about by the reality that nations and people cannot prosper where there is strife. Neither can nations and corporations continue to fast-track growth at the expense of the Earth's natural resources, depleting what generations have assumed will be available in perpetuity.

As the world's population increases, an increasing number of people are migrating to cities in order to access better education, better jobs, and better healthcare. In other words, they are seeking a better life.

According to UN Habitat's 2009 estimation, three million people move to cities worldwide every week. At the 2017 World Cities Summit Mayors' Forum in Suzhou, China, many participants described the challenges associated with coping with the increasing stresses on the infrastructures of cities that stem from such migration.

The stresses placed on cities' infrastructures are not the only challenges in this regard. As populations become more diverse, societies become correspondingly more fractious. Political parties can exploit this situation and base their campaigns on divisive ideology. Almost unequivocally, communities in cities have a key expectation – equality. More specifically, they expect equal access to amenities and opportunities.

In *The Economy of Cities*, Jane Jacobs argues that cities are both the locale and the driver of innovations. Corporations that understand the stresses of cities have learned to unlock the associated business values.

Opportunities exist in terms of designing solutions for the environment, including waste management, energy, mobility, urban planning, and general living services.

Today, most new townships are planned with the best of intentions, with livability in mind.

Close to my home in Singapore, the Housing Development Board's (HDB's) Punggol Eco-Town offers a good example of this intention. The town, the first of its kind, is a living lab for new ideas concerning sustainable development and the integration of urban solutions for livability.

Corporations that are prepared to invest in the co-vision of a city, as well as in the co-creation of solutions, will encounter new avenues for revenue growth and the development of new skills.

Importantly, new skills are constantly being developed and corporate purposes reinvigorated. Nothing attracts top talent more than the search for solutions to some of the world's most complex problems.

Recognition of city transformations on the global stage serves as a form of encouragement and education. The Lee Kuan Yew World City Prize is one such award, which looks at the transformation of a city over the course of a decade. The prize is awarded on the basis of criteria such as the development of sustainable urban communities, leadership and governance, and the endurance of the transformation.

When businesses, governments, and society exert their collective might in tandem, solutions and opportunities with regard to sustainability are abundant. In essence, we get to see SDG 17 in play.

What is Not Measured, Matters

My children studied at international schools. When they came home excited about making a new friend, my first question was generally, "Where is your friend from?" In all instances, they could not answer my question. Instead, they knew their new friends' hobbies, favorite songs, books, etc. Can we learn from our children? Can we leave behind our conditioned norms and prejudices to find the common good within a community of residents who are not like ourselves?

And that leads me to this extract of a speech by Robert Kennedy on March 18th, 1968, at the University of Kansas, just 3 months before his assassination:

> Our Gross National Product, now, is over $800 billion dollars a year, but that Gross National Product - if we judge the United States of America by that - that Gross National Product counts air pollution and cigarette advertising, and ambulances to clear our highways of carnage. It counts special locks for our doors and the jails for the people who break them. It counts the destruction of the redwood and the loss of our natural wonder in chaotic sprawl. It counts napalm and counts nuclear warheads and armored cars for the police to fight the riots in our cities. It counts Whitman's rifle and Speck's knife, and the television programs which glorify violence in order to sell toys to our children. Yet the gross national product does not allow for the health of our children, the quality of their education or the joy of their play. It does not include the beauty of our

poetry or the strength of our marriages, the intelligence of our public debate or the integrity of our public officials. It measures neither our wit nor our courage, neither our wisdom nor our learning, neither our compassion nor our devotion to our country, it measures everything in short, except that which makes life worthwhile. And it can tell us everything except what makes us proud.

Fifty years have passed since Kennedy gave that speech. We can still secure the inheritance of a better world for future generations.

For centuries, humans have evolved and survived calamities and strife. It should not be different for this generation. They may be complex or costly, but solutions are in sight. Willpower is a necessary ingredient.

— *Goh Swee Chen*

The following three changemakers address diverse and equally powerful solutions for making a difference.

Alexander Inchbald explores the need for art, culture, and human expression as an opportunity for communities to come together. His ability to invite the artist within everyone to help create a new and powerful future is inspiring.

Deborah Harris addresses how vital it is for businesses to embed a giving model within the core of their business and thus help to create sustainable cities and communities. But more than advice, she also gives a tried-and-tested three-step plan to implement it today.

And Jamie Selby discusses the importance of meeting the basic needs of every citizen, not just in terms of supplying food, water, and shelter, but also the psychological human needs for love and belonging. He explores an important topic and provokes deep thought and reflection with his insights.

These are fellow citizens with the ability to innovate our future. You can too.

UNLEASH THE ARTIST WITHIN
ALEXANDER INCHBALD

I tried to change the world for seven years.

I worked on each of the SDGs with organizations such as the UN, WHO, UNICEF, UNOPS, The Red Cross, Gavi – The Vaccine Alliance, The Global Fund to Fight Malaria, AIDS and Tuberculosis, and many other NGOs. During that time, I discovered that the greatest impact I had on changing health was on my own — and it was negative.

I spoke to an entrepreneur in Kenya while working on the WASH (Water, Sanitation and Hygiene) campaign. He boldly told me that he didn't want a handout, he wanted a "hand up." I realized that no one wants to be saved by some random stranger; instead, they want the opportunity to change their world — themselves. When I really understood this, I stopped fighting companies that didn't want to change and chose to work with individuals who were already changing. This changed everything, including myself.

Cities represent the melting pot in which we will either achieve the SDGs or we won't, and creativity is the missing ingredient that will catalyze success. We are creative beings in a creative universe. Inside us, two million new red blood cells are created every second, while outside us, 4,500 stars are created in the universe every second. On a very, very large scale, the universe is constantly creating, while on a very, very small scale, our bodies are constantly creating. Our cells are a fractal of the universe. Interestingly, the two ends of this spectrum look surprisingly similar. Try using Google to compare the latest images of the universe with an image of the synapses firing in a neural network inside the human body. They look almost identical. Both networks create trillions of connections every single second. Cities can serve as a hub to further ignite connection and creativity.

More than half the world's population lives in cities. Newcomers are drawn by opportunity and driven by climate change, natural disasters, and agricultural mechanization. Yet, cities experience more poverty, inequality, poor health, poor sanitation, and conflict than the countryside because cities disconnect us from our true nature — our essence, our spirit, our soul — what you choose to call it doesn't matter. What matters is the fact that most of us feel disconnected. As a result, city dwellers are more likely to experience depression, addiction, and a sense of isolation than their cousins in the countryside.

The bright lights and gaudy distractions of cities tend to pull us more toward the world outside us than the world inside us. Every wisdom tradition describes a duality within us. Most of us flip-flop between these worlds without forming a consistently balanced mindset that links them: psychologists talk about the conscious and the unconscious, philosophers talk about the personality and the essence, artists talk about the intellect and intuition, while scientists talk about the Newtonian physical world of things and the Einsteinian metaphysical world of ideas.

I talk about the Inner Game and the Outer Game, based on Bob Anderson and Bill Adam's research involving 50,000 leaders, which they describe in their book, *Mastering Leadership*. They found that those who lead with their Inner Game (creativity, purpose, and intuition) are up to 1,000 times more effective than those who don't.

The Inner Game enables us to dream up a Masterpiece, while the Outer Game enables us to bring that Masterpiece to life. What we create is an expression of our inner world in relation to the world outside us.

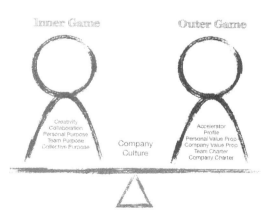

Disconnection stems from relying almost exclusively on our first five senses, which connect us to the world of matter outside us, and ignoring our sixth sense (intuition), which connects us to the world of energy inside us. This disconnection is more likely to occur in cities.

The good news is that humanity has never been as concentrated as it is today in cities, nor has it ever been as easy to connect within cities and between cities. As our innate interconnectedness becomes more obvious, the balance of power will shift away from nation-states and toward cities, since they serve as critical nodes within this emerging network. This shift represents an enormous opportunity. Creativity, in the form of art, has helped us to connect with ourselves, with each other, and with something greater than ourselves ever since our ancestors created the first cave paintings in Lascaux. So, if the SDGs are the antidote to humanity's current symptoms of imbalance, the root cause of that imbalance is disconnection from our essence, and cities are change agents in waiting, then creative cities could be the panacea.

There is an apocryphal story about Winston Churchill during World War II. When asked to cut arts funding to help the war effort, he allegedly replied, "Then what are we fighting for?" Regardless of how true this story is, the reason it resonates is because life is not "nasty, brutish and short," as Thomas Hobbes once claimed. It is an exhilarating journey of creation. We create our world every single day.

Some of the happiest people in the world come from some of the poorest communities. Like children, they focus on the here and now, rather than the longing for this or that. If our actions in the so-called developed world inspire those living in such communities to follow us, we will not survive. Purchasing more washing machines, cars, and computers may improve quality of life in the short term, but it jeopardizes humanity in the long term.

We must inspire a new generation of artists, entrepreneurs, and innovators in these communities to think differently.

That, for me, is the purpose of art. Michelangelo provoked us to think differently about the relationship between God and man. Monet and the Impressionists provoked us to think differently about light. Vincent van Gogh provoked us to think differently about how we create. Today, everyone is an artist. Everyone creates. So, what could an artist in Hanoi, Hanover, Harare, or Havana provoke us to do differently? Have you unleashed the artist inside you? And your children?

More creativity is required to achieve each of the SDGs. Cities, however, tend to suppress creativity, since they distance us from the ecological problems we face. It took me many years to realize this. I grew up in the countryside, surrounded by fields. It wasn't until I went to university in Edinburgh that I lived in a city for the first time. From there, I moved to London. And then, to Geneva. In total, I lived in cities for fourteen years. And that's exactly the amount of time I stopped painting for. In cities, I felt that my creativity was suffocated. Since restarting, I've tried to paint "en plein air" in Paris, Moscow, and Basel, but every time my energy gets blocked. It simply doesn't flow in the same way as it does in the countryside. It's a hangover from an imperialistic past in which man believed, in his arrogance, he could conquer nature.

It's great that some cities have parks and many are surrounded by natural beauty, but in general, cities separate us from our true nature.

Creativity doesn't come from our head when we're sitting at a desk thinking. It comes when we get out of our head and we stop thinking. It comes when we're in our body and present. Whenever or wherever our best ideas come to us, such moments are when we are in creative flow. For myself, this happened one day in a blizzard just outside Geneva, Switzerland. I didn't leave the house intending to paint in a blizzard. It just happened. The snow only started to fall after I started to paint. To begin with, part of me, my ego, resisted the snow. It was making the canvas wet and the paint run. I had no control! And I was concerned about what the painting would look like. There was another part of me, my essence, which was intrigued. So, I let go. After all, snow is just water in another form and the paints I use are water-based, so the atmosphere, which is also water-based, is infused into the painting.

The snow fell more heavily and started to merge with the paint. There was now no separation between the paint and the snow. They were collaborating. My job was simply to enable them to fuse together. I was the facilitator, enabling creativity to flow.

A little later, I looked at the palette and it was covered in so much snow that I could hardly see the paint. Then, the same thing happened to the canvas. I was now painting through the snow. Except who was really painting? Me or the snow? Or something else? It certainly wasn't my ego, which had dissolved into the snow. Who was creating? I didn't care. All I knew was that I felt at one, in pure peace, in total flow …

The moment I finished painting, the sun came out. The snow and ice, which had merged with the paint and held it to the canvas, began to melt. Everything dissolved and the paint started to run. Yet, I had experienced something profound. I realized that instead of resisting the environment and integrating it into the painting, I had stepped into another world, the world of flow. These experiences led me to conclude that flow is possible for everyone, everywhere.

My partners and I encourage others to tap into this universal flow and creativity. We have created a blueprint that draws on ancient wisdom within a modern context to balance the Inner World and Outer World. With the help of communities, we are creating a new, sustainable world, one that is so healthy, wealthy, and wise that everyone who experiences it wants to join in. These programs are designed to combine healing, art, and nature. We facilitate:

- **LIFE:** Three to five-day retreats in the world's most stunning locations (Mont Blanc, Mount Fuji, Mongolia, Maldives, a South African game reserve, the Russian Caucasus, the Himalayas, Norway, Bali, etc.). We use the power of nature, healing, and art to elevate collective consciousness.
- **Creative Communities:** Large-scale collaborative art projects in cities and museums around the world. They are designed to replace the prevailing sense of collective disconnection with a sense of inclusive community.
- **Impact on Purpose:** Helping changemakers (increasingly in cities), their teams, companies, associations, and partnerships to articulate and realize a Collective Purpose.
- **Personal Purpose App:** Helping thousands of changemakers to articulate their Personal or Collective Purpose and then to realize it.

GIVE AND GROW – NEW BUSINESS SOLUTIONS
DEBORAH HARRIS

Having recently traveled to some of the world's largest cities – spending time in Johannesburg, London, Tokyo, Kyoto, Beijing, and Shanghai – I witnessed the challenges facing these megacities, including how they deal with poverty, pollution, and the sheer mass of people in a way that is respectful and caring for all.

However, it was in Cambodia, South Africa, and Bali that I really started to understand the deeper significance of building sustainable communities. In these places, I saw the challenges of extreme poverty, poor sanitation, poor nutrition, and limited access to health facilities.

All the SDGs inspire me because none of them can be fixed in isolation. Choosing to make a community sustainable has to include taking care of its natural environment, namely the waterways, land, and air. It has to include making energy solutions possible. It must also care for the needs of the people, providing opportunities for work, for food and shelter, and for medical treatment and education.

My interest in making our communities inclusive, safe, resilient, and sustainable began when I was in my teens. As a teenager, I volunteered at a center for children with severe disabilities. It was shocking to see how non-inclusive life could be for those children and their families. This realization was reinforced as my sister gradually lost her vision. I started to really see the marginalized and the homeless. Even in First World communities, there are people in dire need.

As a farm kid, I left home at 17 to study. I moved to the city, where the neighbors didn't know me, where I didn't know how to catch public transport, and where I couldn't see the stars, find a quiet place, or even breathe clean air. But at least I could seize opportunities that were previously unavailable to me. After meeting my husband, I never returned to that rural community, except to visit on holidays.

Then came a severe drought in Queensland, Australia. Some of my peers had to leave university to go home and put down their livestock as the animals were starving to death. The opportunities for work in their communities were no longer viable. In some cases, the lives of the farming families were so desperate that it became commonplace in the media to hear of escalating suicide rates among farmers. They chose to use their life insurance policies to give their families a new start.

When I really started to travel, I began to understand the level of poverty in some places. Seeing slums firsthand didn't just give me a picture of squalor, it gave me an insight into how arrogant my thinking was. Prior to that, I sometimes thought, "Why don't they clean up?" and "Why don't they work together?" I had to open my mind to the fact that simply meeting their basic human needs was such a struggle that they had no energy and no ability to think beyond that. In order to improve their condition, they first needed their condition to be improved.

The Best Gift You Can Give

When I started my entrepreneurial journey, I realized that my capacity for thinking and solving problems was the best gift I could give to these communities. While there is definitely a need to contribute financial resources to emergency projects, sustainability comes not from a handout, but from a "hand up." That is, providing solutions that can be replicated to lift communities into safe, inclusive, resilient, and sustainable places.

Having been involved in business for over 30 years, Jeremy and I have come to recognize our desire to contribute more philanthropically. We started the new brand with The Grow CFO Co. to combine our virtual chief financial officer solutions with training in order to inspire teams within purpose-driven businesses to lift their cash flow and elevate their growth and giving initiatives.

We believe that every business can situate giving at the core of their business. If giving is not just part of your ethos, but is rather core to your vision, mission, and values, then it should be the leading key performance indicator for the business.

The Three-Step Metric Plan to Situate Giving at the Core of Your Business

1. Determine who you want to help, how you want to help them, and when you want to help them. Our plan looks something like this:

   By the end of 2019 we want to provide 6,000 women with access to a business development training course through MicroLoan Australia and B1G1 so that they can help their families by making a truly profitable micro business in their community, repay their loans and allow the funding opportunity to be provided to others.

   We set these giving metrics for each of our products and services.

2. Develop your broader business model to incorporate giving. Ours looks a little like this:

   100% Revenue = 5% Giving + 10% Marketing + 10% Sales + 50% Delivery of Product or Service + 25% Growth/Profit and Administration.

3. Set your promotion and project plans to help meet those objectives and then work backwards.

For example, if we decided to give $1,500, we would aim to generate a revenue of $30,000. Then, we would focus on what we can deliver to achieve that revenue target, on time, within cost, and with the giving impacts we aimed for.

Why does this matter? By using this simple three-step strategy, we positioned giving at the core of our business. Our aim over time is to streamline other activities and lift the 5% to 10%.

You can create a legacy business today.

Legacy Businesses

The idea of leaving a legacy inspires me. I want to gift something forward to future generations.

When I was in Japan recently, I visited a beautiful Bonsai garden. The trees were over 1000 years old. An older man was spending up to 15 hours per day tending the trees. He was a wealthy individual, who didn't need to do it for financial reasons. A member of the group I was with asked him why he spent 15 hours every day taking care of the trees. His translator told us that he replied, "How could I not?"

It was there that I realized a legacy was not necessarily about what I create. Each Bonsai tree has had generations of loving hands forming and shaping it. That was when I truly understood that providing a legacy is about being a custodian for the future, about shaping and forming a world in which every person is honored, appreciated, and given the opportunity to benefit humanity.

You don't need to save the world. It's not your job to save the whole world. Your job is to activate others so that together we can save the world. Not one world leader has been able to save the whole planet single-handedly.

To act, you just need to:
- Be conscious of your community, whether virtual or local.
- Recognize a problem that needs to be solved and take responsibility for solving it.
- Contribute to someone else solving a similar problem in another part of the world.

This will connect you to a global community of people who think and act like you. Together, we can inspire each other, and our progress when working together will seem so much more significant.

There have been a number of very specific events that prompted me to choose my current journey in trying to lead an ethical and conscious life as a parent, a business owner, and a global citizen.

We chose a school for our children with an amazing leadership program. In their senior years of schooling, the students tour a Third World country as part of an Antipodeans Abroad program. They spend a week trekking, a week being a tourist, and a week contributing to a program within the community. To date, the students have finished classrooms, built houses, and even funded artificial limbs through money they raised together as a community. Over time, our children have contributed to initiatives in Laos, Borneo, Cambodia, and Vietnam, and our youngest travels to Nepal later this year.

A few years ago, I took one of our daughters to Cambodia, where she connected with the young children in their community while building a playground. I found it amazing to sit with another group of women, without a common language and yet able to communicate our love for our children without words.

Our family has deep connections and memories associated with many special projects. This Life Cambodia contributes bicycles to school children in Cambodia, while we contribute to the village school of Supingstad on the border between South Africa and Botswana through our connection with Tau Game Lodge.

Perhaps the most profound opportunity to connect with projects happened in Bali while we were attending the 10th Anniversary Conference of B1G1 and saw the work of the John Fawcett Foundation. The foundation provides a clinic bus to perform operations in some of the poorest villages. Our family gave the gift of vision that day. I stepped inside the clinic door as a young doctor was taking her first lead in surgery, being guided and advised by the senior surgeon. She carefully removed the cataract, and when it came out whole, her peers quietly applauded. They then put the cataract on a piece of gauze, handed it through the partition, and placed it in my hands. I was overwhelmed.

My sister had three similar surgeries before she was 30, but unfortunately, she faced other vision challenges and remains blind. But there, holding the cataract in my hand, I was making a difference...a life-changing difference. I was giving the gift of sight. And as giving often does, it made my own vision clearer.

This year, we aim to light up the world for Christmas. Throughout the year, we are creating a virtual village with a great group of friends, including Chris Wildeboer from Balance Central, Adam Houlahan from Web Traffic That Works, and Tim Wade from timwade.com. Each time we get together, we contribute to everything a village or sustainable community could need, from water to healthcare. My goal is to light up the world for Christmas. Solar lighting is essential in many parts of the world. It is cheap to produce, and with it families can help their children remain in school and study after hours. Also, they don't create pollution with their kerosene lanterns. Light can extend their day and enable them to take up other opportunities for learning or creating items to sell.

Lighting the world lights up my life, and this type of legacy never diminishes.

THE CITY KID AND THE COUNTRY KID
JAMIE SELBY

I come from a small village. I used to spend a lot of time with my best friend, Marcus. Marcus lived in the city and we spent a lot of time there, ice skating, going to the cinema, visiting fast food restaurants, and at the weekends, playing football.

What I didn't realize at the time was how much Marcus' mother wanted him out of the city. She loved him so much, but she didn't want that life for her son. She almost forced him to stay with us at weekends so that she could get him away from the city. I just thought it was awesome that my friend always stayed over after football.

One day, while alone in the city, I was cornered. A group of hooded youths attempted to mug me at knife point. The incident destroyed my confidence, in myself, in others, and in city life. The experience sent me to a dark place. I was depressed. I wouldn't go into town. I didn't tell my parents. In fact, I didn't speak to anyone about it. Except Marcus.

I don't blame the muggers. I blame the lack of sustainability. I blame the difficult conditions they grew up in. They came from the cities where their parents lived. Their parents worked, but they were not earning enough money to maintain the household. They were forced to seek alternative means to make money. Most turned to drugs or alcohol to numb the pain stemming from the lack of support to solve even the simplest of problems.

I believe these youngsters were forced down a route they didn't want to travel. I don't think for one minute that they woke up that morning thinking, "You know what? I'm going to try and destroy someone's life today. I really want to make somebody feel miserable today." I think they woke up that morning thinking, "I don't know where my next meal is coming from. I don't know where my next loving hug is going to come from. I don't even know whether my friends or family love me. I don't know whether or where I fit in."

The only friends they had were leading them down a destructive path. The destruction they caused was huge. It deeply, deeply impacted me. It's just a shame that it was such a negative thing they put all their effort into. Just think how much good they could have done if they could have chosen a different path, a different lifestyle. Some might say they did have a choice. Yes, they had a choice, but when you feel cornered in life, you make desperate decisions.

Later on, Marcus stopped hanging around with me to keep me away from the city. He was being forced into a life of crime. He became a drug dealer and hung around with the wrong crowd. He dealt drugs in the belief that he was supporting and protecting his family, and ultimately, it was too easy for him. He didn't know any other job where he'd get paid the same money. He said to me, "Jamie, if you can find me a job that pays me over £1,000 a week, I will quite happily quit dealing." He was only 17.

This had a huge impact on my life. I saw the deeper loss that the lack of a sustainable city causes. Racial divisions escalated and social groups formed their own alliances. The perpetual cycle that this causes leads only to further division and disconnect. And that is just not sustainable in so many ways.

Marcus Karringan Atkinson died on January 25th, 2014. May you rest in peace, brother. You inspired me to be myself, to not live in fear, to always have fun, for that I am eternally grateful.

Creating Kinder Cities and Caring Communities

Let's think about you and me for a moment. Consider the last homeless person you walked past and completely ignored. Now ask yourself this question: Why did you ignore them? I am not saying this to make you feel bad, but society has led us to believe that it is OK to just walk past homeless people and ignore their problems. People feel it is OK to see a problem and just ignore it, or if anything, to get out their phone and record it.

Sustainable cities can start with us and with our actions. Next time you see an elderly person struggling with their bags, ask them if they need help. Next time you see a homeless person, engage. Ask how their day has been. Maybe ask why they are homeless.

Here's the truth. People don't wake up in the morning with the desire to make you feel bad or to get in your way whilst going to work. Their cars don't deliberately break down or crash to make you late. No one does that stuff on purpose.

There are no excuses to do nothing, to stand idly by while people suffer. We can create kinder cities and more caring communities.

What we don't see doesn't hurt us — or at least that's what we think. Sustainability is the key word here. We need to think in more sustainable ways. If we are living on our overdraft and spending more money than we earn, is that sustainable? Of course not.

If each one of us reduces our wasteful habits by just 10%, it will have a huge impact on the world. So, can you turn your house into a zero-waste environment? Try turning the lights off, growing some vegetables. If you cook too much, next time drop off some meals at a homeless shelter rather than throwing the food away.

We take from the planet. Now we need to give back.

Sustainability is not only about reducing poor choices, but also about creating new ones. If you have any great ideas, then please share them with others. Again, engage. Don't wait around. You could be holding the key to changing the world.

Community = Communication and Unity

Cities are the fastest growing areas in the world. If they continue to grow, they won't be sustainable.

Consider some of the world's biggest cities. Will you be able to visit them in 20 years' time? Traffic is a huge problem. Even with congestion charging, commuting during the rush hour is becoming unbearable and stress levels are soaring. This is all compounded by rising carbon emissions.

As a parent, I worry about the kind of future our children will face. Will they be able to enjoy cities and experience the buzz and mass of opportunity? Or will they be pushed out due to pollution, overcrowding, and crime? Just think back to 20 years ago and ask yourself this question: How much has your local city changed?

That's why your local city, your local community is so important. And when we break that word down, I get *communication and unity = community.* When we come together in small communities, we can make big changes.

Sustainable cities aren't only about physical needs. Psychological elements are important, too. People need to feel a sense of belonging, a sense of community care and welfare. These emotional needs run deep and provide people in the community with a sense of hope and belonging, a sense of pride. This is becoming so much more important to remember now that technological advances are making people 'replaceable'.

Here are some key focus points that could help us to pave a new way forward.

Needs - Focus on addressing the basic physical and psychological needs of communities. When people don't have their basic needs met, violence increases and living together becomes more dangerous and cramped. Then, people stop caring about their neighborhood – and their world. They stop caring about anything but themselves.

Love - It's hard for people to start thinking about love. Yet the importance of feeling loved, including amongst friends, families, and communities, is a basic human need. Without love, we become angry, sad, and bitter. The flow of love between citizens, cities, and countries is not being spread widely enough. More love is a vital component of leaving a legacy for our children. And when you think of legacy, every moment counts.

Support Small Businesses - If we continue to see small businesses fail, we will see less money in the small business community, and given that the small business community represents over 160 million businesses worldwide, it would be a disaster. Do you think governments can change the world? Or do you think small businesses can? I think they can, if, and only if, they get the correct advice and we see more investment in the small business community. More investment will lead to more jobs, more jobs will lead to more money, more money will lead to less poverty, and less poverty will lead to change.

People First - People's welfare must always come before money. Many large corporate businesses forget this basic human need.

Some people are voluntarily working exhausting hours so that they can make more money, which results in more profit for businesses. If we view life as a bank balance, we give life as a transaction to others.

Wages should be fair. Often, the flow of money is not distributed fairly and we need to stop perceiving jobs as having a "higher" or "lower" status. Many people are currently in the wrong jobs. If we could automate some of the menial tasks, then we could also support others to see the value in transfering themselves to other roles, ones they may enjoy more, and therefore, contribute more personal and community value.

Creating Community Together

We need to value the fact that each job and each person is contributing to society in a beneficial way. We need to recognize the value in what we bring to the world. And every single moment counts.

Community. Communication and unity. The way forward for humanity. Now.

WHAT YOU CAN DO TO CREATE A WORLD OF SUSTAINABLE CITIES AND COMMUNITIES

Lifestyle tips:
- Shop, eat and drink locally.
- Take care of public spaces.
- Travel in a sustainable way – bike, walk or take public transport.

Business tips:
- Invest in renewable energy.
- Adapt new technologies with care and consideration.
- Join initiatives like B-Corp and UN Global Compact.

Giving tips:
- Support a project in a slum for safe housing.
- Help fund projects to improve the livelihood of people.
- Volunteer or fund a project.

CARING THROUGH OUR EVERYDAY CHOICES

12 RESPONSIBLE CONSUMPTION AND PRODUCTION

HOW YOU AND YOUR BUSINESS CAN ENSURE SUSTAINABLE CONSUMPTION AND PRODUCTION PATTERNS.

"You have to hold yourself accountable for your actions, and that's how we're going to protect the Earth."

— Julia Butterfly Hill

THE CHANGEMAKERS

EMPOWERING IMPOVERISHED COMMUNITIES
BRIAN KEEN

Brian lived in Malawi for many years, running several construction, development, and transport businesses. Wanting to help the people in Malawi but unable to find a charity that met his criteria, he founded the Australian branch of the MicroLoan Foundation. Brian and his partner, Prue, also founded Franchise Simply, a world-first cloud-based franchise consulting and training company. Franchise Simply sponsors the B1G1 Worthy Cause MicroLoan Foundation Australia, enabling 95 percent of donations to be delivered to women in need.

microloanfoundationaustralia.org.au

SHOPPING OURSELVES TO EXTINCTION
SIAN CONWAY

Sian is the founder of Ethical Hour, the world's first and largest online support network for people who want to live and work more ethically. She found a way to bring her strategic marketing skills and passion for sustainability together by creating a community of conscious consumers and businesses to achieve positive change. Sian has worked with hundreds of brands to create positive impacts around the world. In 2018, she was named the UK's Green and Eco Influencer of the Year.

ethicalhour.co.uk

CONSCIOUS CONSUMERISM
RICHARD FLANAGAN

Richard Flanagan is a passionate creator and an award-winning entrepreneur. He has founded six businesses and is driven to make products and services that delight customers. His latest venture, Tshirtify, which he founded with wife Kerry, enables creators, influencers, and independent brands to carry their messages directly to consumers. Richard is a Prince's Trust mentor, creating and running enterprise programs in schools across the UK to help young people find their genius and to encourage young entrepreneurship.

tshirtify.com

CARING THROUGH OUR EVERYDAY CHOICES

Children's author, Maurice Sendak wrote — "There must be more to life than having everything!"

The story is about a little dog called Jennie. Jennie's not content with owning everything and goes out into the world to find something she doesn't have. That new something ends up causing much more trouble than she anticipated.

Sounds familiar? The sweet little fable stands as a simple reminder that chasing after the next shiny material object may not get us what we hoped for.

Yet too often, we keep on doing it.

Consumerism across the globe is at an all-time high. We are spending more on "things" and yet not reporting increased levels of happiness and wellbeing. The new cars, the bigger house, the latest tech devices are not doing what we thought they would — they're not increasing our feelings of joy or fulfillment. And in many cases (like in tech, for example), the new "something" is causing trouble.

More and more "buy this" messages surround us than ever before. Media in all its forms is filled with sales strategies, ads and more recently, so-called "influencers" enticing us to consume more and think less.

But we could change the world if we consumed less and thought more.

Consider that millions of people are expected to join the middle class over the next two decades. These socioeconomic and demographic changes are good for individual growth and prosperity, but it puts an increasing strain on our already stretched use of our natural resources such as water, oil, copper, natural gas, coal, and forests.

The surge in consumption has been fuelled by our population growth and advances in technology. Online buying is now a one-click process. And ever faster delivery methods make it easier and easier to get that dopamine "hit" of instant gratification.

However, while adding billions to the world's GDP, the increasing trend is undermining the world's natural systems and enhancing poverty.[1]

Yes, our instant "throwaway society" is causing us do harm to the earth and keeping people in poverty. In essence, it's not just old TVs and iPhones we're throwing away — but our planet's health and the chance for others to get out of poverty.

But it's not only our buying choices that are causing this impact, but also how and what we produce. And what we do with it, or don't.

Consider the following[2]:

1.3 billion tonnes of food gets wasted every year, while almost 2 billion people go hungry or undernourished.

The food sector accounts for around 22% of total greenhouse gas emissions, largely from the conversion of forests into farmland.

Only 3% of the world's water is fresh (drinkable), and humans are using it faster than nature can replenish it.

Should the global population reach 9.6 billion by 2050, the equivalent of almost three planets could be required to provide the natural resources needed to sustain current lifestyles.

We've all seen media reports on developing country exploitation: companies using child labor, insufferable working conditions, and pay rates inadequate to survive on.

We've seen images of the environmental damage caused after natural resources have been pillaged, or from the wars and conflicts that have emerged.

We've seen anti-slavery campaigns attempting to expose the human rights abuses hidden inside global supply chains, or pollution campaigns seeking to tackle the ongoing harm caused to the planet.

But seeing and knowing simply isn't enough anymore. Conscious actions must marry good intentions. Achieving economic

---

1   Mayell, H. 2004. *As Consumerism Spreads, Earth Suffers, Study Says About 1.7 billion people belong to the global "consumer class."* National Geographic.
    https://www.nationalgeographic.com/environment/2004/01/consumerism-earth-suffers/
2   Legacy Maker Content:
    https://www.unenvironment.org/explore-topics/sustainable-development-goals/why-do-sustainable-development-goals-matter/goal-12

growth and sustainable development requires us to urgently reduce our ecological footprint by changing the way we produce and consume goods and resources.

As changemaker Richard Flanagan rightly points out, we all have a role to play. He highlights the fact consumers have the power to change the current situation by making conscious buying decisions. And remaining conscious is the key. The first vital step to a huge change. We must become collectively conscious.

Changemaker Sian Conway did just that. She consciously investigated the world behind consuming and producing. You can do the same, simply by looking into where and how your clothes, furniture, goods are made is important. This helps us make ethical choices and these collective choices will impact the world.

Businesses are at the fore of making or breaking this SDG. Sian says that businesses should exist to solve problems for their consumers, the community and the planet.

Changemaker Brian Keen is part of this change. He points out that reducing poverty and improving the standard of living in developing communities is critical to allowing these countries to meaningfully contribute towards achieving responsible consumption and production. His micro-loan initiatives help women begin their own business journey and become part of the movement toward an ethical business economy. He integrates community action with global change.

If we do it right, growth and sustainability can exist without impacting negatively on each other. But we must do it right – for all.

Together we can investigate things like efficient management of our natural resources, the way we dispose of toxic waste and pollutants, how we can reduce waste and develop sustainable patterns of consumption and production.

Read on and discover how you can help everyone prosper sustainably and not at the expense of our most natural resource — our planet and each other.

EMPOWERING IMPOVERISHED COMMUNITIES
BRIAN KEEN

I first recognized the importance of responsible consumption and production early this century, after spending almost a decade in Malawi, Southern Africa. It was there that I discovered the critical element in relation to achieving this goal: people must raise their standard of living and live in sustainable communities. It is not possible to achieve this goal while people are experiencing poverty, an inadequate diet, no access to basic healthcare, little equality, poor water and sanitation, and a lack of clean energy sources.

It was the population of Malawi and its rapid growth that shocked me the most. When I arrived in the country in 1966, the population was just over four million. When I left in 1975, it had grown by 25%, reaching 5.3 million. It was a significant increase that the county could not support.

Malawi, unlike many countries in the region, has little in the way of natural resources, except for land, and occasionally, minerals. From the mid-70s, the government was severely constrained in terms of its development of the country due to political instability. As a result of periodic drought and flooding, and despite the fact there was plenty of vacant land and forested areas, it was apparent that the country's problems would continue to grow. However, the waterways were still clean and there was enough cleared land to permit subsistence-based families to support themselves, albeit only very modestly.

Nevertheless, it was clear that in suburban towns and small rural villages alike, drainage and sanitation were becoming a major problem, one that would need to be addressed quickly given the staggering increase in the population. By 2005, Malawi's population had reached almost 13 million, and by 2018, the official figure had reached 19 million.

Whilst living in Malawi, I founded and ran several businesses across the country, which employed over 100 Malawians. I spent time traveling widely, including in Zambia and Zimbabwe. Through these travels, I noticed that common trends existed. In order to feed themselves and their large, growing families, communities were over-planting and clearing all the native trees to provide fuel for heating and cooking, which degraded the soil. The vast majority were living in moderately populated rural areas, but people were moving very rapidly to the cities, where the situation soon became chronic due to the lack of employment and facilities.

This urban spread and the associated issues were inevitably going to continue. To my mind, it was a matter of overcoming these problems at the source. The source in this case being the country areas, particularly the remote villages where poverty was rife, where families were unable to feed their children, afford school fees for basic education, provide clothing or suitable housing, or access fundamental healthcare.

I knew that improved circumstances would allow people to raise their standard of living and contribute more meaningfully toward achieving the UN SDGs. In turn, it would enable growth in their economies, while also helping to manage population growth. I believed that if these problems could be addressed, word would spread throughout the country, resulting in high-skilled immigration to urban areas. This would effectively upskill the nation and result in a move toward attaining the goal of responsible consumption and production. However, I was acutely aware that if this situation was going to be addressed, initiatives had to be put in place very quickly and delivered effectively at a grassroots level in the villages.

Unlike many others, I couldn't turn a blind eye to these issues. I felt that something needed to be done, and I wanted to start helping the people I had worked with in Malawi. Unable to find a charity that met my criteria, I founded the Australian branch of the MicroLoan Foundation, which had been established in the UK in 2002 by Peter Ryan.

When the MicroLoan Foundation entered the field, it made an immediate impact in terms of minimizing these issues. To this day, the foundation continues this impact across Malawi, Zambia, and more recently, Zimbabwe. Expansion into Swaziland, Natal, and Lesotho is planned.

The results to date are encouraging. Today, life expectancy in the sub-Saharan countries is around 55 years, compared to 45 years at the turn of the century. Momentum has been achieved, but much more help is needed to raise the life expectancy to a respectable figure that is comparable to that seen in the developed world.

Achieving Impact: Creating a Business That Matters

It's critical that every business organization has a recognized "why," that is, a passion to achieve something beyond its purely commercial activities. The challenge with every business is to determine how to conduct its affairs whilst ensuring that it is also fulfilling its "why."

A business that matters is any commercial endeavor that has a positive impact on other people, communities, or businesses. The reason that creating better businesses matters is because our planet has suffered serious degradation due to generations of poor habits. If this continuing deterioration of the planet is not quickly halted, serious impacts will be experienced by the whole of humanity. The current population levels in many parts of the world will become unsustainable, potentially crippling civilization as we know it.

The potential to reverse this situation lies with businesses that have the power to act, businesses that can stand up to global challenges, take responsibility and harness their power and position to give back to the world.

Operating as a "better business" is not difficult. The key to becoming a "better business" is to take as many steps as possible toward reducing negative impacts and creating positive impacts. This can be achieved by incrementally improving business behavior. At an individual level, this might be as simple as making it a daily habit to seize opportunities to give people a helping hand or to pass on knowledge. As a business, it may be done by making conscious positive decisions that support the SDGs, and where possible, influencing and encouraging other businesses to do the same. For example, requesting that business partners adopt the same practices. You can exert a very powerful impact through leveraging your business for good by quietly encouraging others to follow suit.

The Microloan Foundation Australia is driven by the ultimate purpose of helping communities to develop responsible consumption and production. We have chosen to focus on helping women living in poverty in the sub-Saharan region of Africa by getting involved at the grassroots level and helping women to start their own businesses. This is done by providing business loans, extensive training, and ongoing mentoring and support.

By establishing successful businesses, women can lift themselves and their dependents out of poverty and develop better facilities in their businesses and their homes. In doing so, they learn and implement more environmentally friendly practices, which enables them to improve their quality of life and reduce environmental damage. Due to being seen to be successful by using more sustainable methods, these women become the perfect role models for encouraging others in their communities to adopt the same habits. As this influence spreads, communities and countries will move positively toward playing their part in helping to achieve the SDG goal of responsible consumption and production.

Determining the What, Why, and How of Business

As I edged my way toward retirement, I realized that in order to be happy, I had to be involved in something constructive, something meaningful, something that gave me a sense of fulfillment. The desire to leave a legacy, a meaningful footprint, has always been important to me.

I've always been passionate about providing the tools necessary for people to grow businesses that will create wealth, allow them the time to enjoy their families, and give them the opportunity to spread their knowledge throughout the community, thereby helping others to do the same. My chance discovery of the MicroLoan Foundation in Malawi and meeting its personable founder, Peter Ryan, led to a "flash of the blindingly obvious" and the subsequent birth of the Australian MicroLoan Foundation franchise.

During my early days in business, I recognized that a business needs to be specifically focused if it is to be successful. Business isn't just about making money, although of course that is a key way to measure success. For the Microloan Foundation Australia, this was certainly a serious challenge. However, we developed a process that proved to be sustainable, and it is no different to what every business owner needs to pursue in order to be successful. It is vital to determine "what" the business is going to do, "why" it is going to do it, and "how" it is going to go about doing it.

The golden opportunity that every business has is to create a business that serves not only the owners and the staff, but also helps the local community and the world at large.

The challenge of identifying credible causes and then periodically contributing is often something that small businesses do not have the expertise or time for. This is where the B1G1 portal steps in and provides a remarkable facility for people to do just that. The thorough monitoring of its special causes ensures that contributions end up in the hands of the people who need them the most.

My key piece of advice for all businesses is to get involved. Talk to B1G1, talk with their supporters, talk to their special causes and select those causes that best align with your business. Then, simply use the amazing automated processes to channel your generosity to your causes, giving you more time to both run your business and enjoy life with your family. Join other members in mindfully improving the world in which we live.

And remember, take every opportunity to share these joys with your customers and colleagues.

SHOPPING OURSELVES TO EXTINCTION
SIAN CONWAY

At the end of 2017, 15,000 scientists from around the world issued a stark warning to humanity. Their message was clear: the time we have left to tackle climate change is running out, and if we don't act soon, we will never be able to reverse the negative impacts of global warming.

Unfortunately, our willingness to heed this warning has been limited. Our culture of mass consumption rages on, as corporations deplete natural resources, pump emissions into the atmosphere, and exploit people, animals, and the planet to make a profit. Household consumption accounts for 60% of global greenhouse gas emissions.[1] If we were to change our consumption habits, it would create meaningful change for the planet, but if we don't, we are at risk of shopping ourselves to extinction.

Yet, brands continue to invest millions in advertising to create demand for the latest trends, whipping consumers into a shopping frenzy and increasing their financial bottom line, while the environment pays the price.

The fashion industry is a prime example of our consumption problem. According to the UNFCCC, it is currently responsible for 10% of global carbon emissions, with that figure set to rise by more than 60% by 2030.

High-street fashion brands release up to 24 new collections per year, generally at low prices that encourage shoppers to treat clothes as disposable. Over the past ten years, clothing has become the fastest growing waste stream in the UK, with the average garment being discarded after just eight wears.

---

1   Konstantin Stadler, Kjartan Steen-Olsen, Richard Wood, Gibran Vita, Arnold Tukker, and Edgar G. Hertwich. "Environmental Impact Assessment of Household Consumption," *Journal of Industrial Ecology 20*, no.3 (2016): 526-536.
https://onlinelibrary.wiley.com/doi/abs/10.1111/jiec.12371

Did you know that you can purchase a T-shirt on the high street for less than the cost of the average latte, yet garment workers are living in poverty, risking their lives in unsafe factories, and being exploited in the name of fast fashion?

Things must change. We must transition toward responsible consumption and production if we are to have any hope of a sustainable future. We need a new model that empowers workers and reduces the strain on the environment. Businesses have the power to play a key role in this, thereby helping to overcome the problems we see in society today. Through responsible consumption, we can create a better future, but we must all play our part.

My personal journey toward responsible consumption began with ethical fashion.

From Fast Fashion Addict to Ethical Activist

In the face of significant global issues such as climate change, plastic pollution, poverty, and slavery, it can be easy to feel too small to make a difference. The causes we care about often feel overwhelming, and this can lead to resentment and disillusionment, which is how I used to feel.

At university, I'd been a keen activist, campaigning for "Say No to Sweatshops" and getting involved in charitable projects on campus. So, when the opportunity came up to spend a summer volunteering in Sierra Leone, supporting the construction of an eco-tourist resort, working on rainforest conservation, and establishing a community development program, I jumped at the chance. It was an incredible experience.

The country's troubled history and the devastating impact of civil war remain visible in everyday life. It was inspiring to see how people were working to build a better future, but it was upsetting to think of the trauma they were carrying. When I came home, I struggled to re-adjust to my day-to-day life, which seemed to revolve around consumerism. I searched for ways to do work with more meaning, but with my marketing background, I felt trapped working for corporations focused on promoting mass consumption. I soon fell back into that routine.

It wasn't until I traveled to Cambodia in 2015 that things changed.

Who Made My Trousers?

I had found myself swept up in fast fashion, addicted to chasing the latest style. If I had a bad day at work, retail therapy was my go-to solution. During my coffee break, I would flick through glossy magazines to try and keep up with the latest trends. Fashion had become such a throwaway habit that I didn't once stop to think about how my clothes were made.

In 2015, while traveling in Cambodia, I had a lightbulb moment. As I was getting dressed one morning, I noticed that the label on my trousers read "Made in Cambodia," and it made me pause. Somewhere in the world – in the country I was currently in – someone was making these clothes. Not a robot, but a real person. That's when it hit home: if I was paying less than the cost of a coffee for my clothes, what was the woman who made them being paid?

As I started to research, I became increasingly aware of the exploitation inherent in the fashion industry, of issues such as modern slavery, the 2013 Rana Plaza collapse that killed 1134 people – many of them low-paid garment workers for high-street brands – and the damaging environmental impact of my choices. I decided that I would no longer be part of the exploitation by continuing to purchase in this way. Instead, I would vote with my wallet and align my spending with my values, becoming an advocate for the women working in the garment factories by using my purchasing power.

From Mass Consumption to Meaningful Marketing

Through making small changes to my fashion habits, I began to feel empowered as an ethical consumer, although I knew that I still had much to learn. On social media, I connected with people who offered advice about ethical living, and I felt less alone. Responsible consumption might not be the most common way of life yet, but by bringing together a community of like-minded people online, I realized that others share my vision, which gave me hope.

By starting an online community as a welcoming place for people to learn more about ethical living, I also began connecting with ethically focused small-business owners who were encouraging responsible consumption, upholding ethical and sustainable standards, and representing my vision for how business could be. My corporate career in marketing, which was focused on selling products and services for as much profit as possible, had begun to make me feel uneasy, but through conversations with my new online connections, I came to realize that I could offer valuable skills to these ethical businesses. I could help them to share their stories and encourage others to adopt more responsible lifestyles. I could make a real impact with the skills I already had. That's when I decided to dedicate my working life to supporting them, and in 2017 I left the corporate world.

Collective Action is the Key

Today, I only work with businesses aligned to the SDGs, that is, businesses with ethics at their heart. I believe that the first step toward becoming a "better business" or conscious consumer is deciding on your core values. Businesses and individuals alike must ask the questions: "What kind of world do I want to see?" and "How can I help make that come about?" Once you have formulated your vision, it will act as your guiding compass.

Businesses should exist to solve problems, for their consumers, for their community, and for the planet. To build a business that matters, we need to find a community that we can serve. That way, we can make things that consumers actually want, rather than making consumers simply want more things. That's how the businesses of the future will create a world of responsible consumption.

Consumer capitalism creates a deficiency cycle. The new model of conscious consumerism, which has the notion of giving back at its core, creates a sufficiency cycle where everyone is empowered to make a positive impact. When businesses promote responsible consumption and production, they become more inclusive, create more impact, and achieve more success against a triple bottom line of people, the planet, and profit. This is how we will create a better world for everyone, by working together.

When I first started my journey toward ethical living and business, I felt overwhelmed by the causes and the scale of the issues, as well as by my own drive and passion. The process of aligning my life and career with my values took time. I discovered that my "why," my legacy, is helping changemakers to embrace their voice for change and unlock the power to find their purpose by connecting with their community. I believe that we already have the resources necessary to solve global problems and achieve the SDGs, although we don't necessarily have the connections required to turn our desire to make a difference into meaningful action.

Individually, our actions may be small, but collectively, they are powerful. Everyone has a part to play in achieving the SDGs, and every business, regardless of size, can choose to be a force for good.

Having a positive impact doesn't have to be something extra that you need to make time for. With a little reflection on the values you care most about, you can look for opportunities to embed impact into the things you're already doing.

Around the world, businesses of all sizes are feeling the financial, social, and environmental benefits of operating with purpose and using their values to attract a growing market of conscious consumers. Embedding positive impact into your business serves as the perfect magnet for attracting like-minded customers, gaining their trust, and creating the content needed to grow your relationship with them.

There's a rising tide of responsible consumers looking to vote with their wallets and spend money with responsible companies. The statistics speak for themselves. In fact, 64% of consumers say that simply giving money away isn't enough. They want businesses to integrate social impact directly into their business models (e.g., "Buy One, Give One" campaigns).[2] When it comes to choosing between two brands of equal quality and price, 90% of consumers are likely to choose a cause-branded product.[3] Finally, when quality and price are equivalent, social purpose is the number one deciding factor for consumers worldwide.[4]

Responsible consumption alone won't save the world, but it's a place where all of us can start, and we need businesses to lead the way by becoming a force for good. My vision is to create a world where ethical consumption is the default position for every consumer and where we globally unite for a more sustainable future. A vision I believe is possible through the power of community.

2   http://ppqty.com/GoodPurpose2010globalPPT_WEBversion%20(1).pdf
3   http://www.conecomm.com
4   http://ppqty.com/GoodPurpose2010globalPPT_WEBversion%20(1).pdf

CONSCIOUS CONSUMERISM
RICHARD FLANAGAN

We are all consumers. At times, rampant ones at that.
I'll hold my hands up, too. Everything we consume has been through a production process of some kind. Every buying or trading decision we make, whether it concerns price, convenience, or impulse, affects decisions made at every point and link in the production chain. But only rarely do we give thought to the fact that everything we touch, handle, and use in our daily life has a story to tell.

Right now, that story isn't always a good one.

Take cheap goods, for example. We rarely know how our choice regarding price impacts the decisions made by the businesses and corporations that make the product, which in turn affects the employees, individuals, and environment involved in its production. If price is the driving factor for consumers, then in order to make goods cheaply, someone or something along the way will have suffered.

While many manufacturers are upping their game in terms of providing information for consumers, there is still not enough. For example, we don't know the extent to which raw materials, production processes, packaging, and transport are involved in getting that product into our hands. Nor do we know how many people had to handle it before we received it, including how those individuals were treated or compensated.

The reality is that manufacturing relies heavily on developing nations for many raw materials and base products, which means that we are engaging with processes and people that we know nothing about.

Then, there is the issue of marketing. Often, the consumer falls prey to hype or buzzwords. The word "organic" offers a good example of this issue. This word is often misinterpreted and not a true reflection of the actual process; rather, it is a marketing term that is employed without thought as to its wider implications.

In reality, "organic" means that no chemicals were used in growing the cotton. It doesn't mean that the cotton was grown sustainably or that chemicals weren't used in the production of the actual garment. "Organic cotton" can be used as a marketing term because we don't realize its wider implications.

As a manufacturer exposed to these challenges, I believe that finding a solution to achieve the global goal of responsible consumption and production is important. I'm aware of the challenges involved in being able to prove responsibility in terms of production processes and materials due to the heavy reliance on others. However, I believe in transparency and the ability to fully inform customers, which is why this goal is important. Our consumers will play a key role in the transition to conscious consumerism.

The Power is in the Hands of the Consumer

It was Blockchain that first alerted me to the importance of this goal. When I understood the concept, it opened up possibilities. Blockchain is a decentralized, distributed, and public digital ledger that is used to record transactions across many computers so that any involved record cannot be altered retroactively without the alteration of all the subsequent blocks.

It's very easy in the manufacturing field to isolate our awareness. We're only aware of the production of our products, not what happened to the materials we use in our process before they arrived or once they left our custody. The idea that we can embed awareness into a product and track every touchpoint through a framework such a Blockchain is revolutionary.

Knowledge is power; power that can rest in the hands of the consumer. By creating a transparent environment, the consumer is better informed and so better able to make conscious choices. The sooner this happens, the sooner we can start eradicating harmful processes and unethical treatment that impact both people and the planet.

Rethink the Business You are In

The Japanese word "Ikigai" means "reason for being," that is, where the intersection between doing what you love, what you are good at, what you can be paid for, and what the world needs can be found.

This concept ties in with becoming a "better business." Becoming a "better business" involves having a massively transformative purpose (MTP) that gets to the root of "why" it matters. Once the MTP is identified, it becomes a lot easier to drive purpose into every touchpoint and to create a company culture around it.

At Tshirtify, our MTPs are "build, empower, and grow dreams" and "build, empower, and grow consciousness." Our clients trust us to represent the success of their brands: their dreams. Our business model focuses on helping our clients to build their brands by empowering them with actionable information and offering services to help ensure growth. As our clients grow and achieve success on their terms, they raise awareness and consciousness about the need to naturally begin to look for ways to start to give back, to begin to influence their own customers and the wider community. To support this, we are also creating our own Blockchain blueprint, which will be made available to our clients and customers.

How do we do this?

We've been lucky enough to have found and partnered with B1G1. In doing so, we have created an incredible impact both through life-changing projects and in partnership with our customers and their teams. By using the terms "dream" and "impact" as forms of measurement, we've been able to shift the perception of both the product and the services, thereby helping to build and empower our team. Having a strong team creates a better product and service.

Becoming a "better business" involves creating a culture that can support your team. The SDGs represent one way in which this can be achieved. At Tshirtify, we believe this is imperative. We give each team member a "personal compass" – a guide that illustrates each individual's passions and goals. This fosters inter-team support for their success. They also align themselves to an SDG that they are personally passionate about. As a business, we provide them with the opportunity to contribute to their passion in the context of their role and the vision of the business. Supporting the passionate ownership of team members represents a powerful way to create a better business.

We're all searching for passion and purpose in life. I've realized that life and passion are about being aware that we're always creating and connecting moments that can create an impact.

A lot of businesses underestimate the value of a real connection, particularly in the modern world, where running a solo business can lead you to being "digitally lonely," that is, connected by technology, but not to actual people. Connection leads to learning and learning leads to leveled-up thinking and conscious decision making. Connection is hence one of our core values.

Again, the Japanese have a philosophy for this – "Ichigo ichie" – which means "treasure every moment for it will never occur again." I'm passionate about treasuring moments enjoyed through my time with people. It's that time and connection with others that allows me to pass on what I've learned in the hope that others will learn and pass it on, too. Connection leads to learning, while learning leads to deeper thinking, more conscious decision making, and ultimately, more giving.

At Tshirtify, we believe in informed, conscious decision making.

In addition to connection, I encourage other businesses to start making conscious buying decisions. Ask questions about the products you have in your hands. The easiest way to do this is to use the internet or to download apps, such Good On You and CoGO, to check the ethical and sustainable practices of the brands you wear and use. Conscious decision making leads to contribution and giving back to the world.

We made a conscious decision to build our business differently.

Being a "giving business" during the founding phase of Tshirtify was transformative. As small businesses, our size means we are more agile and hence more able to create an impact and take the lead from corporations. We can be the leaders and changemakers in the world, and leading by example can expose the truth and force transnational corporations to adopt better practices.

I can now fulfill my personal legacy in terms of creating impacts that last.

Be a Custodian, Not Just an Owner

In Japan, I spent time with a Bonsai master, which had a powerful impact on me. Bonsai masters consider that they are a custodian of a tree, they don't own it. They are aware of the decades and centuries before and after their tenure.

Japan has the oldest businesses in the world for the same reason. Because they are custodians, they are running the business for only that moment in time, and they always nurture and care for the business so that it is ready to pass on to the next custodian.

This long-term thinking changed my perception of what creating and evolving a business can mean. Having patience and recognizing your place within the history of the business means that you make different decisions along the way.

Responsible consumption alone won't save the world, but it's somewhere that all of us can start. My vision involves creating a world where ethical consumption is the default position for every consumer. This vision is possible through the power of community.

WHAT YOU CAN DO TO
CREATE A WORLD OF RESPONSIBLE CONSUMPTION AND PRODUCTION

Lifestyle tips:
- Buy from companies you know have sustainable practices.
- Choose reusable products and containers.
- Sell or give away what you no longer use.

Business tips:
- Continuously move to more environmental practices.
- Apply for award programs and certifications that promote social responsibilities.

Giving tips:
- Support recycling and food rescue charities.
- Support awareness-raising initiatives by volunteering.
- Ask others to give to causes instead of buying gifts for you.

PROTECTING THE PLACE IN WHICH WE BELONG

13 CLIMATE ACTION

HOW YOU AND YOUR BUSINESS CAN TAKE URGENT ACTION TO COMBAT CLIMATE CHANGE AND ITS IMPACTS.

"The Earth is what we all have in common."

— Wendell Berry

THE CHANGEMAKERS

THE GREAT OUTDOORS
CRAIG DOYLE

Craig Doyle is the co-founder and director of 90Degrees Global. The company delivers exceptional, transformational programs for business owners, entrepreneurs, and leaders across Australia and New Zealand. Offering the legendary Money & You, as well as Powerful Presentations & You, Creating Wealth & You, and the annual Global Excellerated Business School for Entrepreneurs, 90Degrees Global is a committed Champion Partner of B1G1.

Craig is focused on realizing his dream of building a $100 million global enterprise while also bringing transformation to all those who participate in the 90Degrees Global programs. Both his work and his life are now focused on answering Buckminster Fuller's profound question: "How do we make the world work for 100% of humanity, in the shortest possible time, through spontaneous cooperation, without ecological offense or the disadvantage of anyone?".

moneyandyouaustralia.com.au/lp/money-and-you

NOT FOR PEOPLE LIKE ME
ROBERT LEE

Robert Lee is the CEO and co-founder of Rescuing Leftover Cuisine, Inc. He was a Gates Millennium Scholar and graduated cum laude from the Stern School of Business at New York University. Having come from a humble background, he is committed to doing everything he can to help those in need. After graduating, he worked in Asset Management at JPMorgan Chase & Co. before resigning to pursue his passion for helping the hungry and reducing food waste by co-founding Rescuing Leftover Cuisine. The company has now expanded into over 16 cities across the United States, rescued over 3.2 million pounds of food from over 300 food establishments, and won numerous accolades for its work, including CNN Heroes, Forbes 30 Under 30, and Blue Ridge Labs' Incubator Award.

rescuingleftovercuisine.org

PROTECTING THE PLACE IN WHICH WE BELONG

It is quite common for people to ask us to "think big," to tackle big issues. What if they asked us to think small?

Example: Greta Thunberg.

It's Monday August 20, 2018. Greta is 15 years old. She takes her hand-painted sign that reads 'Skolstrejk för klimatet'. And she sits alone on the steps of the Riksdag in Stockholm.

Her parents tried to dissuade her. Her classmates don't follow.

The first day she sits alone. But people notice.

She recalls it this way: "I sat alone from about 8:30 am to 3 pm — the regular school day. And then on the second day, people started joining me."

Credit: Getty Images. Photographer: Michael Campanella

Her Facebook page on 22 May 2019, says this:

Now I'm not alone anymore! On Friday 24/5 we are striking in 1,387 places in 111 countries. And counting! Share this!! Spread to everyone!!

#FridaysForFuture #schoolstrike4climate #climatestrike

Norwegian MP Freddy André Øvstegård said this when he nominated her for the Nobel Peace Prize: "We have proposed Greta Thunberg because if we do nothing to halt climate change it will be the cause of wars, conflict and refugees. She has launched a mass movement which I see as a major contribution to peace."

The power of small combined with the power of action.

And again, we see the inherent links with the Global Goals — in this case, the *lack* of climate action linking to wars, conflict and refugees.

Changemaker Robert Lee, finds similar parallels in his case, feeding the homeless leading to a reduction in carbon emissions. Who would have thought?

His 2,000 word story here raises so many other wonderful links too.

Fellow changemaker, Craig Doyle, takes a different approach — a "power of small" approach with only 78 well-chosen words — words you may want to pin on your fridge or post on Instagram.

And think about that. Just by that simple power of small *action*, you inspire others.

You may not be Greta Thunberg. But you can take action — action that attracts others, action that inspires them to also take action.

You could decide not to do it alone but to be inspired by the alignment across all goals implied by Goal 17 — Partnerships for the Goals.

As we write this book, another coalition of global Fortune 500 companies has been formed to urge government action on climate change.

Affirming that climate change "is a major threat to the U.S. economy," the CEO Climate Dialogue calls on Congress and the Trump administration to enact a federal policy "as soon as possible to protect against the worst impacts."

The consortium has published six guiding principles for a market-based approach that it proposes as an outline for an effective federal policy.

The 13 companies signed up to the new association are Dupont, Dow, Shell, BP, Dominion Energy, Ford, Unilever, Citi, BASF, DTE Energy, Exelon, LafargeHolcim, and PG&E.

Four activist groups have joined as partners: the Environmental Defense Fund, the Center for Climate and Energy Solutions, World Resources Institute, and the Nature Conservancy.

CEO Climate Dialogue joins several other substantial, executive-led consortiums which are taking collective action to address climate change.

- We Are Still In consists of 2,187 businesses and investors who have joined together to declare their continuing support for climate action to meet the terms of the Paris Agreement.
- The World Business Council for Sustainable Development, a CEO-led association of 200 multinational companies from all business sectors, supports collaborative efforts "to accelerate the transition to a sustainable world." Its roster of member firms represents a combined revenue of more than $8.5 trillion and 19 million employees.
- Climate Action 100 includes 320 investors with $33 trillion in assets under management who engage with a "focus list" of 160 companies to improve governance, curb emissions, and strengthen climate-related financial disclosures.

And of course, we must include small businesses in this picture too.

In the last decade, small businesses working with B1G1 — the initiative that many of the changemakers of this book belong to — have collectively created nearly 200 million giving impacts.

Whether it's Greta, Robert, Craig, you or the collective 'power of large' described above, none of it can happen without action.

Goal 13 is the only Goal with the word 'Action' in it.

Take it.

Now.

THE GREAT OUTDOORS
CRAIG DOYLE

The Great Outdoors,
our present and past.
Yet my prediction is,
that dream is diminishing fast.

No care and attention.
As a collective of one,
we step out each day
living as if it's all done.

Insights and action
to transform the view.
From the rear-vision mirror
to the future anew.

It's about their future,
the one our grandchildren will live.
And never forget, it's not what we want;
it's about time and what we can give.

NOT FOR PEOPLE LIKE ME
ROBERT LEE

I recently re-read some of my journal entries, and honestly, many of them were humbling. Here's one from when I was thirteen:

I hate this. It's ramen every day. Why? I'm sick of ramen, but we're probably going to eat it for breakfast and lunch, or maybe just for breakfast + lunch at 10:00AM or 11:00AM, for the rest of the week. It sucks. I remember when I was like seven and we were still living in Whitestone and I got sick of ramen then, too. But there's nothing else to eat, so I am forced to eat it. Hey, there's one good thing about it though: I'll be a master at cooking ramen!

— Entry from Robert's journal, 4/1/04.

Here's another, from three years later:

Today's my brother's birthday, and we can't do anything. We can't go up to Ithaca, and we can't send presents either. We can't pay electricity bills and phone bills, but we're hanging by a thread. It seems we almost lost that thread when my parents' cell phones wouldn't work last week.

— Entry from Robert's journal, 11/4/07.

Whenever I read reports about food insecurity or hunger around the world, I am reminded of my own childhood. I was fortunate in many regards, and I found employment in the finance sector to help my family, but I was angered when I learned that 40% of food goes to waste in the United States, while 1 in 7 Americans, including 14 million children, suffer from food insecurity. I was inspired to make whatever difference I could when I learned that the world produces enough food waste to feed the planet's entire hungry population three times over.

I know that when I was a child and only had the free lunch provided by my school to eat for the whole day, I could not focus on my homework. I was irritable and uninterested in new experiences such as hanging out with friends, and I could not afford extracurricular activities. Even though I did not know that my situation was not normal, I eventually realized that there was abundance all around me. It just wasn't distributed to people like me.

I grew up the younger of two children of Korean immigrants to New York City who struggled with an unfamiliar language, environment, and culture. My parents ingrained in me the importance of being resourceful and never wasting food. They would often tell me that if I wasted food, then everything I wasted would be collected and I would have to eat it all in one go during my afterlife! Coupled with the fact that there wasn't much food to begin with, this attitude meant that rescuing food was a part of my daily life while growing up. Although my family struggled, my parents emphasized how education would lift us out of our difficult situation. I decided to pursue finance when I was in high school, and I applied to the NYU Stern School of Business so that I could eventually get a job that would ensure that my family would never have to struggle again.

But it was at NYU that I became involved in a club that would change my path in life. The club involved taking leftover dining hall food to nearby homeless shelters, and I was impressed by the idea. I had to get involved. When I came across the club, I was instantly drawn to the elegance of its solution. It was common sense, after all. It also opened up a whole world of learning about legalities, food safety, and the laws concerning food donation. The fact that food waste was such a huge environmental issue made me realize the importance of food rescue as a solution that could solve multiple problems at once.

After four years of being involved with the club, I had learned a lot about the food rescue industry and I didn't want to give up what had become a large part of my life. So, a couple of members of the club and I created Rescuing Leftover Cuisine, Inc. after winning a venture competition during which we combined what we were already doing in the club with more advanced technology, financial incentives for food donors, and a stronger structure for managing volunteers.

Rescuing Leftover Cuisine uses technology to engage volunteers to take excess food from food establishments, such as restaurants, to people who need it at human services agencies, such as homeless shelters. Not many people realize that excess food contributes to climate change in a significant way. According to the Food and Agriculture Organization of the United Nations, approximately one-third of all food produced worldwide is wasted. This wasted food, when it ultimately ends up in landfills, emits methane gases that are more than 30 times worse for the environment than carbon dioxide, since they mount up and undergo anaerobic digestion. We must also account for the natural resources that food waste needlessly uses on a global level. The amount of water used to produce this wasted food, for example, is equivalent to the annual water discharge of the Volga – the longest river in Europe. Additionally, wasted food uses 1.4 billion hectares of land, or close to 30% of the world's agricultural land. In the United States, the transportation of food that is ultimately wasted accounts for 10% of the annual U.S. energy budget. As a whole, the carbon footprint of food waste is estimated to be 3.3 gigatonnes of CO_2 equivalent, which means that it ranks as the third highest emitter after the United States and China.

By rescuing this excess food before it is thrown away and then using it to feed people, Rescuing Leftover Cuisine is eliminating all this waste and preventing the associated carbon emissions. Our company is committed to creating an organization that matters. We partner with restaurants that matter because they donate their excess food rather than throwing it away. Through every single food rescue event, even a small amount of food not going into the garbage reduces the environmental impact. The food rescue might go further and help to provide hope or a meaningful change, or even to turn a food-insecure person's life around, but even if this does not happen, we are at least providing an opportunity for the food to matter, while also directly reducing the environmental impact of excess food.

I hope that my ultimate legacy is making food rescue the universal standard for food waste. I want to help people to realize the potential of excess food and to see past the inconvenience of it to feel the impact of using our natural resources to create something that meets a fundamental human need. Someday, all food establishments will donate their excess edible food and compost their inedible food rather than throwing it all away.

According to the Intergovernmental Panel on Climate Change, we have only 12 years to limit climate change to a maximum of 1.5°C, beyond which even half a degree will significantly worsen the risk of drought, floods, extreme heat, and poverty for hundreds of millions of people. If we can make food rescue the standard practice and stop food waste, we can eliminate the third largest emitter of carbon emissions worldwide.

I am passionate about food rescue because of my personal experiences, the efficiency of the solution, and the absurdity of the problem of food waste. We can all make a difference three times a day. Join the movement and we can ensure that food access is changed so that it can be provided to people like me.

The Part We All Must Play

Climate change is important because it affects every country and every person on Earth, and everyone can do something about it.

In kindergarten, I wanted to be a paleontologist when I grew up. I remember one theory about how the dinosaurs went extinct because a large asteroid that hit the Earth kicked up so much dust that it blotted out the sun, causing global sea surface temperatures to decrease by as much as 7°C (45°F). As a child amazed by such astonishing creatures, I was skeptical that an entire species could be eliminated by climate change, but the possibility that one change to the climate could cause such irreversible damage left a deep impression on me.

Later, while I was in high school, through all the buzz about *An Inconvenient Truth*, I was open-minded about the possibility that climate change could have drastic adverse effects on our society and current food systems, and the mounting evidence of humankind's influence was daunting. However, I did not know what I could do to influence what was happening in terms of climate change. What I failed to realize was that I was already contributing to changing the climate – just not in the way I wanted or intended to.

It was not until I was at college that I started to realize that my decisions reverberated through the systems we are all part of. Every dollar vote I cast with my resources perpetuated a view of the world and supported a system. Although it was gradual, I began to make tiny changes to my routines and habits that would have a small but permanent impact.

After graduating from college, I heard something at a conference that reminded me of the plight of the dinosaurs: climate change is not about saving the world. The Earth will be fine, despite climate change. It is humanity that needs to be saved. Majestic creatures such as the dinosaurs have come and gone, and humanity will be on the same track if we do not act, regardless of the cause of climate change. From the perspective of saving future generations from poverty and extreme weather events, I started to think about how I could make a larger impact beyond my personal actions.

As you can see, my realization of the importance of climate change was gradual – it took some time for me to understand the magnitude of the issue.

Climate change appears overwhelming when you consider research on its current and future impacts. The massive current impact of climate change is already apparent in recent exacerbated natural disasters, record amounts of ice melting, and declining biodiversity. When projecting this impact into the future, whether it is extreme weather conditions threatening more lives than ever before, rising sea levels that will render islands inhabitable and thousands of people homeless, or changes in our ecosystem thatwill affect our food supply, everyone will feel the impact of climate change, regardless of whether or not they acknowledge it. Unfortunately, climate change also disproportionately affects the poorest and most vulnerable across the world.

Although climate change causes long-lasting changes to our climate system and threatens irreversible consequences, it is also an area where we can all play our part every single day. Whether it's by reducing our personal food waste, which would emit methane gases in landfills, limiting our energy usage, or by eating less meat, we can have an immediate and tangible impact.

This SDG is particularly inspiring because the global nature of climate change calls for broad international cooperation. It represents an opportunity for urgent and accelerated action on the part of all countries to make a difference worldwide and to be proactive rather than reactive. We can play our part in building resilient cities, forming innovative solutions for achieving a sustainable low-carbon future, and accelerating the reduction of global greenhouse gas emissions. We are uniquely armed with the knowledge of historical trends, and we can prepare for the future in ways no one in the past could have done. All of us have a part to play in this preparation.

WHAT YOU CAN DO TO
INSPIRE CLIMATE ACTION

Lifestyle tips:
- Eat less meat — beef is more demanding on the environment than plant protein.
- Compost.
- Reduce your use of paper and plastic.

Business tips:
- Measure your carbon footprint and see what you can improve.
- Develop a climate action plan.
- Engage in the global initiatives to underpin and enhance changes in your business practices.

Giving tips:
- Support and fund tree planting efforts.
- Make donations to National Parks and conservation facilities.
- Support environmental campaigns to create a greater awareness.

UNDERWATER BEAUTY

14 LIFE BELOW WATER

HOW YOU AND YOUR BUSINESS CAN CONSERVE AND
SUSTAINABLY USE THE OCEANS, SEAS, AND MARINE
RESOURCES FOR SUSTAINABLE DEVELOPMENT.

*"We forget that the water cycle and the life cycle
are one."*

— Jacques Yves Cousteau

THE CHANGEMAKERS

A WHALE'S TALE
DOUG BARRA

Doug Barra is one of the owners of the internationally recognized ActionCOACH Team Sage business coaching firm in Miami, Florida. After a successful career in software consulting and a stint in corporate America, Doug broke out on his own, building a custom programming and website design company. He then entered the world of business coaching with ActionCOACH business coaching franchise.

Doug has helped hundreds of business owners create successful businesses.

Doug wakes up every morning to work with business owners, to help them make a lasting difference in not only their own lives, but also in the lives of their families, their team members and the community they serve.

actioncoachteamsage.com

THE UNEXPLORED GIFT AROUND US
MATHEW COLIN DAVIS

Mathew is an award-winning marine scientist, Amazon bestselling co-author, international speaker, entrepreneur, educator, mentor, and thought leader. He founded the award-winning Australian Coastal and Marine Ecology Environmental Consultancy, and later also founded the Coastal Protection Core. He is a member of the University of the Sunshine Coast Scientific Industry Advisory Committee and the Moreton Maritime Alliance Committees. Mathew has won a number of awards, most recently the University of the Sunshine Coast Alumni of the Year Award 2017 for his incredible work across local ecological and environmental management within the Moreton Bay region.

In 2017, his company, Coastal Protection Core, won the Moreton Bay Unity Water Innovation Award. Mathew and his companies have been nominated for multiple environmental and marine science awards.

coastalprotectioncore.com

UNDERWATER BEAUTY

It's a majestic, soul-filling scene. The huge Humpback whale leaping out of the blue ocean and splashing back down, leaving millions of white-coloured drops in its wake.

Then there's the magic of a pod of dolphins diving wildly through the waves just for fun. Or freshly hatched baby turtles attempting to make their life-threatening trek toward the ocean waters. And we're mesmerized by the documentaries we see where schools of fish zig-zag in perfect sync through the coral reefs as one.

The ocean really is magical, mysterious and magnificent.

This interconnected aquatic system is home to an identified 200,000 species, with the possibility for millions yet to be discovered. It's a world of wonder and delight.

Geography maps say that Earth has five oceans: the Arctic, Atlantic, Indian, Pacific and Southern. Their names can be found on any map with their "borders" coloured in varied shades of blue. But there's really only one ocean. The world ocean. And not only is it home to a various assortment of interesting creatures, it's also what supports and maintains life on Earth. Yes, life below water affects life on land and vice versa. Together, they are Earth. One. Our home.

Many of us look over the vast ocean and reflect; the great expanse naturally evokes feelings of awe and wonder. And as the waves swell and drop, we are often filled with our own internal waves of peace and tranquillity. Most of us can relate to these feelings, yet it's amazing what we don't know about the ocean.

The ocean covers three quarters of the Earth's surface and contains 97% of the Earth's water. It represents 99% of the living space on the planet by volume, it also holds considerable amounts of precious mineral and energy resources such as oil, gas, salt and precious metals.

Yes, the ocean drives our global systems which makes the Earth habitable for humankind. Our rainwater, drinking water, weather, climate, coastlines, food sources, and even the oxygen in the air we breathe, are all ultimately provided and regulated by the ocean. Oceans are responsible for temperatures and currents, weather patterns and our health — they absorb about 30% of carbon dioxide produced by humans and help buffer the impacts of global warming.

The ocean does so much more than look beautiful. It gives life. It sustains us.

Practically, for many, the ocean also supports their work. In fact, over three-billion people depend on marine and coastal biodiversity for their livelihoods.

It accounts for 200 million jobs in fishing and aquaculture and many more in indirect employment in sea-related activities such as distribution of food, shipping, tourism, sea mining, marine military activities, science research and leisure activities.

Staggeringly perhaps, shipping accounts for the transport of 90% of the world's international traded goods.

So ... what happened? Although we depend on the ocean for just about everything — our health, our weather, our transport, our jobs and our way of life — our collective neglect, our use (and abuse) of the ocean is mind-blowing.

80% of ocean pollution comes from the land — yes, we are the major problem — from individuals, industry and improper waste management and infrastructure. The remaining 20% is the result of ocean-based sources, such as the fishing, shipping, and cruise ship industries.

Of course, most people wouldn't intentionally destroy the ocean but our lack of awareness often results in this very thing. Littering, sewerage, ocean mining, oil spills, agricultural runoff, toxic chemicals, air pollutant and maritime transportation all contribute. Most people don't know that not all sewage that enters our waters is treated. In fact, 80% of sewage[1] that flows into the Mediterranean Sea is actually untreated, which leads to disease and pollution.

As Blaise Pascal said, "The least movement is of importance to all nature. The entire ocean is affected by a pebble."

---

1 http://wwf.panda.org/our_work/oceans/problems/pollution/

It's true. Throw a pebble in water and it ripples. So why do we throw plastic and trash and chemicals into our life-sustaining governance? What results is a ripple effect of mass proportion — and not a good one.

Here's a few harsh truths about the ripples we have created.

- Research estimates anywhere from 15 to 51 trillion particles of floating micro plastic[2] are in our oceans. That's approximately one truckload of plastic[3] that enters the ocean every single minute. And sadly, this waste in the ocean takes a long, long time to decompose.[4] Styrofoam takes 80 years, aluminum takes 200 years, and plastic takes 400 years.
- Over 100,000 marine animals die every year from plastic entanglement and ingestion. At least two-thirds of the world's fish stocks are suffering from plastic ingestion.[5]
- There are now close to 500 dead zones covering more than 245,000 km[2] globally, equivalent to the surface of the United Kingdom.[6]
- There is an island of garbage twice the size of Texas inside the Pacific Ocean: the North Pacific Gyre off the coast of California is the largest oceanic garbage site in the entire world. It's here that the number of floating plastic pieces in the water outnumbers total marine life six to one in the immediate vicinity.[7]
- Chemicals in our polluted waters can make their way back to us and cause serious health issues like reproductive problems, hormonal problems, kidney damage, and nervous system damage.[8]

These are just a few facts; the true list is extensive and rather depressing.

But as author and marine scientist, Mat Colin Davis points out, we can change it. We can act differently NOW. We can look

2 https://www.coastal.ca.gov/publiced/marinedebris.html#vansebille
3 https://www.greenpeace.org/usa/key-facts-about-plastic-pollution
4 https://plasticoceans.org/infographic-ocean-pollution-affects-humans/
5 http://oceancrusaders.org/plastic-crusades/plastic-statistics
6 http://www.unesco.org
7 https://www.rubiconglobal.com/blog-ocean-pollution-facts/
8 https://plasticoceans.org/infographic-ocean-pollution-affects-humans/

after our oceans before it's too late. But we must act now. We must get sober about the reality and unite to find new ways forward. And time is important.

That's because, currently, around 50% of the world population lives on the coasts, and it's estimated that it will rise to 75% in 2025. That's a lot of people living on the shores. So, careful and smart management is a vital key feature to building a sustainable future for our ocean.

True sustainability can only be achieved through international cooperation to protect the ocean and its vulnerable habitats. Already, around 20% of the world's coral reefs have been effectively destroyed and show no sign of recovery. About 24% of the remaining reefs are under threat of collapse through human involvement.

Doug Barra shows us here that each and every one of us can contribute by adhering to the 3 R's: *Reduce, Reuse and Recycle.* Entire families can and must get actively involved in caring about our ocean and the life within it.

We want our children and grandchildren to know the majesty of our underwater world. To be able to stare in awe as a whale drops back into the deep blue sea. To delight in the beauty of our coral reefs as vibrant colored fish flourish in healthy habitats. To see turtles, penguins, dolphins, sea horses, stingrays and the full spectrum of exotic sea creatures. To witness pristine, clean oceans and enjoy them.

This legacy is priceless.

It's tempting for some in positions of power to place a dollar value on what it might cost to clean up the ocean. Here's a better question: what does it cost us to not clean it up, to not protect it, to not act?

It costs us our health, our planet, and eventually our lives and those of our marine family.

Simple united actions can restore and replenish our waters and our previous ignorance. Let's swim in the ocean of change together. Let's not think of land and ocean as separate. As science writer, Arthur C. Clarke, pointed out, "How inappropriate to call this planet Earth when it is clearly Ocean."

A WHALE'S TALE
DOUGLAS BARRA

One day, I was walking along the waterfront with my wife, Jody, and we saw this huge statue in the distance of a whale's tail, as if it was about to do a tail flap. I was drawn to it because I love whales and it had an interesting multi-colored look about it. I don't remember exactly where we were, as during our 14 years with ActionCOACH we've traveled to many different places. But as we approached the statue, I realized that it was immense; it stood about 15 feet tall and was about 10 feet around the base. On closer inspection, I gasped! It was made, entirely, from plastic trash that had been fished out of the ocean. As I stood there looking at the individual pieces of plastic that it was made from, I couldn't help but be both awed at the immense amount of work and effort that it took to make the statue and appalled at all that trash!

Without healthy oceans and ocean life, there won't be any life left on this planet. This is an area that has been ignored for way too long because of the sheer size of it. Since most of the planet is covered by water, we have always considered it something that we do not need to be concerned about. What's one small load of garbage in this vast expanse of water? However, due to our vast numbers and years of disregard, this extremely important resource for life is now showing signs of danger. We must start to take care of our oceans and what lives within them.

I remember the first time I heard that cruise ships dump their garbage overboard. I was appalled. I don't think they do it anymore, but I'm sure that there are plenty of ships, of all types, that still do. Recently, I heard about an island-sized mass of floating garbage! I am so glad we are now, as a community, starting to develop awareness and to get involved in the plight of our oceans.

I was super excited when I heard that Sir Richard Branson was creating a competition for young entrepreneurs to create a viable way of cleaning up plastic from our oceans.

The first time I truly recognized the importance of this goal, or at least the need for it, was about 15 years ago. I was at the beginning of my relationship with my wife, Jody. Her son, Ron John, who is a fisherman, was talking about how important it is to cut up plastic six-pack rings because of all the animals he'd seen tangled up in them.

Recently, I heard about a whale that had washed up on a beach and it turned out that the whale had died because its belly was full of plastic! That is completely unacceptable!

As the years passed, I heard more and more things that really appalled me: governments deciding that the ocean was the best place to dump garbage, the slaughtering of whales, oil spills where so many animals perished, and more. Then I started hearing about the massive amounts of plastic being found in the ocean. This showed me how important and scary our situation is.

"Water and air, the two essential fluids on which all life depends, have become global garbage cans."

– Jacques-Yves Cousteau

The Three Rs Anyone Can Do

There are a few ways in which I personally contribute to cleaning up our oceans. The primary way is that I am very strict about recycling. I work to not use plastics, or if I must, I use plastics that are recyclable and then recycle them. The more we recycle, the less trash we generate.

I think the most important thing that people can do is to reduce the amount of waste they produce. Cut down on plastic use, especially single-use plastics. Recycle, recycle, and recycle some more. Don't buy products that come in non-recyclable plastics. Do buy products made out of recycled plastics. Ultimately, be present and aware of what you are throwing away.

Remember the three Rs:

- Reduce
- Reuse
- Recycle

Small Business = Big Impact

In our business, we are committed to making a difference. In fact, our business is all about making a difference to the lives of business owners and their families, teams and communities. For me, that is a business that matters, a business that makes life better for others — isn't that what business is for?

For me, the legacy that I will leave behind in the world is to have made a lasting, positive impact on people's lives. More specifically, to have transformed what it means to be a small business owner and the impact that they can have on their lives and the world. I see small business owners as a force for change in our world that can make a difference for all the SDGs intended to create a sustainable future for our planet.

Unless my business, or any business that I am part of, is doing something that makes life better for others, I can't really get behind it and I don't think most other people can either. We also like to make a difference to others worldwide through our giving. This is why we love B1G1, since it allows us to make giving part of our everyday business activities.

During my years as an ActionCOACH, I have had the opportunity to visit many amazing places and to meet many amazing people. One of the most memorable trips was when we traveled to Bali, which was an incredible opportunity for many reasons. While we were in Bali, we got the opportunity to be driven around by a couple of local people. Although we did want to see some of the "sights," we also wanted to experience the "real" Bali — at least a little. Here were people who, by our standards, were incredibly poor, but who were also incredibly industrious and happy. We learned that true poverty did not really exist in their culture, since it was part of their culture to take care of everyone.

Another incredible thing to come out of our trip to Bali was that we met Paul Dunn, one of the founders of B1G1. He is a man who is so giving that it defies description.

Let me explain why I say that. At the time we were heading off to Bali, back in our home town of Miami, Florida, Jody was putting together a summit called "What Will it Take to End Hunger in Miami?"

The summit was scheduled for a couple of months after we returned home and Jody was still working on how to create the right list of people to serve as the catalyst for the conversation. After hearing Paul speak at our conference, Jody asked him to join her for breakfast to talk about her project. He accepted, which was amazing enough on its own. During breakfast, as Jody explained what she was creating, Paul said, "Do you think it would make a difference if I came and spoke at your event?" Can you imagine! He's from Singapore, we're from Miami, we're talking in Bali, and he's offering to come to Miami to speak for someone he's only just met simply because he likes the cause! It was the start of an awesome friendship with this amazing man, and eventually, his equally amazing wife!

I am passionate about helping others and being of service. To me, the most important thing in life is to help others. I'm not a big believer in handouts, but I am a true believer in "hand ups" and I will go out of my way to help someone up. That is a big part of why I became a business coach. I tell people what could be done better all the time — I get up every day and help people to be more successful and to achieve the things they want in their lives, and I get paid for it. I also contribute my time and my money to causes that make a difference for people, whether it's in their personal lives, their work lives, or the community in general. What a life!

THE UNEXPLORED GIFT AROUND US
MATHEW COLIN DAVIS

As a marine scientist, I've been in the industry long enough to see a growing trend toward people caring about our oceans and environment. I have worked on billion-dollar infrastructure projects and also community-based projects. I've seen how things are done on both spectra. However, although we are becoming more conscious of our role in the bigger picture, some damage has already been done. I look around and see how human interference has already completely destroyed rivers, estuaries, and some ocean areas. It hurts me to see it.

The good news is that we now have more knowledge about both our oceans and the consequences of humanity's actions than ever before.

Only 5% of our oceans have been explored thus far, and scientists estimate that 91% of marine species have yet to be found. Oceans cover over 70% of the Earth's surface and contain about 97% of the plant's water. The remaining water is either found in polar ice caps and glaciers (almost 2%), held as groundwater (about 1.7%), flowing as liquid freshwater in creeks and rivers, existing as water vapor and clouds in the atmosphere, or found in living organisms. We all depend on water; it's vital to life, *for* life.

Life under water is a new world waiting to be explored. We are going into space, we are exploring planets millions of kilometers away, while the deepest part of our oceans, the Mariana Trench, is only 10,994 meters deep and we are yet to fully explore it. Imagine the undiscovered gems hidden in our most precious resource. What medical advances can we make from the thousands of species living on the Great Barrier Reef?

I am excited about our future, and about my children's future. There's no doubt that we can create a sustainable world for future generations, that is, so long as we act responsibly. We must treasure what we have and seek to protect our most precious resource.

On land, our environment is visible and everyone can see if there is a major (or minor) negative impact, but life under water, that is, in our marine and freshwater environments, is almost invisible to the majority of humans, although we all rely on water for our very survival.

Our bodies are comprised of about 70% water and we need to drink water to survive, but in developed society we disrespect water. We flush our toilets with water every day, while in some areas of the Earth people are struggling to find drinking water. It's an unbalanced paradox.

We are a global ecosystem and we need to tackle this problem as a species. Both the Australian Coastal and Marine Ecology and the Coastal Protection Core teams dedicate their entire existence to preserving, conserving, researching, managing, educating, connecting, collaborating, and inspiring in relation to the future of our oceans and our environment.

I believe that we are at the crossroads of a significant breakthrough, with humanity at last awakening to the impacts our predecessors have had on our natural ecosystems.

We have one chance, and the time to act is *now*.

Natural Beauty that Money Can't Buy

Growing up in Australia, I had an amazing opportunity to experience some of the best environments and natural ecosystems in the world, including the Great Barrier Reef, one of the most incredible locations on Earth; Fraser Island, the largest sand island in the world; the Daintree Rainforest, an incredibly diverse rainforest in the tropics of Queensland; and some of the best surf beaches in the world.

I grew up on the coast of Queensland with this wonderland of magnificence on my doorstep. One day, while surfing on the Gold Coast, I looked across the coastline and thought, "We really need to do this better." I saw a coastline littered with high-rise buildings on the foredunes and I knew that we could develop things better. I wanted to create a more sustainable future and I knew there were unexplored options available to do this in a better way.

Since then, I have gone on to have children and I want them to experience what I did growing up. To feel the clean sand, to taste the salt in a clean ocean, and to breath fresh rainforest air. To touch the essence of real beauty.

Just recently, I was on the most northern tip of K'Gari (Fraser Island) at the sandy cape. We were searching, satellite tagging, and relocating the eggs of the majestic loggerhead (Caretta Caretta) and green sea turtles (Chelonia mydas) in effort to conserve these incredible species.

In Queensland, Australia, loggerhead turtles are classified as endangered, which is an incredibly sad situation. In a relatively isolated stretch of beach and key nesting areas, you would assume that during nesting season turtle sightings would be abundant. Yet, for every 1000 eggs laid, only one tiny hatchling survives to maturity, which takes 30 years!

Generally, the clutch size is around 110 eggs and about two to eight nests per season. This means that for the species to persist in Queensland, we need at least ten clutches per season from at least two turtles. Due to the predation of eggs by dingoes, loggerheads have little chance of survival, which is why we relocate the eggs to dingo-proof cages.

This is a perfect example of creating harmony between land and ocean, and how what we do on the land affects our oceans and the species inhabiting those oceans. What is fascinating is the energy transfer across this ecotone (the area between two different habitats, for example, land and ocean), as well as how some species rely on input from the ocean for their survival. If we alter this system, particularly through plastic pollution, it causes a significant impact through the food chain.

We, as a species, have an incredible opportunity to act now and to create a sustainable and clean future we can be proud of for future generations. Recently, airlines in Portugal have ditched plastics, and you can do the same in your personal life and business. It's one of the easiest changes that makes a huge difference to our marine life.

Our oceans are one of the most important ecosystems. We are dependent on them. What we don't see does affect us.

Near Death Can Equal New Life

There was a point where I thought I had it all. I had a successful business; our company was really making an impact. Life was great. Then, I realized that something was missing. I searched my soul for answers. Was it my passion? No, I have always loved the ocean, whether SCUBA diving, fishing, surfing, or just being on the water. Was it my life's purpose? No, I had no doubt that I was living my life's purpose. Was it my home? Or family? Or friends? Absolutely not.

I met Paul Dunn at a business presentation, and he explained the importance of giving back in a different light. I'd also heard Tony Robbins talk about the importance of giving back. He said that if you're not giving 10% back when you're earning 25k, then you definitely aren't going to give back when you're earning millions! So I began to explore ways to give back to key causes benefiting our oceans and environment. Something as simple as giving back makes a huge difference, but it's often overlooked in business models. Now, we are not only making an impact through our day-to-day business, but we also are making waves across the globe on key projects. We give back a portion of profits to key causes.

One of my proudest moments (aside from marrying my soulmate and our kids being born) was when I launched our first research vessel, Whoppa, which was one of my life-long dreams. It means that every day I live to make a positive impact on life under water, to develop solutions to marine construction that will minimize the impact on our precious ecosystems. This is an example of research that gives.

But none of these magic moments prepared me for the moment that changed my life, the moment where my passion and soul collided in a sudden, life-altering way.

I was in New York after a whirlwind trip to Sir Richard Branson's home on Necker Island. After joining Sir Richard in the Caribbean, I was invited to join 34 other entrepreneurs after winning an innovation award for my company, Coastal Protection Core, located in Moreton Bay, Queensland, which was set to become a global game-changer for the future of our environment. We were also due to meet the United Nations team, but I felt unwell and was unexpectedly rushed to hospital, although I was later released. Unfortunately, I missed meeting the UN team, which was something I was really looking forward to.

I had to fly back to Los Angeles and then board a plane to Brisbane, a thirteen-and-a-half-hour flight, 33,000 feet above the Pacific Ocean. During the flight, I stepped out of the tiny bathroom and my head began to spin. I called out to my wife, "Eva, I'm going to pass out," but she was blocked in the aisle by the dinner service.

That was the moment I had been warned about while back in hospital in New York. In that moment, my life literally flashed before my eyes, although it wasn't a flash, it was more like a movie reel of my life. It happened in an instant, but it also felt like an eternity. The movie of my life was incredible.

- Dinner and red wine with Sir Richard Branson – ✓
- Meeting one of my life-long idols, Arnold Schwarzenegger – ✓
- Marrying my soulmate – ✓
- Having the two greatest achievements of my life, my two sons, Reef and Marley – ✓

"No way," I muttered, thinking I was about to die.

As I prepared to lay down in the aisle some 33,000 feet above the Pacific Ocean and die, I saw a spiral of energy — light, intense, and powerful, but full of pure love. A rapture of pure love swept over me. I felt safe. I felt loved. I felt nurtured. And I was not alone.

Just as these intense emotions were pouring through me, something somehow came from the energy and whispered to me, *"Do it for them. Do it for our future generations."* My sons' faces appeared right in front of my eyes. As this happened, a man held me on the shoulder, Dr. Chris from Proserpine. I had leaned on his mother-in-law's seat as I stopped in the aisle and she got his attention.

Dr. Chris gave me saline through an IV. I began to feel slightly better, but we still had ten hours on the plane to go. Dr. Chris recommended that the plane be diverted to Honolulu, Hawaii, because I might not have made it to Brisbane. He was right. After an ambulance trip to Poli Momi Hospital in Hawaii, they began the search for the internal bleeding that had been happening for the past four or five days, but to no avail. I initially declined blood transfusions, but on day four, the doctors explained that without an immediate blood transfusion my life was at risk.

After a blood transfusion and six or seven procedures later, they finally found the bleeding in my small intestine and patched me up. The explanation was that it was "just one of those things."

I returned to Australia a new soul, driven to "inspire future change." I was driven to help create a sustainable world for future generations. My purpose was crystal clear. And I now live my purpose and my passion every day, knowing that the only way to achieve an ecologically balanced future for my children and future generations is through connection, collaboration, and education.

WHAT YOU CAN DO TO
SUSTAIN THE WORLD BELOW WATER

Lifestyle tips:
- Put rubbish in bins – don't litter.
- Eliminate single-use plastic as much as possible.
- Make ocean-friendly choices when buying products or eating food derived from oceans.
- Eliminate the use of plastic water bottles.

Business tips:
- Don't pour chemicals down the sink or into our waterways.
- When hosting events, request hotels and facilities to provide jugs and glasses instead of bottled water.
- Encourage people to use their own reusable bags.

Giving tips:
- Support marine life protection organizations.
- Volunteer your time to clean up beaches.
- Sponsor or support marine life research programs.

BECOME A GOOD STEWARD OF THE EARTH

---

15 **LIFE ON LAND**

HOW YOU AND YOUR BUSINESS CAN HELP TO PROTECT, RESTORE, AND PROMOTE THE SUSTAINABLE USE OF TERRESTRIAL ECOSYSTEMS, SUSTAINABLY MANAGE FORESTS, COMBAT DESERTIFICATION, HALT AND REVERSE LAND DEGRADATION, AND HALT BIODIVERSITY LOSS.

"No matter how few possessions you own or how little money you have, loving wildlife and nature will make you rich beyond measure."

— Paul Oxton

THE CHANGEMAKERS

THE FORESTS ARE OUR LUNGS. THE ANIMALS ARE OUR HEART.
DEANNE FIRTH

Deanne Firth FCA is the director of Tactical Super, a chartered accounting firm specializing in conducting audits. She is also a regional councilor with the Institute of Chartered Accountants. Deanne was named Auditor of the Year both in 2017 and 2018 by SMSF Adviser, and Tactical Super was named SMSF Audit Firm of the Year in 2018.

Aside from being an audit specialist, Deanne is the director of Effective PD, a professional development company, where she presents on taxation and superannuation. She is also a board member of B1G1. In this role, she assesses charities that want to be added to the approved list of B1G1 worthy causes.

Deanne is currently writing a new book, *Effective Giving: How to Do the Most Good*, as part of her NFP Auditing for Good.

tacticalsuper.com.au, effectivepd.com.au, auditingforgood.com.au

BECOMING COSMOCENTRIC
DR. ANDREW BACHOUR

Dr. Andrew Bachour is a dentist practicing in Brisbane, Australia. He has a passion for health, life, and knowledge. In relation to his interest in sleep as well as nutritional and environmental medicine, Dr. Andrew is passionate about getting to the origins of problems rather than only treating their downstream symptoms. His ideal future consists of both a world living in harmony with the environment and a world in which all the fields of healthcare are bridged, with the primary focus being on health. In his spare time, Dr. Andrew has a love for astronomy and philosophy. Alongside B1G1, Dr. Andrew and his team are making people smile all over the world.

drandrewbachour.com

BECOME A GOOD STEWARD
OF THE EARTH

Picture Africa – the land of sweeping desert plains, rugged mountain summits and breathtaking waterfalls. Wild animals parading their exotic beauty in wonderful display – zebras, giraffes, elephants, lions and rhinos are all part of the natural African majesty.

Now imagine the lush green Amazon rainforest. A 55-million-year-old ecosystem, home to more than 30 million people, 1.6 million of those belonging to over 400 different indigenous tribes. Not to mention the 40,000 unique plant species, 16,000 tree species, 5,600 fish species 1,300 birds, 430+ mammals, 1,000+ amphibians and 400+ reptiles that reside in this natural wonderland.

Next, imagine the summit of the Himalayas. An awe-striking mountain range encompassing over 50 snow-capped mountains and comprising over 10,000 species of plants, 1,000 species of birds, 300 species of mammals and home to millions of people.

Life on Land is precious, beautiful and diverse.

Now, breathe.

Consider that every single minute, the earth – *we* – lose masses of forests, the equivalent of 27 soccer fields.

Reaching the goal for SDG 15 means that the world's forests, mountains, dry-lands, and wetlands will be conserved and restored by 2030. What a legacy that will be!

It's legacy that stops deforestation, protects natural habitats, protects endangered species and supports our fragile ecosystems. Like all other goals, urgent action is necessary and here's why:

Those 27 soccer fields of forest we are losing every minute. Well, if current deforestation levels proceed, our rainforests may completely vanish in less than 100 years.

Farming, grazing of livestock, mining, and drilling combined account for more than half of all deforestation. Forestry practices, wildfires and urbanization make up the remaining portion.

In some countries, for example, Malaysia and Indonesia,

deforestation to produce palm oil destroys not only the forest, but decimates the orangutan environment so they are now an endangered species. Sadly enough, palm oil is found in many general household products like cleaning products, shampoo, cosmetics and candles.

But it is possible to produce palm oil sustainably. In fact, companies like Unilever now only use palm oil from sustainable suppliers.

Forests are home to more than 80% of all terrestrial species of animals, plants and insects.

Rainforests are often called the lungs of the planet for their role in absorbing carbon dioxide and producing oxygen, upon which all living creatures depend for survival. Rainforests also stabilize the climate and produce nourishing rainfall all around the planet.

And much like the orangutans mentioned earlier, loss of forests equals loss of wildlife. Add to this, illegal poaching and wildlife trafficking and our wildlife species are disappearing at alarming rates.

Within the last 500 years, human activity has forced over 800 species into complete extinction. And in May 2019, a landmark United Nations report warned that, thanks to human pressure, 1 million species may be pushed to extinction within the next few years, with serious consequences for human beings as well as the rest of life on Earth.

Changemaker Dr. Andrew Bachour brings this into sharp focus. He states that on the International Union for Conservation of Nature's Red List for Threatened Species, there are more than 96,500 species, with over 26,500 listed as threatened with extinction. That's an enormous number to fathom.

To put this in perspective, between 2014 and 2017, more than 100,000 African elephants were killed for their ivory. There are less than 70 amur leopards in the world today due to them being hunted and killed for their beautiful unique fur. Rhinos continuously get slaughtered every day for their horns. And poaching also kills humans.

In Africa, nearly 600 rangers were killed by poachers between 2009 and 2016. In the Democratic Republic of the Congo's Virunga National Park, one of the continent's most dangerous parks, at least 170 rangers have been killed during the past two decades.

Poaching accounts for around $20 billion dollars of illegal "goods" each year.

As changemaker Deanne Firth points out, sustainable practises can be formed with the right knowledge. "All businesses," she says, "can take one united approach toward changing industry practices and standards. All can look at their supply chain and demand ethical and environmental practises."

Dr Andrew Bachour highlights the immediate question we must ask. He says, "My question is, why do we need to wait for critical times to change?". Let's ask ourselves that question now...

The answer is: we don't. We mustn't. In fact, waiting is the problem.

Let's take action. Swift and groundbreaking action. Reading what follows is part of that process.

Let's save our forests, our wildlife our lands and ecosystems. Let's leave the legacy of our natural diversity so that future generations can savour the exquisite beauty of our glorious landscapes and exotic creatures.

Chief Seattle, the Suquamish and Duwamish chief after whom the US city is named, was attributed to saying:

"The earth does not belong to man, man belongs to the earth.
All things are connected like the blood that unites one family.
Man did not weave the web of life, he is merely a strand in it.
Whatever he does to the web, he does to himself.
The earth is sacred and men and animals are but one part of it.
Treat the earth with respect so that it lasts for centuries to come and
is a place of wonder and beauty for our children."

THE FORESTS ARE OUR LUNGS.
THE ANIMALS ARE OUR HEART.
DEANNE FIRTH

When I was six years old, I lived in outback Queensland and there was a big flood. Australia is known for its weather extremes – droughts and flooding rains – and this was the flooding rains. We were being evacuated from school due to the floods; our parents were on one side of the water and we were on the other. We took our sandals off, checked for snakes, and with our hearts pumping, we were passed across to safety.

It was the animals that intrigued me the most during that period, especially the snakes. People were using brooms to sweep snakes off their doorsteps (understandably so) and they swam past us desperate to find a higher, dry place to be safe.

It struck me then that we all need to co-exist in this environment. Yes, even the snakes. The environment makes us all flourish or perish.

Consider the bees: while collecting pollen and nectar for their food, they also pollinate plants, fertilizing them so they can grow and produce food. Without bees, many plants would die. In fact, it is estimated that one-third of the food we consume each day relies on pollination.

Go outside and take off your shoes, let your feet feel the earth beneath you. Look up at a tree. What does a tree do? It provides a habitat and food for birds and other animals. It absorbs carbon dioxide. It stabilizes the soil to prevent erosion. There is nothing more amazing or uplifting than nature.

Inspiration comes from the beauty of what you see. From the ruggedness of Alaska to the beaches of the Maldives. Life on land is simply beautiful and we need to do all we can to protect it.

The Choice Made by One Man from Borneo

Have you ever looked into an orangutan's eyes? Or watched an orangutan look at its child? Do you know that you can buy one hectare of rainforest in Borneo for just $500 US? Buying that hectare protects the rainforest from destruction for palm oil plantations. It also provides food for villagers and animals.

Visiting Borneo in 2018 was a life-changing experience for me. Villagers who were once illegal loggers now work on rehabilitating the rainforest and looking after the orangutan habitats. These villagers could earn more money by illegally logging or working for palm oil plantations, but they love and care for the environment. They want to protect it. Even if it costs them financially.

The land is sold to palm oil plantations because the people are poor and need the money. The only way to protect it is to buy it. The charity I visited, the Friends of National Parks Foundation, does just that. It buys the rainforest and employs villagers to manage it. However, funding is tight, wages are low, and keeping staff is hard, but we can help by donating to them and visiting the orangutans. We should be inspired by them not just to help the orangutans in Borneo, but to help life on land all over the world.

In Borneo, we saw such amazing wildlife. My ten-year-old son loves taking wildlife photos, so I bought him a good camera with some great lenses. I saw our tour guide's eyes light up when he saw it. The guide, who works for an NGO, clearly knew about cameras and lenses, whereas I only knew how to point and shoot. I had no idea how to adjust the shutter speed, light, or whatever else was needed to take a decent picture. I just put it on auto and pressed the button.

After the first day, we got back to the little wooden boat we were staying in and I gave the guide the camera to take some shots along the river. He was so happy. The next day I didn't take any photos. Instead, I gave him the camera and told him he could take the pictures. The orangutan and monkey photos he took were amazing.

He told me that he was a photographer and showed me some photos on his phone. His photos were simply incredible, and he gave them away for free to promote the protection of orangutan habitats. They are on posters, websites, and t-shirts all around the world. I asked him where his camera was. He told me that he had to sell his camera to pay for a family member's medical situation. My heart sank.

We live in a world where my ten-year-old son owns a professional camera, but a talented photographer doesn't own one, just because of where he was born. Does this make sense to you?

This man could have earned more money by illegally logging forests or working on a palm oil plantation. He could have insisted on payment for his photos rather than allowing them to be used to raise awareness. Instead, he works with a reforestation organization. He loves the orangutans – he knows them all by name, where to find them, their family trees. By choosing to do the right thing, he is financially worse off than if he chose to do the wrong thing. Yet, he still chooses to do right, every day of his life. That is inspiring.

That day, I promised him I would come back with a camera for him. And this year, I will be visiting him again, with that camera in hand.

This is one choice made by a man from Borneo. An integral choice. A global choice. He chose to honor life on land and his love for the animals and forests over his personal desires. This is a choice we can all make. The question is, will we?

Auditing for Good – How to Tell if a Charity is Effective or Not

My goal in business has always been to have my business run itself and make enough money so that I can focus on doing good. I am not there yet, and I still work many hours in my business, but I am working toward that goal so I can put more time into Auditing for Good.

It can be difficult when looking at the annual reports and websites of charitable organizations to determine where the money is going and how effectively it is being used. This is where Auditing for Good comes in. I break down the numbers and assess charities, not just based on their admin ratios, but also on their effectiveness, to ensure transparency in giving. You see, it isn't just about admin ratios, it's about overall effectiveness.

For example. I could give 100% of my money to you to

build a well. In that case, my admin ratio would be 0%, since 100% of the money is going to build the well. But what if you have never built a well before? Do you know how to build the best well? Do you have the skills necessary to negotiate the best price? Do you know what the best materials are? Do you have the expertise to know where to drill?

What if, instead of giving you 100% of the money, I spent 20% of it on training you? In this case, only 80% of my donated money goes toward that well, but the materials are cheaper, you drill in only one place rather than five before finding water, and the design and quality of the well mean it will last longer. Even though less money went directly toward building a well, the outcome and overall effectiveness of the money increased. So, looking beyond the numbers is important.

It's important that we take a wider view of the world and think beyond our own front door. We need to consider the impact of our actions and the effectiveness of our decisions. It's something I think about. My aim is much like everyone else's, that is, to leave this world better than I found it. I also want my children to love and respect each other and to treat others with respect.

My motivation in both business and life is to deal fairly and honestly with everyone and to treat everyone with respect, to go the extra mile and make their day, and to put people before profit.

Sometimes, it's the little things we can do that matter the most. For example, if someone owes you money, it could be that they are dealing with something you don't know about. Maybe they have just had to put their mother in an expensive nursing home. If someone on the street asks you for money, don't judge them, since we are all just one or two bad decisions away from where they are now. These simple attitudes help to create a better life, a better business, and a better world.

I hope that my ultimate legacy is a smile when someone mentions my name.

BECOMING COSMOCENTRIC
DR. ANDREW BACHOUR

If Not Us, Who? If Not Now, When?

Life on land.

Say that slowly. There is your inspiration. I remember being in primary school and learning about the many challenges that we, as humans, will face in the future: pollution, climate change, deforestation, overpopulation, animal extinction. It scared me, but I would selfishly reassure myself that such things would not happen in my lifetime.

I am older now (and hopefully a little wiser) and have a beautiful family of my own. I want my children, my children's children, and the generations thereafter to enjoy the full beauty and biodiversity this Earth has to offer. In just my short time on Earth, the negative impact we are having on the planet has become vividly evident. As a civilization, we are living unsustainably on all fronts, and unfortunately, we are leaving a trail of immeasurable destruction behind us, not all of which has made itself evident yet. We need to consider the full consequences our actions have for both the seen and unseen environments, and we must learn to live in harmony with our surroundings.

As humans, it is natural to grow and slowly develop over time. However, we tend to make significant changes during critical moments or times of immense pain. My question is: Why do we need to wait for critical times to change? We shouldn't wait until the point of no return, until sickness plagues us or species go extinct, before we open our eyes. It is natural to evolve and develop; however, we must do so sustainably.

Gaining the understanding I have today did not result from a single "aha" moment, but rather it was something built block by block. As a child, I loved watching documentaries about nature, Sir David Attenborough was always on the television. I'd heard of the threat humans pose to the Earth, about habitats being destroyed through urbanization and deforestation, and news of some animals going extinct and others being placed on the endangered species list. Now, in hindsight, without having an appreciation of the "bigger picture," simply knowing about this goal and believing it to be important is not enough.

During my first year at university studying for a science degree, I was introduced to subjects concerning animal biology and ecosystems. I was so fascinated by the projects undertaken by the university, looking at the health and preservation of marine life, it started to feel "closer to home." Since that moment, I have understood that, whether it's our own microbiome, a forest, or the Earth in general, ecosystems are of incredible importance. We know that changes in our own microbiome can have significant impacts on the health of our body. When species are removed or introduced to an area, the effects they can have are widespread. The eradication of the gray wolf from Yellowstone National Park during the early 1900s caused a trophic cascade. Their reintroduction in 1995 saw stability and diversity return to the ecosystem, vegetation regenerated, animals came back, and rivers were carved. After such a catastrophic event, it remains questionable whether the ecosystem has fully recovered, which serves as an important lesson.

I realize that everything we have done, myself included, has caused harm to life, whether directly or indirectly. We need to ask ourselves: What impact is something going to have after it becomes extinct? According to the International Union for Conservation of Nature's Red List, there are more than 96,500 species, with over 26,500 listed as being threatened with extinction.

There are species of bees on the critically endangered list. If certain species of bees were to become extinct, the consequences would be catastrophic, since a significant amount of our global food supply is pollinated by bees. We know that even strains of bacteria are going extinct. With what we know about the human microbiome, it is possible that one particular strain of bacteria could someday protect us from a particular disease, but what if that strain has already gone extinct? Given the changes that occurred in Yellowstone National Park due to the eradication of one species, what would happen if we were to lose 26,500 species?

Forget the Symptoms - Treat the Origin

I used to be very "traditional" in everything I did. In school, I was an "A" student. I received university commendations and I graduated in dentistry with honors. My family was always very proud of my constant achievements and accolades. I loved competitive sports (when I could steer clear of injuries), I ate "healthy," and I otherwise felt quite fit. I was living my life as if it was too easy. I had no reason to question anything or do anything different. Why would I? I knew everything. And therein lies the problem.

My "turning point" came when I began experiencing severe headaches, which would send me home from work and wipe out many weekends for me. This went on for years. I tried all the traditional avenues taking medications, seeing multiple specialists, and undergoing a lot of diagnostics. Nothing helped.

I started attending courses, seeking to learn more about the body. The two things I most remember about sitting through those courses was the constant throbbing headache, and at the same time, how invigorated I felt after them as I knew I was inching closer to an answer. That answer was given to me by Dr. Steven Olmos, who opened my eyes to the world of posture, breathing, nutrition, environmental medicine, and most importantly, the concept of treating origins, not symptoms.

As simple as that sounds, it does not happen often enough. What I mean is that in conditions such as chronic pain, for example, where it hurts or where "the symptom" is rarely accounts for the origin of the problem. Unlike, say, an acute trauma, where it hurts at the source. In the case of chronic conditions, we need to locate and treat the source rather than focus on the symptom if we are to achieve complete resolution. The late Dr. John Beck, an orthopedic surgeon, devised methods for locating the origins of chronic musculoskeletal pain and said that the traditional approach whereby the doctor investigates patients based on their symptoms is like "letting the dumb lead the blind." With this in mind, the approach of the future should be based on finding and treating origins rather than symptoms, and it should be focused on going toward health rather than away from sickness.

Strength in Numbers

So, where is business in all of this? A business that matters refers to a business that is a force for good in this world. A business that is not a force for good will likely ultimately become unsustainable. The same principle can be applied universally. If we don't live harmoniously and thoughtfully, then ultimately, life won't be sustainable. As Simon Sinek says, all great businesses have a why, a purpose, a belief. We believe that we can change the world for good. This principle can be applied in all areas. Always know your "why," and only focus your energy on good intent. In this way, you will resonate with all that is positive.

Our business is focused on improving what we do and how we do it. That is an important step for any business, since change is inevitable. What's not changing though is our "why." As most people would agree, dentistry and healthcare have changed for the better, and thankfully, we are not practicing like we did 100 years ago.

I hope to see a future in which treatment is not focused on symptoms, but rather on origins. I hope to see a future in which the focus is on moving toward health, not away from disease.

Most people would agree that all the systems of the body work together as one rather than working independently of each other. We believe that the way of the future will involve bridging all the fields of health and merging dentistry, medicine, and all the other health professions. Not one philosophy can dominate.

The World Health Organization has shown the rates of cancers, diabetes, neurological diseases, and other conditions to be increasing at an unprecedented rate. Given the prevalence of disease that we are now facing, the search for cures is crucial, but it is arguably matched by the need to pursue prevention, to pursue health. If we continue in the same way, disease will unfortunately become the new norm. We must change.

Whether it be in business or in life, we may not yet have all the answers, but they do exist. We just need to keep searching. Just because we cannot see something, doesn't mean that it doesn't exist.

Be the Change You Want to See

I am sure we have all seen or heard of ecosystems being destroyed, wildlife entangled in plastic and poisoned by toxic chemicals. But what about the significant rise of disease in humans? It would be imprudent to say that the same is not happening to animals due to the significant increase in chemicals and airborne pollutants found in the environment, amongst other things.

Simply put, taking immediate action is actually quite easy. You can still live your life; you just need to make adjustments where you can. What chemicals are we allowing to go down the drain? What are we eating? What are we disposing of? Where is it going? Be thoughtful in all your actions.

The change we want to see in the world starts with us, with the power of one. We just need to speed things up a little. We all have the responsibility to live in harmony with our environment. Be curious. Show gratitude. Live with mindfulness. Love the universe, since the same force that governs the universe runs through all of us.

WHAT YOU CAN DO TO
SUSTAIN LIFE ON LAND

Lifestyle tips:
- Visit your local animal shelter and adopt an animal there.
- Avoid using pesticides and chemicals when growing plants.
- Avoid buying products that are tested on animals.

Business tips:
- Insist on fair treatment of animals in your supply chains.
- Reduce the use of harsh chemicals.
- Become a certified Business for Good via B1G1.

Giving tips:
- Give to environmental causes to protect natural habitat.
- Volunteer with street animal organizations or shelters.
- Join an existing clean-up event.

GOVERNANCE FOR A PEACEFUL WORLD

16 PEACE, JUSTICE AND STRONG INSTITUTIONS

HOW YOU AND YOUR BUSINESS CAN HELP TO PROMOTE PEACEFUL AND INCLUSIVE SOCIETIES FOR SUSTAINABLE DEVELOPMENT, PROVIDE ACCESS TO JUSTICE FOR ALL, AND BUILD EFFECTIVE, ACCOUNTABLE, AND INCLUSIVE INSTITUTIONS AT ALL LEVELS.

"Our hopes for a more just, safe, and peaceful world can only be achieved when there is universal respect for the inherent diginity and equal rights of all members of the human family."

— Phumzile Mlambo-Ngcuka

THE CHANGEMAKERS

LET NO ONE BE A SLAVE
CHERYL ANGELA

Cheryl Angela is a transformational coach, healer, award-winning musician (harp and voice), and composer. Cheryl works with leaders, entrepreneurs, creatives, healers, and philanthropists. Her music has been described as "music from the angels." She has performed healing concerts across the globe and also released three original albums and numerous collaborations on film, DVD, and CD, including the multiple award-winning film soundtrack, *The Omo Child*. Cheryl serves on the executive team of the non-profit Global Prosperity and Peace Initiative and is the director of the Voice Advocacy Foundation.

cherylangela.com

THE LESSON OF A LIFETIME
SUSIE HUTCHISON

A visionary entrepreneur and passionate philanthropist, Susie Hutchison blends her flair for commerce with her love for humanity. She equips the next generation of social entrepreneurs with the skills, experience, and inspiration needed to impact others. She is the executive director of a leading global travel technology business and an advisory board member of a number of charities, including SevGen Indigenous Corporation and Antardristi Nepal.

susiehutchison.com

ACTIVISM WITH AWARENESS
JODY ANN JOHNSON

Jody Ann Johnson started her ActionCOACH business coaching firm with her husband over a decade ago. She believes working directly with small businesses to help them grow can have the greatest impact for good, since when people have their needs met, the next most natural thing for them is to be of service. The mission of Jody's business is to transform the economic landscape so that, together, we can create a world that works for everyone.

actioncoachteamsage.com

GOVERNANCE FOR A PEACEFUL WORLD

On 25th May 1969, John Lennon and Yoko Ono were in bed at the Fairmont Queen Elizabeth Hotel in Montreal, Canada.

And that setting became the venue, or "the studio" in a sense, for Lennon's "Give Peace a Chance," recording. That's more than 50 years ago. And yet we're still trying.

Peace is perhaps the paradox of our time.

People pray for it. Leaders commit to it. And beauty pageant contestants are well-versed in wishing for it.

Peace, Justice and Strong Institutions are unlike other SDGs. They aren't impacted by the weather nor are they at the mercy of climate change. They are entirely within our control. Control equals power. So this SDG is an open field entirely up to us to create it.

To put it simpler — we are the answer.

But the list of problems is long. Too long. The obstacles to creating a peaceful and just society are complex and often stem from other related issues like poverty and hunger. For example, if there were no poverty and hunger would Victor Hugo's Jean Val Jean have been thrown in prison for 19 years for stealing bread for his starving sister? Justice indeed.

According to a 2019 report by the Task Force on Justice, the justice system is failing to resolve problems for 1.5 billion people. The report points to a hidden and unjust epidemic running through the globe. It confirms what we've always suspected — that the poorest people are hit the hardest. It also provides the first estimate of the widening gap that exists in our global justice sector. The report identifies the need for a new justice model. One designed to provide justice for everyone.

The Task Force identifies a global justice gap with 3 dimensions:

- At least 253 million people live in extreme conditions of injustice — they are modern slaves, stateless, or their countries or communities are engulfed in conflict, violence, and lawlessness.

- 1.5 billion people cannot resolve their everyday justice problems — they are victims of crimes they do not report or have a serious civil or administrative problem they cannot resolve.
- 4.5 billion people are excluded from the opportunities the law provides — they lack legal identity or other documentation related to employment, family, or property, and are therefore unable to access economic opportunities and public services, or the protection of the law.

Stop for a moment and consider. That is two-thirds of the world's population who lack adequate access to justice.

Mostly it reflects the structural inequalities and differences in power. For example, statistically speaking most of the injustice happens to women, children, and other vulnerable groups.

Re-examining and building a just system is a logical place to start. After all, how can we hope for world peace if two-thirds of our population are not given access to justice? But it's a big job to unravel an old system because, according to the UN, the institutions most affected by corruption are the judiciary and police sectors.

How can we hope for justice if we are plagued by corruption from the very institutions that are supposed to protect us?

Threats of violence, human trafficking, sexual exploitation and homicides will continue without a change in our global justice gaps. What goes unreported doesn't get the chance for justice. As Martin Luther King Jr. said, "Injustice anywhere is a threat to justice everywhere."

We see it. We hear about it. We know it's there.

Take human trafficking as an obvious example. Changemaker Cheryl Angela is doing her bit to stop it in all its forms. Not only does she provide us with some dark and confronting statistics but she urges us to not accept them. To say, "I'm not okay with that," and do something real to reduce them. Or better, eradicate them completely.

An institutional way to start protecting children and individual rights is to implement birth registration around the world and to create more independent national human rights institutions.

For example, whilst 73% of children under 5 have obtained registered births, only 46% of children in Sub-Saharan Africa have had their births registered. This makes them especially vulnerable for trafficking and exploitation.

Our modern world brings with it new problems and new solutions. So, if there's a good time to re-examine our system it's now. New laws are thankfully being created every day - for things like cyberbullying, social media online abuse, threats of violence.

We are at the cusp of a new era and we must take the opportunity to demand reform, equality and justice. In all its forms, for everyone.

Changemaker Jody Ann Johnson has always done that. She encourages us to be both aware and active. Then we, as active citizens, can demand change for everyone, not just for our community or our children. But for all communities and children everywhere. It's in our hands.

Susie Hutchison is another shining example of making things happen. She says that, "Peace is not just a word, but an action and an attitude." As you read her story about her connection with a young Nepalese boy you'll experience those qualities in action. And you'll see that indeed we are the solution to this global situation and that one caring person really makes all the difference.

We have been waiting for world peace since long before John and Yoko were in that bed. Again, we're given the opportunity to do things differently — to choose to give peace a chance again. And choose we must.

In his address before the United Nations in 1963, John F. Kennedy said, "Peace is a daily, a weekly, a monthly process, gradually changing opinions, slowly eroding old barriers, quietly building new structures. And however undramatic the pursuit of peace, that pursuit must go on."

Gradually changing opinions. Slowly eroding barriers. Quietly building new structures. That pursuit must go on.

Let's keep on doing that.

LET NO ONE BE A SLAVE
CHERYL ANGELA

Human trafficking is modern-day slavery.
It represents one of the most horrific assaults on humanity and the dignity of human life. Everyone has the right to a life of happiness and freedom and to live life to the fullest. Human trafficking is a crime against humanity.

The statistics concerning human trafficking are astounding:

- The International Labor Coalition estimates that there are 40.3 million people currently enslaved through human trafficking.
- One in four slaves are children, 71% are girls.
- According to the US State Department, 600,000 to 800,000 people are trafficked across international borders every year. Some 80% are women and half are children.
- Criminals who enslave other humans are profiting to the tune of an estimated 32 billion US dollars each year. Within this multi-billion-dollar industry, 2 million children, mostly girls, are exploited sexually for profit.

I am not OK with any that! A world that treats other human beings in this way, especially children, is not acceptable. As part of my efforts to make a difference in this situation, I have talked firsthand to individuals who were themselves trafficked for sexual exploitation. The scars and trauma that this has left them with are deep and often lifelong. It takes a tremendous amount of healing to overcome the trauma and to be able to live a fulfilling life. The effects are beyond devastating.

I have also talked to a number of men who have gone undercover at great risk to themselves to rescue children who are enslaved and being exploited. They have described with great emotion and pain the tragedy of finding children who are drugged and chained to a bed being sexually assaulted by those who pay the traffickers for use of a child's body. This is an ugly, harrowing subject. Many people do not want to acknowledge that it exists, but unfortunately it does. My goal in shining a light on this dark situation is that people worldwide join forces to eradicate slavery and the abuse of others in all its forms.

My first exposure to this issue occurred ten years ago. A coaching client came to me for healing and support. She described how she had been sexually trafficked as a young girl. She had also been sexually exploited in ritual worship. The daily trauma she suffered due to this experience greatly impacted her life. It really made me realize that this was a real and not a fabricated or exaggerated situation going on in the world. This had happened to her in a small town in the Northwestern United States, a place where you would not expect such a thing to occur. I hadn't previously known that human trafficking for sex and for labor was a worldwide issue. I didn't realize that there is more slavery in the world today than there was back in the 1600s–1800s when slavery was practiced in the USA.

Not long afterwards, I moved to a very high-scale neighborhood in California. This was a classy neighborhood and yet I was surprised to learn that my neighbor had gone to jail for child pornography and the trafficking of young girls. It was clear that human trafficking is a very lucrative business for a criminal. You can keep recycling a human for work, for sex, etc., whereas drugs and illegal weapons are a one-time only deal.

Over the last few years, I have met a number of people who have been trafficked. I have also met people who have gone on rescue missions to free the victims of trafficking from slavery, and I have become involved in a number of non-profits that are active in rescuing children and adults from trafficking and take measures to prevent and stop such enslavement. They are all very brave people, kind people, people giving so much of themselves to help others experience a life of joy and freedom.

So many people fail to realize the vastness of the human trafficking industry, which is why awareness is so important. Many people think that it does not happen in the Western world. They dismiss it as something that only happens in certain parts of the world, such as the Caribbean and Asia. It does indeed happen in these regions, but what surprises people more is how much it is happening in the most developed countries in the world, and even in the most upscale of places, just like the neighborhood I described.

Every life is precious and must be treated as such.

The Crusade to Ease Suffering

I first became conscious of the suffering of others when I was 5-years-old. My brother was born with a heart condition. I would travel with my mother to his doctor's appointments and I witnessed all the stress and concern that my parents went through. When I was 5, he had to go tothe hospital for open-heart surgery. It had a 50% success rate. Seeing his challenges and my parents' challenges opened my eyes to other people's pain. What impacted me further was seeing other children at the hospital, some even younger than me, with illnesses and diseases. It was from that moment on that I was determined to help others and to ease suffering in the world.

As I grew up, this desire led me to various activities, including volunteering to help other children, teaching other children, volunteering in hospitals, and going and serving seniors who needed help with getting groceries, cleaning, and mowing the lawn. I also started doing alternative healing as a young teenager to help people and their pets move out of pain and illness and into health. My desire to ease suffering in the world has guided my activities throughout my whole life since my experience as a five-year-old.

Before I was born, my parents lived in Nigeria. Our home was full of African items. I was keenly aware of the different conditions in which children in other countries grew up in when compared to my own. This fueled my crusade to not only cease to take my own blessings for granted, but to be an agent for change for conditions such as hunger, poverty, and strife in the world. Therefore, as both a child and an adult, I have worked with many organizations and people to make a difference in the areas of hunger, poverty, education, health, social justice and equality, clean water, and sanitation.

Being Involved Matters

For the majority of my working life, I have been either in the non-profit sector or an entrepreneur. I am a firm believer in social entrepreneurship, social enterprises, and businesses for good. I truly believe that businesses for good and social enterprises have the ability to change the world.

I have seen a lot of non-profit organizations struggle for funds. Businesses that partner with these non-profits can make all the difference in terms of accomplishing the goals of the organization.

I believe that a business must provide value and benefit to all its customers, not be purely profit-driven, and use a portion of its profits to help causes that are changing the world. This is what I seek to accomplish with my business. If I can help others to make more of a difference, then everyone wins. So, my business is itself cause-driven. I also seek to give back through B1G1 and other causes. In this way I can grow and increase the impacts for charities and causes and thereby impact more lives and make a difference to issues facing the planet.

In addition, I share my business model with my clients and many others, encouraging them to adopt a similar business model of giving, being a business for good, and being a social enterprise. Giving is contagious. Love is contagious. It brings great happiness to give, to be of value, to feel of purpose. If more businesses adopt a genuine practice of giving, of being impact-driven, we can totally transform the world.

I believe that we can accomplish the 17 SDGs by 2030 if we all work together. With more enlightened leadership, dedicated NGOs, heart-driven social enterprises, socially responsible corporations, and passionate individuals, we really can achieve these goals.

Human beings are designed for peace and for love. We thrive on those positives, not on war and strife. It may seem like some of these goals remain far for being achieved, but I believe that they are attainable, and as long as I draw breath, I will do my part.

THE LESSON OF A LIFETIME
SUSIE HUTCHISON

Many years ago, I met someone who had the most amazing influence on my life. He was only ten years old, sitting on the sidewalk, obviously homeless, and begging for money in Pokhara, Nepal. His name was Vatsal, which means love and affection.

I am now a well-traveled trekker, but back then I was a first-time tourist to Pokhara and my heart broke when I saw him. Vatsal was a couple of years younger than my son.

We sat in the gutter together and shared a laugh. Over the next week, we swapped Nepali lessons for food. On the day before I left, Vatsal begged me to take him home with me, saying that he was in danger if he stayed on the street.

What could I do? Although I had witnessed many children with troubles, I was totally unprepared for this situation. This was real poverty and I found it heart-wrenching. All I wanted to do was to hug him and give him the love and guidance he deserved. This wasn't to be the case. I sadly explained to him that taking him with me was not possible, I was totally unprepared for the connection we had formed.

The next morning, I saw Vatsal passed out in front of my friend's shop. He had been sniffing glue all night with the older street kids. It was in that moment that I understood the value of giving and providing a "hand up" rather than a handout.

I stayed with him until he dried out and we spoke about his situation. It was devastating. I felt helpless as I had to leave the next day. Before I left, with the help of my local friends, I organized meals for him in return for him doing a little work at a local Nepali restaurant. We also organized a place for him to stay.

I saw him twice more over the next two years. He was well and had moved into a home. He had started to care for the next generation of homeless kids. This brought home the power of a "hand up" and how it can inspire a person to make extraordinary changes.

Although people assume that it was me who changed Vatsal's life, it was in fact Vatsal who changed mine. He took an opportunity and made something from it.

I have since shared many stories about this life-changing experience with the Nepali children I have met. Meeting Vatsal prompted me to start supporting amazing, kind, dedicated, local organizations that really make a difference. They create hope and a better quality of life for the next generation.

I am not alone in this quest. There are many organizations worldwide working to ensure the safety of the next generation. Today, and driven by the Nepalese government, most of the homeless children in Nepal are now off the street and living in orphanages.

I continue to work with Antardristi Nepal to create change in terms of eliminating child sex abuse in Nepal, a difficult issue. Our aim is to create a healing environment and an awareness program so that these kids start to feel peace, support, and understanding. The hope is that they will start to speak about what heals them and feel empowered to continue their life in a proactive and peaceful way.

Our cause, Antardristi Nepal, is conducting a "Break the Silence" campaign throughout Nepal. The aim is that by 2030, and in line with the SDG, all children in Nepal will be able to live in a safe and happy environment. Times have certainly changed and people are now willing to speak out against sexual abuse.

Peace is Not a Privilege, it is a Human Right

Everyone has the right to peace, to live in a peaceful place in an environment that is just.

Peace is not just a word, but also an action and an attitude. I often ask a simple yet powerful question to "reduce" peace to a daily action and attitude.

The question is: What would LOVE think, say, and do?

Let's break it down according to my model:

Peace: Can You Be It?

- If peace is what you desire, even in business, then will you

choose peace? Every day?
- Acknowledge your thoughts, are they of kind intent?
- Listen to your words, are they what love would say?
- Observe your actions, are they what love would do?
- If not, are you OK with your negative thoughts, words and actions?

Justice: Law vs. Lore

There was a time when I didn't really comprehend that "true" law is in fact ancient lore, and that this body of ancient knowledge and wisdom is at the core of our foundation, that is, it's in our DNA.

With this knowledge, I now comprehend that one can police or govern only oneself, and that doing so is the basis for ensuring a happy, loving, and peaceful life. No more, no less. We can NEVER control another, but we can control ourselves.

The current civil and penal laws used by society represent a fear-based system of rules that, if not adhered to, result in punishment. It's odd to think what we humans will do to each other!

The divide is becoming increasingly bigger, with some people enjoying sustained levels of peace, security, and prosperity, while others fall into seemingly endless cycles of internal conflict, resulting in terrible greed and violence.

For me, SDG 16 is all about governing oneself and being comfortable with being peace. This will lead to strong institutions and create "true" justice rather than justice enforced through man-made fear-based laws.

Without policing ourselves, we cannot live in peace, enjoy stability, or care for human rights and personal governance, all of which are required to build effective, accountable strong institutions.

It would be wonderful if we were all able to **stop and police ourselves**.

Only strong discernment regarding your thoughts, words, and actions will work.

The One Question that Needs Answering

If we get the first two things right, then life will respond and allow individuals and institutions to be strong as well as to be what they ultimately wish to be.

Real wealth comes from within. When we, as individuals, step into our peace and govern our thoughts, words and actions, we can really start to comprehend what it takes to create a strong institution in this new Earth.

If you really want to make a difference, there is a strong chance that you already are, but that you just can't see it! You are giving every day in every way by just being you. Just take a moment now, offer gratitude, and acknowledge YOUR thoughts, words, and actions.

Are they serving you, your community, and humanity at large? If they are not, give thanks for the lesson and let them go.

You are present to everyone. It is your choice, so why not make your presence beautiful? And what about building strong businesses?

A business that matters is one concerned with *trust*, which is traditionally defined as consistency over time. It is trust, as well as the business of our customers and partners, that we seek. But it is still important to question why we even have a business or company.

In my case, it is wonderful to be able to share, to work in a team, and to support meaningful projects. I am a great believer that abundance is given so it can be shared. Through these funds, businesses are able to support projects and worthy organizations, to support the fundamental rights of humanity.

Good businesses today have giving embedded within their business philosophy, not only through donating funds, but also through seeking enjoyment when sharing skills and time, "being of service," and helping to create sustainable change.

My friend and colleague Terri Waller from SevGen shared a wise indigenous Australian decision-making process, which is always to ask:

"How is this decision going to affect the next seven generations?"

To me, the above question really says everything necessary about decision making for a sustainable future.

ACTIVISM WITH AWARENESS
JODY ANN JOHNSON

Perhaps the reason why this goal is so important to me is because I grew up in the 1960s and 1970s in Miami. It was the time of the civil rights movement and of both the Vietnam War and the Cold War here in the States. Those years were sprinkled with events that have shaped our world. Shortly after I was born, Fidel Castro came to power in Cuba, and our nation's relationship with Cuba and the plight of Cuban refugees became a huge part of Miami's evolving story. It was the time of Martin Luther King's "I Have a Dream" speech, his marches for black voter registration, and his subsequent assassination in 1968. It was a time of forced desegregation and racial riots.

I had a friend named Warren Butler. He was the only African-American student in our small Catholic school of 300. Our principal, Sister Anthony, was also an African-American, and she took us on field trips to the migrant farms to take food, clothes, and books. My parents, who were people of strong faith and action, had dear friends who were an interracial couple. I didn't grow up with the fear or prejudice others had. On the contrary, I had the direct personal experience of comradery and acceptance.

Other significant events during those decades included President Kennedy being assassinated in 1963, just months after passing a sweeping civil rights legislation. Martin Luther King and presidential candidate Bobby Kennedy were both assassinated within months of each other in 1968. I remember my parents being deeply shaken by these events, and by that time, I was old enough to also have been deeply affected by them. I feel inspired as I reflect on how far we've come and the significant difference the UN's Millennium Development Goals made from 2000 to 2015 in terms of making the world a better place for all.

As an idealistic teenager who marched against the Vietnam War and was appalled by the injustice the civil rights movement sought to address, I prayed for peace and justice. I truly believed that we could change the world; that our protests were very important; that war was stupid, cruel, and destructive; and that it was mainly politically motivated.

As I entered my 20s, I had a child and I began to work. I became less and less involved in the social and civic activism of my youth. I guess I was just consumed with my daily life. At that time, Miami was a city in the throes of drug use, smuggling, and violence. Emerging somewhat under the radar was the gay rights movement and the unfolding AIDS epidemic.

Injustice still abounded in different forms, from domestic violence to wage inequality, from genocide to the exploitation of another country's resources and people, and so on. I just had less time to focus on these things as I worked to establish myself as a single mother.

Still, things bothered me, such as an incident at a church service I attended in South Carolina. The priest said that HIV and AIDS were God's punishment for being gay. One of my dearest friends, Jess, was HIV+. I knew Jess was more a man of God than almost anyone else I knew, so I got up and walked out. Jess died of AIDS in 1998, before the antivirals were mainstream. I created a public service announcement in his honor. A small gesture, more personal.

I'm older now and I'm becoming more like the idealistic teenager I once was. Our planet is becoming a kind of world city rather than individual countries and states. We're more aware and it's much easier to collaborate on solutions. One of my favorite quotes from Martin Luther King states, "there is no deficit in human resources, the deficit is in human will."

In the absence of peace and justice human beings can be wounded. Sometimes, they are wounded in ways that may seem irreparable, impossible to overcome. People can be wounded inside even through just witnessing injustice, and this includes the effects of war at the nation-to-nation level, as well as the effects of things directly witnessed inside the home on a person-to-person level.

Before going into business, I was the clinical manager of the emergency department of a large teaching hospital. One night, a woman walked in complaining of pain from a burn. When we brought her into the treatment area as she undressed, to our horror we saw that she had numerous burns all over her body from an iron of the kind used to press clothing.

The man she was living with had been torturing her in this way for a long time. One night, while he was out, she climbed out the window using a sheet and walked several miles to our ER. We called the police; however, she wouldn't tell them where he was or what his name was; she was terrified of him finding her. She told me that both she and her mother had been severely beaten for most of her life. It took a surgeon and I the better part of the night to debride her infected wounds. Mercifully, we gave her a medication known for its sedative and amnesic effects so she wouldn't feel anything.

That night represented a kind of existential event for me. I wanted to go home and drink that sight away, drink those feelings of helplessness and hopelessness away, but I knew it wouldn't work. I decided to go home and paint instead, rather than doing something self-destructive, even if the end result was terrible, it would serve as a way to get the feelings out. This led to the creation of a project, and eventually, to a non-profit called "Healing Thru Arts" with my sisters and some friends. The premise of the non-profit was to use art as a means of healing what people couldn't or wouldn't talk about. We worked with sexual abuse victims, with domestic violence victims and their children, and with teenage girls who were both in jail and pregnant in a maximum-security women's prison and in a juvenile detention center.

Even when we finally achieve peace and justice, there will still be work that needs to be done to heal the wounds of the spirit. It will take institutions strong enough to stay the course of what we're building through these SDGs. It is my hope that we will sustain our will.

On a positive note, the patient I described went into a shelter and began healing in terms of her mind, body, and spirit. She became a leader for the other women there and put her life back together. Years later, one of the police officers involved that night told me that the man who had tortured her for all those years had been brought to justice. Never give up hope regarding the strength of human beings to overcome and turn the most adverse circumstances into something good.

Small Business is the Backbone

Small business is the backbone of the global economy. Most small business owners have a skill or a passion and then go about creating a business around it. However, while skill and passion are important, many lack the knowledge required to run a successful business.

A successful business contributes to the community in many ways. Of course, it has team members whose wages are paid, vendors whose supplies are purchased, and a product or service that meets people's needs and/or wants.

Another dimension of a business that matters concerns the involved business leaders and the ways in which they model leadership and stewardship in both their business and the communities they serve.

Today, many businesses are becoming more focused on the triple bottom line of people, purpose, and profits, as well as on the concepts of sustainability and giving back. There is a growing distaste for waste of any kind and a growing appetite for sustainability. The ideas of making profit and doing good aren't at odds, they can coexist. As Peter Diamandis states, "The best way to become a billionaire is to solve a billion-person problem."

Business leaders and their teams have this sort of ability and power on a very small, local scale, as well as on a global scale. People in business are now combining their values, beliefs, creativity, and energy with the spiritual dimension of something bigger than profits, bigger than themselves. We became certified giving partners with B1G1 several years ago, and we have found it to be an ideal vehicle for making a difference through our routine business practices. It's an important aspect of creating a more conscious business, one that is aligned with our values and purpose in life.

My ultimate legacy is to be peace.

I read Pema Chödrön's book *When Things Fall Apart* some years ago, and while she's amazing, there are times when I read something and I had to stop and put the book down. The following was just such a sentence. "Moment by moment you have to ask yourself, am I going to practice peace, or am I going to go to war?" That sentence really messed me up when I read it because I knew there were times when I chose war, especially with my husband. Today, I'm clear that the dynamic that causes war in my home is the same dynamic that causes war in the Middle East. Practices for peace here in my home are the same practices that bring peace around the world. Having read that sentence, I can never not be aware of the fact that, ultimately, I am responsible for channeling peace so that it spreads.

"You never change things by fighting the existing reality. To change something, build a new model that makes the existing model obsolete."
– Buckminster Fuller

The global partners of the UN's Sustainable Development Goals and B1G1 are building new models that can render the dysfunctional models of the past obsolete. The more we think, discuss, raise awareness, collaborate, and take action, the more we create a world that works for everyone.

WHAT YOU CAN DO TO
CREATE A WORLD OF PEACE, JUSTICE AND STRONG INSTITUTIONS

Lifestyle tips:
- Know your rights.
- Peace and justice start within.
- Vote. Take advantage of your right to elect the leaders.

Business tips:
- Create a collaborative and peaceful workplace.
- Stay educated about changes in local regislations.

Giving tips:
- Support programs that prevent abuse and human-trafficking.
- Sponsor legal cost for those who cannot afford them.

YOU ARE A
GLOBAL PARTNER

17 PARTNERSHIPS FOR THE GOALS

HOW YOU AND YOUR BUSINESS CAN STRENGTHEN
THE MEANS OF IMPLEMENTATION AND
REVITALIZE THE GLOBAL PARTNERSHIP
FOR SUSTAINABLE DEVELOPMENT.

"Alone we can do so little; together we can do so much."

— Helen Keller

THE CHANGEMAKERS

CORPORATE SOCIAL RESPONSIBILITY: WHAT IT REALLY MEANS
LINDA SADDLEMIRE

Linda is the principal in charge of the Glendora, California, office of CliftonLarsonAllen (CLA). She has thirty-six years of experience in public accounting. Her expertise includes managing hundreds of audits and overseeing investigations concerning government fraud, public corruption, and other white-collar crimes. Linda is also a certified public accountant (CPA), a certified fraud examiner (CFE), and certified in financial forensics (CFF). Linda teaches accounting and finance and has a doctorate in organizational leadership.

claconnect.com

THE NEW ERA OF ENTREPRENEURSHIP
MONTY HOOKE

Monty Hooke is a serial entrepreneur and business mentor from Australia. Monty has decades of experience understanding what it takes for small businesses to scale. Residing in the Philippines, Monty runs his business consulting and offshore staffing company, The Exponential. The Exponential enables SMEs to scale globally by building their teams, systems, and technology. Monty is a highly sought-after speaker and educator. He is also on the boards of several companies as a trusted advisor.

exponential.business

BEHIND EVERY STATISTIC IS A PERSON
KAREN LONGWITH

Karen is the founder and director of 21st Century Podiatry. Karen learned about the lack of truly effective treatments for a variety of foot conditions when her mother underwent a double amputation. She searched for a treatment that offered a 90 percent chance of success and her first business, Eliminaser was born. With patented laser treatment serving as its backbone, this pioneering business has now grown into a full-scale podiatry clinic: 21st Century Podiatry.

21stpodiatry.co.uk

YOU ARE A
GLOBAL PARTNER

It's not unusual for people to have a great idea based on a strong belief or a conviction they hold. And frequently they want to "go it alone," to do it themselves.

Yet, almost always, the real key to making our individual endeavors highly successful is to know how to involve others; how to create effective partnerships towards our goals. There are all sorts of reasons for that; others might bring important new perspectives, perspectives that help us see obstacles or opportunities we could never see on our own.

Yves Daccord, the Director-General of the International Committee of the Red Cross (ICRC) in Geneva creates and maintains extraordinary partnerships around the world. He has held this significant post as a global leader since 2010 and his ICRC career has spanned more than two decades in a variety of posts and challenging contexts – including Israel and the Occupied Territories, Sudan, Yemen, Chechnya. And as a former journalist, TV producer and international relations expert, he possesses a deep understanding – and an extraordinary sense of optimism – of the intricate social, cultural and human conditions that play a part in creating new directions.

Because of those experiences, it's perfectly fitting that Yves helps begin the dialogue for us to explore the 'Partnerships for the Goals'. Here he is:

The pathways we've set ourselves for the SDGs, like many pathways, have hazards or obstacles in the way to achieving them.

The obstacles don't prevent achievement of the goals; being aware of them now helps us find ways over, round and through them, to bring all of humanity into realising and enjoying the promises of the goals. So let's look at how we can deal with the obstacles that conflict and violence bring up.

The SDGs will undoubtedly face their biggest test in countries affected by conflict and violence, where development gains are often very quickly reversed. Take Yemen, for example. Four years of armed conflict was all it took to set the country back to its human development index of 20 years ago. In Syria, a similar reversal took even less time: just two years.

These are precisely the sorts of countries where humanitarian organizations like the International Committee of the Red Cross (ICRC) are most active, working to protect and assist affected people and communities. As wars drag on for longer and longer, the needs become broader and deeper. The response becomes ever more challenging, making the line between emergency relief and longer-term development more blurred.

The SDGs are designed to serve as the basis of a new global contract between and within nations, between leaders and people, to ensure that "no-one is left behind." Yet, real change in this regard – harnessing the power of humanity - will come from the ground up.

Take my own organization, the ICRC, for example. We have many extraordinarily talented and committed people, each making a valuable contribution in their own right.

People like my colleague Alberto, a physiotherapist, who has spent the past three decades in Afghanistan, setting up orthopedic programs that have helped many thousands of people with disabilities. Like Claudine, a psychologist caring for people with mental health and psycho-social need in Mali. Liliana, a forensic specialist in Colombia. Mira, visiting people in detention in Iraq, helping to ensure they are treated humanely. And the more than 16,000 other colleagues in over 80 countries around the world, often working in extremely challenging environments.

And as the circle widens, so the reach – and strength – of response deepens. The ICRC is part of the Red Cross and Red Crescent Movement, a global humanitarian network with many millions of volunteers.

Beyond the movement, we work with a diverse range of partners, including the private sector, seeking and co-creating innovative solutions to a range of humanitarian challenges. Examples include the use of mobile technologies in improving humanitarian access in remote and conflict-affected locations; energy solutions for ICRC health structures in the field and the development of innovative finance mechanisms for the delivery of aid.

Such partnerships are about much more than just money. They're about pooling ideas, expertise and resources to help some of the world's most vulnerable people. They're about making a stand for the basic principle of humanity in the face of suffering on a vast scale. With the World Bank predicting that in just over 10 years from now, 46% of the global population will be living in fragile and unstable situations, they're about trying to tip the balance in the right direction.

Given the enormity and complexity of the challenge, collaboration, partnership and reaching out to join forces with like-minded people or organizations is vital. When taken together and properly channeled, each individual contribution, each humanitarian gesture – no matter how small – be it from a volunteer or a corporation, amounts to a potentially massive force for good, a force for alleviating suffering.

Movements like B1G1 help focus the combined power of businesses worldwide to make it happen. This book and the people who helped write it are a great example of the collaboration needed to provide a much bigger impact than each one of us can make alone.

And of course, each one of us who reads Legacy can be inspired to act on just one seemingly small thing. And in today's world, that seemingly tiny thing can be amplified through Global Partnerships like never before.

— *Yves Daccord*

Yves' inspiring words are another example of how all of us can be the real changemaker, a global partner to drive our future direction together.

We can often think of ourselves as alone, yet we belong to a much larger species.

Psychologists remind us that one of our core human needs is to belong. To feel part of a collective tribe. To have a sense of being included. Yet on the flipside, society also honors the rebel, the hero, the leader who is willing to go-it-alone and step ahead of the masses.

Changemaker Linda Saddlemire reminds us of the unique South African, Nguni Bantu term "Ubuntu" meaning "humanity." This term is often translated as "I am because we are." That we only exist fully in all our glory and potential because of each other.

Archbishop Desmond Tutu discussed Ubuntu in his book, *No Future Without Forgiveness*. He wrote:

A person with Ubuntu is open and available to others, affirming of others, does not feel threatened that others are able and good, based from a proper self-assurance that comes from knowing that he or she belongs in a greater whole and is diminished when others are humiliated or diminished, when others are tortured or oppressed.

Ubuntu and its deeper meaning isn't meant to be isolated to a single group or one particular culture. The essence of Ubuntu is humanity. And the principles of *Unbuntu* can be applied everywhere. In partnerships, in life and in business.

Imagine if there was a global movement toward this. Imagine that local communities, nations, governments and organizations didn't attempt to battle each other but instead formed healthy partnerships. Imagine we changed our thinking.

There are situations (sometimes personal tragedies) that arise that change our thinking. Extraordinary changemaker Karen Longwith has done what many preach but often fail to do, and that is – she stood up to be the change. She took a personal tragedy and dedicated herself to ensuring others wouldn't have to endure the same fate. She helps us remember what, or more accurately *who* is behind every statistic we read.

Entrepreneur and changemaker Monty Hooke focuses on *who* as well. He provides us with a fresh look at business partnerships and also the deeper connections that happen within business. Monty is a boss with heart, he shows a new way forward and offers a perspective that so many business leaders could follow. He shows that employees are people not numbers or robots. He is what this chapter is all about – A Global Partner.

Now it's time for you to become that too.

CORPORATE SOCIAL RESPONSIBILITY: WHAT IT REALLY MEANS
LINDA SADDLEMIRE

My awareness of this goal began during my education and expanded through a personal interest in the topic. About fifteen years ago, I enrolled in the executive MBA program at the Peter F. Drucker and Masatoshi Ito Graduate School of Management in Claremont, California. This program introduced me to the concept of corporate social responsibility (CSR). I was struck by the power of the connection and influence that the business world can have in terms of addressing societal needs. This sparked my interest in strengthening my own 'company's community involvement activities and I became the leader of our CSR program.

Several years later, I attended a doctoral program in organizational leadership at the University of La Verne in Southern California. It took my interest further and I chose corporate social responsibility as the topic of my dissertation research. I was deeply drawn to the work of J.E. Liebig, who states that "business has become the most pervasive and influential institution in world society."[1] The conceptual framework for my research was based on, and supported by, his empirical research concerning visionary leaders, which defines the common threads of social responsibility as "their local and global concerns for 1) enhancing social equity, 2) protecting our natural environment, 3) enabling human creativity, and 4) seeking to serve higher purposes."[2]

Although my research was specific to my profession of public accounting, the depth of my learning about this topic heightened my awareness of the importance of strategic partnerships between business, government, and non-profit entities. Mackey and Sisodia's

---

1 J.E. Liebig, "The merchants and their visions," in *Leading organizations: Perspectives for a new era*, ed. R.G. Hickman (London: Sage, 1998), 499-502, 499.
2 J.E. Liebig, "The merchants and their visions," in *Leading organizations: Perspectives for a new era*, ed. R.G. Hickman (London: Sage, 1998), 499-502. 500.

concept of conscious capitalism also resonates with me in that, as business leaders, our businesses' purpose can and should go beyond creating shareholder wealth to include working toward having a positive impact on the world and the environment.[3] As a business leader, I am committed to this concept, while as a citizen and a consumer, I tend to support like-minded businesses. This SDG supports the notion that it will take more than donations of money to achieve change, it will take real strategic partnerships.

"Partnerships for the Goals" resonates and inspires me because it supports the deep connectivity we have with one another across the globe as well as the power of what we can achieve if we work collaboratively on enhancing social equity in our world. As reported in the United Nations Global Compact's (2013) *Global Corporate Sustainability Report*, there are currently 1.2 billion people living in extreme poverty, millions of young people with no prospect of employment, and one-third of the population living in countries without access to clean water. It will take a joint effort between businesses, governments, non-profit organizations, and individuals to address and make positive changes in these areas. As both a business leader and a global citizen, this goal is one of extreme importance and value to me and to humanity in general.

My travels to South Africa in 2006 probably had the most profound impact on me. I was a guest on the University of La Verne – "Violence, Resistance and Reconciliation: Women's Perspectives on Apartheid in South Africa" program. We visited Robben Island (where Nelson Mandela was imprisoned), the CSVR (Centre for the Study of Violence and Reconciliation), community centers, and Mandela's home. But the most memorable visits were to the townships.

Here I witnessed unimaginable living conditions. No running water, no electricity, floors and beds made of dirt, roofs made of battered tin. I will never forget the smells. I have such a vivid memory of looking into the eyes of the children and feeling the

---

3   John Mackey and Raj Sisodia, *Conscious capitalism: Liberating the heroic spirit of business* (Boston, MA: Harvard Business Review Press, 2013).

tightness of their grip as they held my hand. It was at that moment that I felt our deep connection to each other. It brought to life the meaning of the African term "Ubuntu," which is often translated as "I am because we are."

I remember that after visiting Kayamandi, we returned to our very nice hotel in a vineyard overlooking the township. Experiencing such an obvious and stark inequity, many of us experienced an emotional collapse that evening. When I arrived home, I knew that I needed to find a way to better conditions like these. I just didn't know how.

Shortly after I returned home, I met Paul Dunn and Masami Sato. They were introducing the concept of B1G1 at an AICPA conference in Las Vegas. It was there that things converged: my place as a business leader and my deep desire to be connected to global needs. I immediately presented B1G1 to my Partners, and we became one of the first, US mid-sized accounting firms to join B1G1. It was a dream come true.

Shortly after we sent three employees on a B1G1 study tour to India. This proved to be a transformational experience for our employees. Listening to their stories when they returned has been one of the highlights of my career as a business leader thus far, and it had nothing to do with accounting.

Let me share a very personal story with you. In 2015, my father was diagnosed with bone cancer. Together with my mother, my five siblings and several of the grandchildren, I was by his side as we said goodbye. One day later, our mother, who was grieving the loss of her husband of 61 years, had a massive heart attack and also died. Losing both parents in a two-day time frame was heart-wrenching and almost unbearable. Extraordinary circumstances stirred an extraordinary response on the part of the employees of Vicenti. In memory of our parents, they contributed 27,500 days of medical support for Ethiopian nursey school children through B1G1. This had special meaning for my family, since one of the grandchildren was adopted from Ethiopia. Giving to others was a wonderful way for them to support us.

CARE = Community – Action – Responsibility – Environment

A business that matters is one that has a purpose beyond making profits. My dissertation research showed that aligning a company's commitment to community involvement is a way to add to the company's purpose and demonstrate the authenticity and motive behind such efforts. Having the purpose stated clearly also serves as a signal that there is sufficient infrastructure to meet the objectives.

At Vicenti, our purpose was "to make a positive difference to our clients, people, and the world in which we live." Our infrastructure included a CARE (community – action – responsibility – environment) committee that had a partner-liaison and that was led by employees. Vicenti sponsored two local initiatives per year, one to support a social need, such as food pantries, educational support, or medical research, and the other to support environment needs; things like beach clean-ups, planting trees, adopting a park, or recycling events. Of course, these events had the added benefit of building teams and helping employees to get to know each other.

In addition, our global giving was done through B1G1. Every year, employees chose a project during tax season, and we gave to that project throughout the season as we completed the returns. We provided water, education, and vitamin E pills to various countries. We also tied B1G1 giving to recruiting activities, new clients, our 60th anniversary, and other public presentations.

In 2017, Vicenti became part of CLA. The purpose of CLA is "to create opportunities for our clients, people, and communities." With such similar purposes, the merger was a good fit and we now added 20 hours of paid time for volunteering as well as a wellness program tied to keeping healthy emotionally, physically, and financially. When an employee logs activities that support this conception of wellness, they earn kudos, which the firm turns into donations to an organization selected by the employee from a set list of entities. One employee earned $1,200 for the humane society just by logging his running for the year.

Through its own foundation, CLA has the goal of providing $1 million per year in grants to non-profit entities that support education, employment, and entrepreneurship for diverse populations. With the nominations for grants coming from CLA employees. CLA partners with Junior Achievement and with American Corporate Partners and provides hands-on volunteering, mentoring, financial literacy training, and financial support to these organizations throughout the country. These are examples of SDG 17 at work.

The Final Legacy

I hope that my leadership as a business owner has inspired others to keep the spirit of doing business for good alive. I hope that the infrastructure around local and global community involvement continues to grow after I retire. I hope too that I can be influential in establishing a robust CSR infrastructure through my role as a consultant to a team that is currently developing a new CSR program. Social partnerships will be a key factor in this plan.

As a new member of the board, I am excited and honored to be part of the B1G1 movement in the United States.

Finally, I hope that linking business to the common good provides a framework for you and, of course, my family – my siblings, nieces and nephews, and great-nieces and great-nephews – as they live their lives. My hope is that caring for people and our planet will be the light that guides them.

THE NEW ERA OF ENTREPRENEURSHIP
MONTY HOOKE

We live in a new era of entrepreneurship. The most successful businesses should not be measured by profit, but rather by impact. The amazing thing is that it's those businesses that are empowered to impact that have now become the most financially successful.

In 2019, I made my boldest business decision yet. I decided to take a business that was already successful and turn it purely toward making an impact. The Exponential was born to help impart as much energy and light to the UN's SDGs as possible.

On its own, each SDG is an amazing platform for businesses to be able to channel their purpose, energy, culture, services, and products to help solve the world's most meaningful problems. But for myself, I feel a responsibility to bring light to the goals themselves. It inspires me to show businesses the importance of not merely waiting for abundance before giving, since it's the giving that brings you abundance.

I didn't always understand this on a deep level. I've spent a lifetime in business, and for most of that time, I felt like I was chasing my tail. I was doing what I thought I was supposed to do, that is, to build a business for money. Of course, there's nothing wrong with that, but I felt unfulfilled.

I launched my first business at only eight years of age. It was born not out of any kind of love for entrepreneurship, but rather out of pain due to needing to fend for myself. Some of the best entrepreneurs, and the high achievers in any arena, have the same innate determination to succeed, often driven by some sort of unconscious pain or feeling of lack.

But at some point, the driving force needs to flip. It needs to move from avoiding pain and toward creating joy, kindness, and abundance for yourself and those around you. Inevitably, bringing abundance to the world.

I believe that every business owner has some positive force that they can tap into, not just to create greater success, but also to foster joy and fulfillment. Having a cause greater than ourselves is actually our responsibility as entrepreneurs. It's something we hear about a lot, but when you have responsibilities and bills to pay, it's another matter to embody it rather than to just understand it.

For myself, it has taken a long time to foster the courage to live in a way that embodies this desire to use my business as a force for good and to give myself fully to helping others build businesses that allow them the opportunity to do the same. But the time is here and the journey has been worth every mile.

More than Just Business

Living and working in the Philippines has been both humbling and eye-opening. Having a team in a developing country where there's a lot of poverty and hardship has allowed me to experience firsthand the contribution that a profitable business can make simply through employing people in the Philippines.

We look after our staff, pay them above-average wages and also pay for health insurance and other benefits to make sure they are being looked after. Here in the Philippines, the salaries of those we employ pay to look after multiple generations of families. It's not like in Australia, where everyone fends for themselves. Life in the Philippines is tough, and many people have a huge responsibility to provide for many others.

Staff members have often invited me to their family home for dinner; usually because they want to express their gratitude for helping them to provide for the family. It's a great feeling to know that we do not just provide jobs for individuals, but also help to support whole communities via those jobs.

It's that feeling that stirs my entrepreneurial heart and makes me want to spread further contributions through as many channels as possible. Not just by providing more jobs, but by being inspired to always check the compass of purpose to ensure our business is headed in the right direction.

For many years, "Ezy VA" (prior to the pivot to The Exponential) did a great job in terms of helping business owners to scale and become more successful through building offshore teams. But the issue was that the service we provided didn't match the product. Our product was offshore virtual staff, but what we delivered was in-depth consulting, planning, systems, and mentoring, in addition to the offshore staff.

It was great in the sense that those clients who valued what we delivered really loved us. But the value went missing with a lot of clients, which was frustrating, although it was no fault of theirs that our business model didn't match our value.

I think this is a valuable lesson for entrepreneurs. It's easy to get caught in the trap of bending your business model to the mold of what you think the market is willing to pay for. However, this will ultimately lead to frustration, as it did with me.

There is boldness in understanding your value and creating a brand and suite of products or services that are congruent with your highest value. This is the energy and culture of purpose, innovation, and abundance. This is the new paradigm of better business, which will ultimately open up bigger and better opportunities, ones that you didn't know existed while you were trapped in the mindset of keeping your business safe and simply paying the bills.

This upgraded paradigm is a "business of purpose." It becomes the springboard to using your business to make a social contribution. This is the beautiful thing about the B1G1 movement. It's not just about giving businesses the platform to "give," since it's also a movement of businesses of purpose – at a time when the world needs it the most.

At The Exponential, our vision is to create a world of impact-driven businesses, thereby bringing abundance and positive change to the world. Our mission is to empower and enable entrepreneurs and small businesses to do their "life's biggest work" by providing mentoring, tools, and resources. Together, we can create a life and legacy of positive impact.

While we pride ourselves on providing the best staffing services, offices, and resources in the Philippines, our objective is to scale mission-driven businesses. Our purpose is to help bring this new paradigm to as many businesses as possible, enabling such businesses to partner with the SDGs so as to facilitate change through their own purpose.

Give Before You Can Afford It

It might sound counterproductive to give when you're still building your business. In fact, taking resources away from more measurable activities related to your business growth, such as marketing and advertising, might seem silly. But giving now, rather than waiting, changes the game. It changes your culture. It changes your persona. It changes how you interact with the market and deepens the relationships you have with clients and customers.

It's not about the amount you give. It's the habit of giving that's most important. Pick a cause that you are passionate about and commit to something you can do each week or month. Involve your team. Get them to help you be part of the process and witness the positive effect it has on the business.

Don't wait until you're enjoying abundance to give. It's the giving that brings you abundance.

My ultimate legacy is to help build as many mission-driven businesses as possible, either through my own companies, other businesses that I'm partnered with, or those that I mentor. I love helping businesses to scale. It's what I'm great at.

Yet, the key to a better life and business is fulfillment. We all want happiness. We all want abundance. We all too often skip over the "why" and "purpose" while looking for the next tactic that will bring in more leads and money. It is a poor attempt to fill the human need for fulfillment.

The best tactics in the world mean nothing if your life doesn't have meaning. Business can be an amazing vehicle with which to create a life of meaning, but it can also get us trapped in a cycle of chasing money.

But with the right purpose and the right meaning for the business owner, huge things are possible.

Changing the world will take a lot of us all playing a small part. But what if we played a bigger part? What if we thought bigger and built bigger? Not for the sake of looking bigger, but rather for a *better business*, a *better life*, and a *better world*.

BEHIND EVERY STATISTIC IS A PERSON
KAREN LONGWITH

Everyone's reasons for starting a business or committing to a specific cause are, quite naturally, individual.

My mother had what most people would consider to be a small health issue, the worst-case scenario of "nasty toenails." For a fit and healthy individual, the condition is generally just unsightly – a fungal infection that causes discoloration and thickening, and if nothing is done, usually nothing more severe than losing a toenail (or two, or a few!).

Unfortunately, my mother was not in the best of health. She was mobile only via a wheelchair owing to a stroke that had caused permanent left-side paralysis some years earlier. For my mother, unsightly nails resulted in a double amputation, with the surgeries occurring a painful (or rather, agonizing) eight months apart.

At the time, I didn't change the course of my career. I did so a couple of years later after reading more research. But rather than my reading about the treatment of various foot issues, or the health service itself, it was a footnote that galvanized me into action.

The footnote told the reader that major amputations came with a known three-, five-, or seven-year mortality rate. My mother had died a little over 2.5 years after her first operation.

My mother's suffering was not a footnote. It was not a strike mark making up a statistic. A statistic that showed this was happening thousands of times every year. And the literature said that the incidence of this issue, while declining throughout most of the First World, was rising in the UK.

Tracing the need for amputation back to a specific condition (those nasty toenails), I found out that new technology was about to be released in the coming months that could hopefully – painlessly and non-invasively – eliminate the initial complaint, which had developed into a terrible secondary issue requiring an operation.

The technology worked.

However, there was little uptake in the use of the technology because of its price tag. So I bought a machine! And since 2014, and with much trialing of protocols, I am now successfully treating those "nasty nails." Since 2017, I have been training other medical professionals to do the same. I have also expanded the number of services we offer that provide non-surgical treatment pathways, are pain-free, are non-invasive, and have no side effects. Such services are suitable for even the most at-risk individuals.

I haven't yet been able to stop others from undergoing operations, but I am starting to be invited to the table. I have become part of the networks that are also looking to bring about a change, such as Diabetes UK and trial forums. I have been making information about what works more easily available, providing more and better support, and allowing other practitioners to learn about better treatment options. Kinder options. More effective options. I am creating an environment in which care is paramount and affordable.

I wouldn't have it any other way.

When I first thought about starting my own enterprise, I knew it had to be something that contributed more than was already available. If all I was going to do was offer the same thing that you could get at any other practice, I simply wouldn't have done it. I was lucky in that a new solution was becoming available for a specific health problem that I was looking to provide more effective treatment for, and I was able to be a pioneer in the field.

In short, I had to have a business that mattered. There didn't seem to be any point in starting otherwise.

Offering the most effective and non-invasive treatments that we've sourced from across the globe gives us the confidence that we are providing the best care available in our niche. With that as a foundation, we can look outside the clinic for other ways to be useful to our community as we continue to work toward attaining our main goal, which has never wavered. We are now starting to make real headway toward our goal of reducing amputation rates in both the UK and worldwide, and our success is visible for all to see via our "Impact" page, a completely separate and dedicated page on our website.

Now that the enterprise has grown, so too has our ability to engage and partner. For instance, we have signed up to the Armed Forces Covenant, thereby committing the clinic to working out a route to employment for ex-services personnel. We have also engaged with Diabetes UK and several other health initiatives to expand knowledge of the successful remission of Type II (or "Lifestyle") Diabetes. The more we do, the more we can do. For me, that's what makes a business matter. And how it continues to do so.

Real Solutions Demand Engagement

SDG 17, "Partnership for the Goals," is particularly important because it makes a person think bigger. As such, it is an inherent component of the make-up of our clinic, and it is applicable at every level of operation.

For instance, when we're looking to onboard new clinicians, learning what they believe to be their role in solving population-level problems is something I believe to be a necessity due to the nature of contemporary healthcare.

Being aligned with the SDGs provides a deeper connection with our clientele. Our clients are always interested when we bring up the wider initiatives the clinic is involved with. In turn, we learn more about where their passions lie and the activities that they, their children, and their other loved ones are engaged in.

Suppliers and industry contacts immediately realize that a bigger game is being played. We've been asked to take part in the trialing of new equipment and technology, and we've been invited to participate in what would normally be "closed-door" conversations and arenas. This is directly related to the scope of application and the commitment that discussion of the SDGs infers.

SDG 17, "Partnership for the Goals," is always an inspiration, because it demands a broader, longer-term vision. You cannot simply pay lip service or use it as a marketing tool. It requires passion and commitment, as well as local and global awareness, to be a goal and principle discussed with integrity.

It means that we provide the best services and tools available to tackle some of the hardest problems, and that we achieve the best outcomes for the individuals we treat. It makes us responsible for enabling more people to live better lives because our business exists than they would if it didn't.

For a long time, this goal seemed far out of reach. But by reaching out to others who were also working toward affiliated and parallel goals, determining where our visions aligned, and becoming partners, the road to achieving those goals became clearer and linked in with other, wider initiatives.

It seems that this goal is both separate and all-encompassing. It asks for more engagement. It takes more patience and perseverance. But aligning with this goal and facilitating increased efforts with other professionals, national bodies, forums, and sectors in order to meet the 2030 deadline, is a true legacy objective.

The ultimate legacy for me would be to reduce amputations stemming from lifestyle illnesses. Year after year. Across the globe. First as a result of better intervention by the medical world for those who are currently suffering. Then, as more and better information and engagement programs are created, because the alarmingly high incidence of lifestyle illnesses in First World countries declines.

Partner with Pride

I encourage all enterprises to remember that what they're doing locally is contributing both nationally and globally. Seeking out others who have a similar reason for doing what they do has helped in so many ways.

Not only as a means of contributing to your cause, but as a way of drawing strength from finding such a network or making those connections, as well as thinking laterally and reaching out to affiliated industries regarding education or charity work already being conducted. I believe that the more niche your route to your goal, the more this will apply.

Have a voice. Even if it's small and tiny at first. Start to hear yourself, whether written online or offline, or spoken on a stage or in a meeting room. Get used to talking about what matters to you so that you can then have a comfortable conversation with possible business partners, think tanks, or policymakers.

Injustice inflames me. I'm simply not OK knowing that these things are happening in the world. That's my passion!

The other side to this is that I look to inject time into my interactions. To consider, to enjoy, whether with other people, flora, fauna, or any part of the natural world. I want to find the spaces where nurturing and dignity reign.

Partnership really is a cornerstone belief for me.

That's my sunshine.

WHAT YOU CAN DO TO
CREATE A WORLD OF
PARTNERSHIPS FOR THE GOALS

Lifestyle tips:
- Use your connections to empower changemakers.
- Engage in dialogues with others. Actively exchange ideas.

Business tips:
- Choose one of the SDGs and do your best to make a change.
- Inspire your team, customers, clients and suppliers to become changemakers.
- Participate in sustainability education events and programs.

Giving tips:
- Belong to a like-minded community or a movement.
- Support and fund a variety of change-making programs.
- If you run a business, join B1G1 and make a difference.

THE FINAL CHAPTER
A journey of a small one

As you close this book, let me assure you of this: you've made a difference. Simply by reading this book, you've helped create these amazing impacts:

- You've helped build one well in a community in Ethiopia to give people access to clean water which prevents water-borne diseases and helps people have more time to pursue greater opportunities.
- If you purchased a paperback book, one tree gets planted to preserve our natural eco-system.
- If you purchased a digital version, at least one child received educational support for a day.

If you purchased this book from one of the co-authors, another impact got created with a project that the author selected.

The moment you connected with this book and resonated with any one of the chapters, you became part of this special new direction. No matter how ready (or not) you feel to do what you believe in, you are already on track.

Whether you are a business owner, planning to become one or whether you're a team member of a business, government, NGO or family, you can help create great change in your surroundings. And as you do what you do with a genuine intention to care and share your gift, you make a difference today and tomorrow.

When the idea of B1G1 was conceived in 2006, a group of business owners asked, "imagine if every time business was done, something great also happened."

Let's imagine that world together now.

- *Imagine if every time you buy a coffee, someone receives access to life-saving water.*
- *Imagine if every time a book is sold, a tree gets planted.*
- *Imagine if every time someone goes to a doctor, someone else receives much-needed care.*

This was the world of B1G1 (BUY1GIVE1) we imagined. It seemed like a very simple yet impossible idea.

In 2007, a social enterprise, B1G1, was founded as a global giving initiative. And since then, one by one, thousands of businesses have chosen to join and make it a reality. Today, B1G1 works with more than 2,700 businesses creating over 180 million giving impacts.

And as we venture out to do even more, projects like this book have come about to spread the message together – not just about the stories of B1G1 but also even more about 'how small really matters'.

We are grateful for all the B1G1 members who've taken the initiative to participate in this book. We're also grateful for the global leaders who kindly offered to share their perspectives in this book recognizing the power of small businesses in the world.

After all, it's about you, your small steps and your commitment to use your life as a real force for good. We look forward to connecting with you as we explore our own endeavors to create a world where every person is lifted to their greatest potential.

Paul Dunn and Masami Sato
The B1G1 Founders

THANK YOU....
To find out more about the B1G1 initiative, visit: **b1g1.com**
To find out more about the Sustainable Development Goals, visit:
sustainabledevelopment.un.org

Share this book with your friends and make a greater impact together:
b1g1.com/legacy-interactive

PUBLISHER'S NOTE

Susan Dean

I once read a quote by H.E Luccock that said, "No one can whistle a symphony. It takes a whole orchestra to play it."

Such is the case with this book.

The unique assortment of authors, voices, ideas and suggestions are much like the orchestral instruments of woodwinds, strings, brass and percussion — all playing their specific role in perfect harmony with the whole. All different, yet blending together as one symphony for the sake of an even grander intention: to change the world one reader at a time.

And this book can change the world. That's because this book is crafted not just to be a read but a book to inspire action. A united action, a plethora of actions that truly can alter our future and create a sustainable world. In this sense, the title *Legacy* couldn't be more fitting.

When I think of leaving a legacy, I think that my part in the grand scheme is to publish books like this. To amplify messages with meaning and distribute them all over the world. To give authors and speakers a platform and a product that can change the lives of others near and far.

I am proud to publish the collective voices in this book. They are not only inspiring and unique people but their advice, their experience and their practical suggestions are tried-and-tested. They are people who have lived, loved, learned. And they are determined to leave this world in a better state than they found it. They really are changemakers.

As a conscious publishing group, our team is also part of the change. We too are B1G1 members and part of the giving movement. Our business aligns with the Global Goals and supports all 17 of them in a multitude of ways: tree planting, literacy programs, hiring practices, gender equality, global partnerships and many more.

As Masami and Paul have mentioned, for every book sold, something great happens. Just like the SDGs require a united effort to achieve successful outcomes — so did this book.

Without the dedication, passion and effort of my amazing team this book would not be the life-changing read it is. Behind the glamour of international book publishing there are many hard-working people that bring a book to life, especially a book with this many authors. And for their incredible efforts I would like to acknowledge them.

Editor-in-chief and writer, Natalie Deane. A woman whose professionalism and dedication to creating world-changing books is second to none. She's not only our chief editor but also a gifted writer who penned many of the chapter introductions.

Creative designer, Jazmine Morales. Her creative flair and design skill made this book shine. She is the humble genius behind the striking cover and formatting design. A very talented woman indeed.

Marketing and media director, Monique Dean. A multi-skilled woman whose incredible energy and organization is paramount to our success. She never wavers from our united goals and is a consummate professional in all our publishing operations.

I'd also like to acknowledge Paul, Masami and the entire B1G1 team for their collaborative support and the amazing Dean Publishing team as a whole. I would specifically like to mention Mauraid Clayton, Chloe Dean, Michael Dean for their dedication, support and efforts across the board: accounts, proofreading, events, book launches and media.

I have always known that books can change the world. Of course, it's not the book itself, it's the words that come alive on the page. It's the poignant messages that trigger action and change perceptions.

Please don't just read this book and stuff it back in your bookshelf. This book is not just in print. We want to keep its powerful message alive and active. Evergreen. And because of this, as stated on page 160, we have made this book interactive in the Dean Library.

This means that you can *experience* the book, not just read it. Join the movement today.

Susan Dean
Founder and CEO, Dean Publishing
deanpublishing.com

Printed in Great Britain
by Amazon